CHINA MEMOIRS

CHINA MEMOIRS

Chiang Kai-shek and the War Against Japan

Owen Lattimore

Compiled by Fujiko Isono

UNIVERSITY OF TOKYO PRESS

Publication of this volume was assisted by subsidies from Daido Life Foundation and the Keizo Shibusawa Memorial Fund.

ISBN 4-13-027025-7
ISBN 0-86008-468-X

Printed in Japan

CONTENTS

Chapter Five
THE TWO SIDES OF THE UNITED FRONT

Chapter Six
THE WAR YEARS

Chapter Seven
BETWEEN THE WAR AND THE STORM

PREFACE

When anyone asked him: "Why don't you write your autobiography?" Owen Lattimore would reply: "Oh! I'm not yet *that* old." Unfortunately, however, years passed much more rapidly than he had foreseen. By the time he finally decided to write down the story of his long and eventful life, he found it impossible to organize into coherent sections and chapters the rush of memories flowing out of the past.

He was then living in Cambridge, England. Like the nomads whom he loved so much, Lattimore moved many times even after his retirement from Leeds University in 1970. He and his wife Eleanor had planned to go back to the United States to settle down in a new house that she had designed, but she died quite suddenly in March, 1970. Consequently, after about one year in Virginia, he moved to Paris to have easier access to Leeds, where he had at long last started a post-graduate course in Mongol studies two years before his retirement. In 1980, however, he finally decided to return to England again.

His frustration at not being able to write his full autobiography led me to suggest that he might concentrate on the period when he was working for Chiang Kai-shek, since he had written almost nothing about his life with the Generalissimo and people wonder why Owen Lattimore was chosen by President Roosevelt to serve as the personal adviser to Chiang, and what he was actually doing in Chungking.

Although he turned down the title I proposed, "Chiang and I," as sounding too much like a musical, the idea pleased him and he started writing drafting a memoir which he called "Working for

Chiang Kai-shek." He began with how he received a most unexpected telephone call from the White House. The writing went very well at first, but after about half a dozen pages he could not go on any further.

At this point I suggested that perhaps it would be easier for him to organize his memories if I asked him questions and recorded his answers. This was in the spring of 1982. I had started to work with Owen in the early 1970s but exclusively in the area of Mongol Studies. My knowledge of modern Chinese history was limited. There was, however, no specialist available who could come to interview him often enough: it was too tiring for him to be interviewed for hours at a stretch. I had no choice but to undertake the task myself with occasional help from my Sinologist friends.

At first I tried to draw up a general outline of the whole book and to pose my questions according to the plan. It was very difficult to stick to the rule, however. I soon realized that Owen could remember very few details about events and people mentioned in the questions suggested by the specialists. What he talked about primarily was his personal experiences. He answered questions straight out of his memory, without any preparation and only rarely consulting any records or documents.

I decided to let him go on talking as he liked, which he did with many deviations and side-stories. These turned out to be more informative and charming than straightforward responses. I had worked with him long enough to put to him such impertinent questions as "But didn't you feel uncomfortable living among the deprived Chinese as a member of the privileged white society?" or "Wasn't Chiang Kai-shek disappointed when he discovered you were not the kind of adviser he had wanted to have?"

In the course of these interviews, we agreed that for the readers it would be necessary to know what in his background made him the choice of President Roosevelt. So, we went back to his birth, and still further back to his parents. The story of his early years grew so long and rich in information that I suggested "Chiang and I" might become his *China Memoirs*. In this way, the part which was originally to be a flashback ended up as Chapters 1 and 2 of the present book.

Over a period of about two years, we recorded more than thirty hours of interviews. The recordings were made at irregular intervals and included a considerable number of overlaps. Our conversations tended to jump from one subject to another according to what came to his mind in association with what he was talking about.

Then the tapes had to be transcribed and the fragmentary information had to be put into coherent order through a jigsaw-puzzle-like process. I managed to do the job only because, after all, I knew what he was talking about. I faithfully retained his own expressions except for inserting connecting words where necessary and amalgamating different versions of the same story. In addition, I made use of interviews which he had given previously to some Sinologists who came to visit him. In such cases, I gave more weight to the earlier versions unless there was other evidence to show that the later one was correct, for his memory was sharper when he was younger.

Even though the draft of the whole manuscript was ready by 1984, Owen's health did not allow him to work on it. I had to call upon Professor John DeFrancis, one of Owen's former colleagues at Johns Hopkins University, to edit the manuscript. A Chinese-language specialist now retired from the University of Hawaii, he kindly accepted the corvée.

In the autumn of 1985, Owen returned to the United States, to live near his son David in Pawtucket, Rhode Island. There, his health recovered to a remarkable degree. When I went to see him in September, 1986, he was fully capable of revising the first five chapters during the two weeks I stayed with him. Drawing upon his refreshed memory, he inserted a number of passages and crossed out some sentences which he deemed too colloquial.

Even though he appeared lively and in good humor, he could sit at his desk for no more than an hour at a time. At the end of my stay, the last two chapters were still untouched. Owen said he would revise them and send them to me in Japan. In fact, I did not really expect that he would do so without his "slave driver," as he used to call me, sitting at his side. Nevertheless, he looked so well and worked with such lucidity that I felt quite optimistic about leaving the remaining chapters until my next visit the following year.

Unfortunately, in the early summer of 1987, Owen suffered a stroke which deprived him of the ability to speak and write, though he continued to read his favorite weekly magazines and even serious books, and seemed to understand the contents. In spite of his great handicap, he remained surprisingly cheerful, thanks to the devoted care of his housekeeper, Emma. His condition gave us hope that he might once again get well enough to do some more work. A year later, although he had maintained his outwardly healthy appearance, his speech showed hardly any progress. There was no alternative but to go ahead with publication plans.

By an unexpected stroke of good luck, however, the travel notes which Owen had jotted down during the 1944 Wallace Mission turned up among his papers. As they contained details of his visit to Chungking, including conversations with Chiang Kai-shek and Madame Chiang, of which Owen did not remember much, I decided to incorporate important passages of this notebook into the draft of Chapter 6. It was also fortunate that Professor Robert P. Newman of the University of Pittsburgh, whose fully documented biography of Owen Lattimore is going to be published soon, was kind enough to read the draft and to point out slips and confusions concerning facts and dates.

As this book was neither written nor dictated by Owen himself, those who have read his writings will miss his unique style. I should like to emphasize that these memoirs are not meant to be a source of precise historical data. Efforts were made, however, to correct obvious errors and identify individuals whose names Owen had forgotten. This is an account of *what* Owen Lattimore remembered and *how* he remembered it. It is not realistic to expect anyone to recall offhand the details of what happened more than forty years earlier. It must also be admitted that Owen's lively imagination sometimes made a story more picturesque than it really was.

This book will contribute to historical understanding not so much through factual precision as through evocation of the atmosphere of the epoch. For example, it brings to life the interplay of forces in the United Front between Chiang Kai-shek's Kuomintang and the Communists. Because of the reticence of both sides to discuss this period, the crucial significance of the United Front for the U.S. war effort as well as for Chinese resistance against the Japanese invasion is now sometimes forgotten.

Some readers may interpret his account as a continued defense against the accusation of communism levelled against him during the McCarthy period. It is of course possible that unconsciously, if not consciously, Owen felt the need to state once more his own case. It is also possible that the public image of Owen Lattimore which underlies such interpretations reflects the portrait created during the time of McCarthyism.

Chinese place names in the text are transcribed according to more or less traditional spellings. In order to facilitate identification of personal names I have followed the *Biographical Dictionary of Republican China* (4 vols., 1967–71, ed. H.L. Boorman and E.R.C. Howard).

I wish to express my gratitude to all those, too numerous to mention here, who have helped to bring Owen Lattimore's memoirs to publication. Special thanks are due to Professor Akira Iriye, who encouraged me at a very early stage and strongly recommended publication; and to Professor Koji Kobayashi and Professor Masahide Shibusawa, through whose assistance publication subsides were obtained from Daido Life Foundation and the Keizo Shibusawa Memorial Fund. My appreciation goes to the University of Tokyo Press, especially to Nina Raj, for editorial and other professional assistance, and Alice Thorner, another old friend of Owen, who, with John DeFrancis, helped me write this preface. I am indebted to Robert P. Newman for assistance in securing the photographs.

Owen Lattimore died on May 30, 1989, while the manuscript of this book was under consideration by the publisher. He left all his books to the Mongolian and Central Asian Studies Unit of Cambridge University. The director of the Unit, Dr. Caroline Humphrey, was one of the first three students who attended the Mongolian course at Leeds, and Owen believed that his work would be continued and developed there.

Fujiko Isono

Owen Lattimore in Paris in the late 1970s.
Photograph courtesy of Raymonde Black.

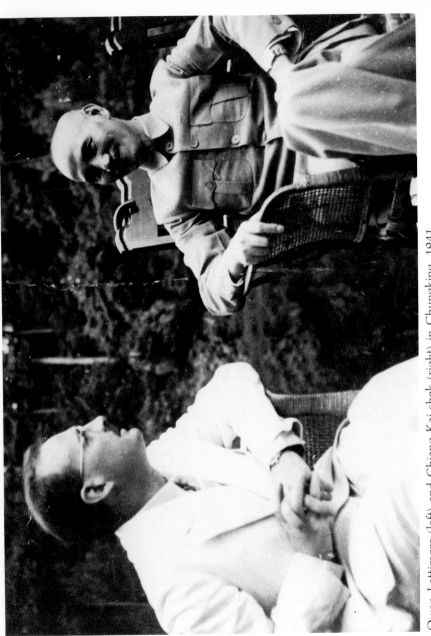

Owen Lattimore (left) and Chiang Kai-shek (right) in Chungking, 1941.
Photograph courtesy of David Lattimore.

The Wallace Mission, 1944: (left to right) Henry Wallace, Owen Lattimore, John Carter Vincent, and John Hazard. Photograph courtesy of David Lattimore.

(Left to right) Philip Jaffe, Nym Wales, Owen Lattimore, Mao Tse-tung, Arthur Bisson, and Agnes Jaffe in Yenan, 1937. Photograph from T.A. Bisson, *Yenan in June 1937: Talks with the Communist Leaders* (Berkeley: Center for Chinese Studies, University of California, 1973). © 1973 by The Regents of the University of California. Used by permission.

Fujiko Isono (left), Owen Lattimore (center), and Chou En-lai (right) in Peking, 1972.

CHINA MEMOIRS

I was brought up mainly by my father and mother. Like
er foreigners, we used to go on summer vacations to
n the seaside near Shanhaikuan. That was the time when
ost of the other foreigners. I can remember how, on more
occasion, we would be sitting on the veranda of our sum-
ge, and my mother would say: "Oh, there are some people
. They might want some tea. Run out and tell the cook to
or some guests." Then I would ask: "What should I say to
she would give me the Chinese instructions which I was
the servants. As I did not know the language, I would
ask her all over again the next time the same thing
.

g Chinese spoken around me, however, I seem to have
to understand the general idea of what people were talk-
t. The summer before the 1911 Revolution, I remember
children were playing on the veranda in Peitaiho and the
nurses of the younger children were sitting watching
uddenly a violent storm broke out, and we took refuge
e roof, looking out on the pouring rain and lightning. The
ere frightened and were whispering to each other that this
onvulsion of nature must be the omen of a coming catas-
They spoke about "messengers going to the villages, warn-
people that trouble was coming."
the Revolution started, there was a fear that it might turn
oxer-like anti-foreign movement, and the foreign legations
g called in their nationals who were in the interior. We were
refugees in a small temple called Sankuan Miao near the
n wall. I was eleven years old, and I knew why we had taken
n Peking, but this did not give me any special fear of the
. As Yuan Shih-k'ai pretty soon took over, there was no real
ance in the capital. I went to the canteen of the U.S. Marines
re stationed in Peking, with other foreign troops, to defend
tion quarter, and for the first time in my life was introduced
dog, which I found to be romantic as well as delicious; and I
e home to astonish the other children, but they were not so
elmed as I had been.
s also during such visits that I watched with amazement the
e Cossacks performed on horseback. In Peking we made

Chapter One

■

THE EARLY YEARS

Childhood in China and Adolescence in Europe

My mother used to say, "Owen crawled across the Pacific," because
before I was one year old my parents took me to China from the
United States, where I was born (in Washington, D. C., on 29 July
1900). My father had had no college education or university
degree. Owing to his family's financial difficulties, he had had to
drop out of school at the age of sixteen or seventeen. In those days,
however, the qualifications for schoolteachers were extremely lax,
and my father, being a good pupil, was immediately taken back as a
junior teacher, probably in the same school, where he taught
English grammar. He was primarily self-educated and made himself a very good scholar in Latin and Greek. He also had an excellent knowledge of French and of German, though his approach was
that of a grammarian.

My father had an elder sister in China who was a pupil and dis-
ciple of Alexander Graham Bell. This famous inventor of the telephone had a deaf and dumb wife who was very intelligent as well
as beautiful. He worked out a method to talk with her and used
some of his wealth to promote the education of deaf and dumb
children. My aunt had the idea of taking this teaching to China. She
did not regard her job as teaching deaf and dumb Chinese children
to become Christians. Under the Treaty System, however, the only
way to pursue her work was through the Treaty privileges of missionaries. She made an arrangement with the American Presbyte-
rian Church, so that it became her cover, so to speak, in China.

Nineteen hundred, the year I was born, was the Boxer year. Even the stupid Manchu government realized that unless China got some modern education, it was pretty well doomed to being dominated by imperialist nations. China needed engineers and scientists and other men with modern training, but since it did not yet have suitable schools for higher education in science and technology, Chinese students had to go abroad. Shortly after the turn of the century, the Manchu government opened the first modern school for higher education in Shanghai. My father received an appointment there, and later in Paotingfu and Tientsin. These appointments were all associated with technological and scientific universities, where his job was to teach young Chinese primarily English, but also French and German, to prepare them to go abroad for their real higher education.

I know a great deal less about my mother than I do about my father. I know that her father was a captain of artillery in the Civil War, and his battery took part in breaking the famous Confederate charge in the battle of Gettysburg. On the field of Gettysburg there is a monument to his battery with his name as captain. I do not know what this grandfather did immediately after the Civil War; but then he ran away with a Spanish dancer and went down to Central America. In those days as today, the U.S. authorities were extremely lenient with war veterans, especially if they had good war records, so he was actually made the U.S. consul in this country to which he had run away. Eventually he came back to the United States and rejoined his family. This is the end of the story as far as I know it.

My mother, one of his several children, including two sons, became a schoolteacher and that was how she met my father. She also did a certain amount of free-lance writing about family life and children. I suspect that my father's family thought he had married a bit below him, but I am not sure of this at all. My mother did know French fairly well and a certain amount of German; and she helped my father in our family school. Later, when we were in Europe, from 1912 to 1914, she ran the family flat in Lausanne and got on well with the neighbors.

I grew up in China from the age of one to the age of twelve. My memories between one and five are very dim. I only have the image of enormous numbers of crabs swarming in the mud of a creek (in Shanghai, as I later found out) that terribly frightened me. My father moved from Shanghai to Paotingfu, to the south of Peking, in

---

1905, and we lived in an old tem
had to go back to the United Stat
who had been working in the sout
Mother was away. I remember he

Here is something unknown to
lived in that period of Chinese his
the privileges of the foreigners an
concessions in the Treaty Ports, wh
ity, but what I remember in Paotin
their own form of exclusion. Their
"We have hired you to teach Engl
does not mean that we need to acc
Therefore, I grew up having no Chir
a little world of our own, though t

I respected my father for his learni
because she was practical. Actually b
kept their distance from their childr
close, affectionate relationship. My m
younger brother, but not so much to
five or six, we were not left to the care
did not believe in that, but it seems to
more like children with their teachers
ably my impression is not fair and is
age of fourteen to the age of nineteen
of the family. While their lives were d
was marked by cleavages with each su
blur the memory of what had gone

Because of my father's conservative
to grow up speaking Chinese and identi
though he himself not only learned flu
became a good scholar in the Confucian
he told me that if we had learned Chine
the servants, and if we grew up speak
would grow up with a servant mentality
was that if, when we grew up, we want
could make the decision for ourselves ab
in the meantime we should be brought u
would fit us to live in the United State
wanted to live.

Though I had a Chinese nurse in Sh

Paotingfu
many oth
Peitaiho o
we saw m
than one
mer cotta
coming u
prepare f
him?" an
to give t
have to
happened

Hearin
been abl
ing abou
that we
Chinese
them. S
under th
nurses w
violent
trophe.
ing the

Wher
into a B
in Pekin
living a
souther
refuge
Chines
disturb
who w
the leg
to a ho
took o
overw

It w
feats t

friends with some foreign children, and we would be put in rick-shaws and sent to the compounds where these friends lived. As Yuan Shih-k'ai was ruling with a very heavy hand, when we went along the big streets we would see human heads nailed up on tele-phone posts to intimidate the people of Peking. Seeing these heads did not bother us. It simply strengthened the idea that we were liv-ing in one world and the Chinese were living in another, that this was the kind of thing that Chinese did to Chinese and had nothing to do with us. I think my father's attitude of white superiority had influenced me, not in the sense of my having anti-Chinese preju-dices, but just in the feeling that they were different people.

By the time I was twelve years old, I had two younger sisters and one younger brother. My father decided to send us children to Europe for education, and my mother took us to Switzerland. When our steamer arrived in a port in Italy, my elder sister came running down to my mother who was in our cabin, crying, "Mother, come up and look! There are white men *working!*" I had seen in the marine barracks that not all white men were being served by Chi-nese servants, but for the girls it was an entirely new experience to see white men doing "hired" work.

In Switzerland I was put in a school, not an expensive, fashion-able school for foreign children, but a school for Swiss boys, where I did all my studies—Latin, German, math—in French. As my father had taught me French as well as other subjects at home, I did not have much difficulty at school. In the summer of 1914, my mother and the younger children were in the Black Forest, as my next younger sister was suspected of having turberculosis. My elder sis-ter was staying with an American friend in Switzerland. I was in England where my uncle was preparing a place at Oxford for a young Polish prince whom he tutored. I was there for the summer holidays, arriving only two or three days before the outbreak of the First World War in the beginning of August.

When the war broke out my mother immediately gathered up all the children and concentrated us all in England, until she found a Japanese ship back via Suez to China, where my father was still teaching. But it was decided that as there was no suitable school for a boy like me in China, I had better been left in England. That was how I came to be at St. Bees, a public school in Cumberland. I was quite happy with the arrangement. I liked to be on my own.

When I entered this school for the first term of the year 1915, I was fourteen-and-a-half years old. Naturally, I was affected by the general British wartime atmosphere and believed that the Germans (we called them Huns) were reverting to barbarism and Britain stood for democracy. In a British public school of that period, we did not have classes in economics or sociology or politics, and my class studies were almost entirely Latin, Greek, history, and literature. My house, the biggest one in the school, had three housemasters, and I became very friendly with one of them, who was a historian, J.E.A. Jolliffe, later a don at Keble.

He recognized my interest in history and encouraged me by lending me books and so on. My interest was already more in history than in classics. He did not, however, want to take me under his tutelage. The senior housemaster, F.C. Ceary, afterward a don at Corpus Christi, Oxford, was my classics master in the sixth form, and Jolliffe, being the second housemaster, did not want anybody to think that he had poached me, since I was, so to speak, the classics master's property. I entered the school below the English level of specialization, and the master with whom I started in Greek recommended me to the classical side as a promising youngster. So I was automatically put in the classical stream. This did not bother me, for I myself wanted to be a poet.

By that time I was already writing poetry, and some of my poems were printed in a school magazine which I was editing with two other boys. Though one of the earliest ones was a rather bloody poem on the Vikings with a line such as "Kill, kill, kill!" I never wrote anything heroic on the 1914 war. I was writing more in imitation of Alfred E. Housman's *A Shropshire Lad*, which was my great introduction to poetry. I think a lot of this book is a poetry of adolescence and I was in late adolescence. Actually it was all a combination of the joy and sadness of a young lad. A boy and a girl fall in love and they get separated and both of them die, or something of that kind. Of course, there is a certain amount of war association: the young soldier gets killed and so on; but that traces back to the Boer War, not to the Great War. I had no suspicion at all that Housman was in fact a homosexual. As a boy I was also attracted by G.K. Chesterton and read a lot of him, and Hilaire Belloc as well. They both represented a sort of a romantic effort to idealize the Middle

Ages. There was a great deal of talk about what was called "guild socialism," and I was influenced by that.

By the time I was sixteen or seventeen and capable of thinking politically, I was, like almost everybody of my generation, no longer really concerned with the idea of democracy against German militarism. There were already appalling casualties in the trench war. Our class of people going to that kind of school had had reports of brothers, cousins, and others being killed. The romance of the beginning of the war reflected, for example, in the poetry of Rupert Brooke, had been killed off. The war was now a dirty but necessary business that you had to go through with. You could not win favor if you were a conscientious objector, but neither did you go out to win medals and be a hero. It was something you had to do.

When I reached conscription age, the United States was also in the war. There was an agreement between Great Britain and the United States that young Britons in the United States or Americans in Britain could have the choice of being conscripted into either army. The age of conscription was eighteen, and I would be eighteen at the end of July, 1918. I had been in England more than four years, and I had no connection with the United States. To go into the U.S. Army would have been a double trial: how to learn to live with Americans and be like Americans, as well as how to become a soldier. It seemed to be much more logical to go into the British officers' training school where I would be with people some of whom might be from my own school, or at least from schools like mine, so that the break from boyhood to soldiering would be a single break and not a double one as it would have been if I had gone into the U.S. forces.

I am not sure in my memory here, but I think the conscription procedure was that as a first step you received a notice to report to an officers' training school. I received a notice and I reported. As I recall, if they decided that your continuing in school for another year would qualify you better as an officer, they would give you a deferment. I received such a deferment to 1919. Not burning with desire for glory, though not a pacifist, either, I was glad to have it. If you went from a school like ours to an officers' training school, when you left that, you got the lowest officer rank in the Army, that of second lieutenant; and this was the class that had the highest casualty rate in the whole army. I had seen it printed several times that the average life of a new officer at the front was only a few weeks. So to get a second lieutenant's commission and be ordered to the front was a kind of death sentence. But by 1919, the war was already over.

In fact, in the latter part of 1918 and the first half of 1919, my principal concern was neither war nor politics, but to try to win a scholarship to Oxford. I never thought of Cambridge. My school had a historically strong connection with Queen's College, Oxford; and the tradition of the school was that though the small number of science candidates mostly tried to get a Cambridge scholarship, the qualified humanities students tried to get into Oxford. Competition was very stiff, and my handicap was that the whole standard was Greek and Latin. My early years in Switzerland had made me fairly competent in French and not too bad in German; but in those days, these two languages did not count at all for getting into Oxford or Cambridge.

My father had started me in Latin, but he had not had time to start me in Greek. From the point of view of winning a scholarship to Oxford, by January 1915 when I entered St. Bees, most of the boys of my age had had a year or two of Greek as well as Latin in their prep school, or had come to St. Bees a year or two younger than I had. So by the sheer quantity of what they had read, by the time it came to sitting for competitive scholarship examinations, they were much more deeply soaked in the classics than I was. In those days, for example, an important item in winning a classical scholarship to Oxford was whether you could or could not write Greek and Latin hexameters, and I was no good whatever at this.

My father was able to start my brother Richmond in Greek when the family returned to China at the outbreak of the war. Richmond later also profited from going to Dartmouth College where my father was a professor, so that in his spare time my father was able to coach him over and above the formal instruction he was getting in class, and helped him mature early and well in the classical tradition. He had a career very different from my own and became a celebrated classical scholar. My difficulty was that in my family it was accepted that Richmond was the clever one, even when we went to Europe. My brother would have been six then, and already at six he was much more intelligent than I had been at that age.

I think if the housemaster who was a historian had taken me over and coached me, I might have succeeded. He was a very good coach for boys who were going up for history scholarships. If I had taken the initiative and asked to be transferred from the classical side to history, I would very likely have been accepted. Or if my parents had been in England and had written to the school that they would like me to be transferred, I am sure it could have been arranged; but being alone at the age of seventeen or eighteen, I just did not have that initiative. For years I regretted that I had not gone to Oxford; but if I had gone there, it would have been at the opening years of the twenties, and I would have fallen under either extreme right-wing or extreme left-wing influence. I did not yet have enough maturity to have a steady opinion of my own.

At that age I was definitely to the right of center, and by going to the university, I might have reacted against that and shifted to the Left. English society was still elitist, and by going to Oxford or Cambridge, you won the God-given right to be either elite of the Left or elite of the Right. Which way you went depended largely on the people you met in those years—the people with whom you associated in the particular College to which you went. These were the years of, for example, people like Aldous Huxley and Evelyn Waugh. I would have come out an insufferable young aesthete. Looking back now, I think that by not having gone to a "real" university, I escaped from acquiring any set ideas about things.

Return to China

Having failed to win a scholarship to Oxford, my sole ambition, I had to go back to China. At the end of the war the value of the Chinese dollar fell sharply; and as my father was paid by the Chinese government in Chinese money, based on the value of silver, he could not afford to finance my university education in England. So, when I returned to China at the age of exactly nineteen, I was a very frustrated young intellectual of the type that was to typify the New York, Paris, London intellectuals of the 1920s. As I had to work to earn a living, I got a job in a firm in the British Concession in Tientsin. It was an old-fashioned British-China coast firm that dealt with everything. As agents we bought for buyers in Europe and the United States everything that China exported and imported everything that China imported. I was put in the department which dealt with the import of British cotton textiles into China. This was a dying trade, because during the war years not only the Japanese but the Chinese themselves had developed their textile industries, and they could supply the China market more cheaply than the British could.

Soon after joining the firm, I met a man who was an employee of the head office in Shanghai; he was in charge of the department, acting as agent of British insurance companies. This was a much bigger business. The insurance man said to the manager of the Tientsin branch: "Can I have Lattimore?" I was very willing to go and spent a year in Shanghai working for the insurance branch. This involved a certain amount of travel in the interior. A Chinese firm would want to have insurance on its factory, usually fire insurance; I would go to have a look at the factory to see if I thought their fire protection precautions were good enough.

Another thing that was growing in China at that time was Chinese flour mills so that the Chinese could buy grain and make their own flour instead of importing white flour from the United States or elsewhere. In a flour mill, if it is not kept properly clean, there is a danger of explosion because of very fine flour dust in the air. When I went to look at a factory, even a novice like myself could easily tell whether it was being intelligently or sloppily managed; among other things I could also sense the attitude of the workers. Psychologically, this was a key to developing an ability to understand the Chinese and get along with them. In a new industrial city, you could check up things like: Did it have a reputation for having a lot of fires? You could also pick up the gossip among men in other businesses, like stories that a firm was running into trouble financially so it had resorted to arson to get the insurance money. This is the kind of unofficial information you learn to pick up when you are in business. Some learn to do it, and some never get the knack.

When I was about twenty-one years old, my father was invited to become a professor at Dartmouth College, and this made it possible for the whole family to go back to the United States for the education of the younger children. So I went up to Tientsin, where my family still lived, to say good-bye to them. There I met H.G.W. Woodhead, who was the editor of the *Peking and Tientsin Times*, the most influential English-language paper north of Shanghai. I do not remember the first meeting with him, but in a small community of foreigners at that time everybody met everybody. Both my father and Woodhead had been in Tientsin for years, and probably my father had said to Woodhead: "This is my son Owen." And Woodhead probably said: "Oh, well, young man, what are you interested in?" and so on. In the course of time, after one or two more meetings, he said: "How about coming to work for the newspaper?" I immediately had visions of myself writing articles and thought, "Oh, this is much better than chasing around doing fire insurance!"

So I joined the paper, but I stayed only for about a year. I was disappointed with the work, because I found that instead of going out and discovering stories on my own, I was really a sub-editor, largely doing proofreading of both news material and editorial opinion coming out in the paper, which was very conservative. The Allied Intervention in Siberia after the Russian Revolution was then coming to an end. Many of the British in China were rather in favor of the Japanese establishing a position in Eastern Siberia, although at the same time they were worried by the extent to which Japan had taken advantage of the British engagement in the First World War to improve its position in Northeast China (Manchuria) and on the Chinese coast at the expense of British enterprise.

On the other hand, the Americans were divided in their opinion about what was going on. There was a rapidly growing fear of Bolshevism, but American opinion was not particularly in favor of the restoration of Tsarism; and it seemed to me that U.S. policy was largely to prevent a too great territorial expansion of the power of Japan. I do remember that while people were anti-Bolshevik, almost everybody was against Ungern-Sternberg, the White Russian officer who had retreated from Siberia into Outer Mongolia and whose reputation as the "Mad Baron" had already been established.

Refugees were coming down from Siberia through Mongolia. There were also White Russians and other Europeans who were running away from the Mongolian Revolution of the summer of 1921. I remember in particular a Swiss, who had been a dairy expert in Urga (present Ulan Bator), who escaped and came to Tientsin. He wrote an article in German about his experiences and observations in Urga and his escape to China. I knew enough German so that with a dictionary I could make a rough translation, which we published in the newspaper. At that time, however, I had never seen a

Mongol and never thought that I would take any interest in Mongolia and the Mongols.

I made one big mistake. Woodhead said: "There is an old man living in a suburb of Tientsin, an Englishman who came out to China a long time ago, in the 1880s. He was in China during the events leading up to the Boxer Rising and lived through it; and he went on living in Tientsin through the Chinese Revolution of 1911. Why don't you go out and call on him, and persuade him to tell you his life story?" My arrogant young intellectual response was: "Oh, another stupid old China Coast man!" I made excuses and did not do it. I think he had been an engineer in a Tientsin arsenal established by Li Hung-chang or somebody like that. Now everybody knows from books that there was a period when foreign engineers were working in Chinese arsenals. These men were close to military thinking, military planning, and the successes and failures of the Chinese in trying to modernize their army. Today, looking back, I realize that I could have got an autobiographical story of real historical importance.

The man from the trading firm who had asked for my transfer to Shanghai came up to Tientsin again, in the course of touring round the branches of the firm. He said: "Why don't you come back to the firm? I'll see that you are placed in charge of the insurance work in the Tientsin office." So, I went back. The insurance work did not take up all my time, and I worked hard, especially in the evenings, studying Chinese. Though I had lived in China as a boy, this was the first time I began to learn the language, both spoken and written. It seemed to me that business circles in Tientsin were hopelessly philistine. There were not many people who were interested in poetry and literature and other things that interested me; and there I was stuck in Tientsin.

While I was working for the trading firm, I had an opportunity to meet the Manchurian warlord Chang Tso-lin. In 1924 there was a civil war going on between him and Wu P'ei-fu, and the railway connection had been interrupted. The foreign international Chamber of Commerce in Tientsin had an interview with Chang and asked me to be their interpreter. We said to him: "Look here, if you want to continue to occupy North China and to draw revenue from it, you must not destroy trade. A great deal of the trade depends on the export of cargoes coming down from Manchuria into Tientsin to be shipped abroad by foreign companies. So, can't you see to it that special permission is granted for our cargo trains to come down from Manchuria to Tientsin?" The old man saw the sense of that. We did not, of course, go into delicate subjects like the balance between Chang's connection with the Japanese and his interest in other foreign trade. Though I was quite ignorant of Chinese politics in those days, my impression of Chang Tso-lin was that he was a tough old soldier who was also agile in politics.

Under the Treaty laws firms like ours could operate in the concessions, but we could not have branches in the interior. There we had to work through Chinese agents. As I wanted to get out of Tientsin as much as possible, not only on insurance business, I made myself into the firm's principal Chinese-speaking trouble-shooter, and I managed to get sent up into the interior on all kinds of missions. This was in the 1920s before the Northern Expedition of Chiang Kai-shek. Warlords were banging each other on the head all over China, and there were many parts of the country where the central government had no real power. The local warlords raised their own troops and levied their own taxes, and they were grabbing cargoes and holding them up for illegal taxes on trade in order to meet their expenses.

I remember one case I worked on in which we had a whole fleet of canal barges loaded with peanuts that were to come to Tientsin to be shipped to the United States. The local warlord had held them up and was demanding a totally illegal tax to allow them to move on. In such cases I would say: "Let me go up there and see if I can fix things up." I would go to the nearest railway station and then proceed from there by mule cart, or whatever the local form of transportation was, for a day or two to arrive at a place where there were no foreigners and the people had seldom seen one. I would then get in touch with our Chinese agents who had been responsible for the deal to discuss with them what we should do.

The handling of such cases provides an amusing footnote to the Unequal Treaty situation. The Chinese quite rightly resented the treaties; but for merchants of the kind I was dealing with, their profit lay in their dealing with foreign merchants. They would say: "The local warlord politicians did this and this, all of which is quite illegal. You must go back and get your firm and the British Legation in Peking to protest and send orders to this warlord."

Then I would have to say to them: "The days of gunboat diplomacy are over. Nobody has that kind of power to apply to the Peking government; and Peking does not have the power to discipline its own warlords. What we have to do is this: You tell me the local conditions. You brief me on the kind of warlord with whom we are dealing. You work out what you think can be done. In this case the deal has already been made, and if we don't ship the goods, we will have to pay damages to our customers in Europe and in the United States for the delay in shipment. So, we lose money. This time we are willing to pay at least some of this illegal tax, in order to get the cargo released, but *you* have to put it to the warlord that this can't go on indefinitely. We can pay at a rate which enables us to make new contracts in the future. No profits, no trade. So, if you want to save the trade and the profits, you tell me what to say to the warlord, or his delegate, when we have an interview. In other words, it is not a foreign imperialist giving orders to you, but you the Chinese, the new rising Chinese middle class (though I did not have this English vocabulary in those days), who have to exert your local influence. We have to think of tomorrow's business as well as today's. So does the warlord. If he wants to have something to tax, he has to tax it within limits that still enable us to make a profit." This appealed to the Chinese merchants' mind, and time after time I was successful in dealing with them.

In the same way, I went up to try to get a trainload of wool from Kueihua (Old City of Huhehot, now the capital of the Autonomous Region of Inner Mongolia) through a Chinese civil war. By dealing with Chinese merchants who had their own troubles with Chinese warlord politicians, I began to learn the structure of the Chinese society of that time. I got wider and wider experience and met Chinese from different provinces. I learned that imperialism was not a simple thing—that in a country which was at a general disadvantage in the imperialist system, there were some who did make a private profit out of the same system. This gave me some idea of class difference; but the fact that these Chinese merchants were making money at the expense of their own working-class people just did not come into my mind. I was not thinking according to any theory like democracy or humanitarianism. It was a matter of the concrete situation.

From my American inheritance, and having heard, in my childhood, adults talking about it, I did have the idea that the European nations and Japan were imperialists, and we Americans were not. Nevertheless, as an English public school boy, the way I looked out on the world was much more like an Englishman than an American. That is to say, the colonial administrators and men doing business in countries like China were an elite. We were, of course, working for our own profit and benefit, but the result of what we did was to improve conditions for the "natives," and therefore there was a beneficent aspect to the white man in Asia as well as the heavy-booted imperialist aspect. This was the sort of divided view I had when I went to China. But later, in the course of working at my job, I encountered problems to solve; and in solving them, working with Chinese employees, not just as a boss but as somebody who had to know how the Chinese employees felt about things and how they reacted, I began to think of my Chinese associates as *we* and not *they*.

Thus it came about that my first approach to China was simply one of dealing with problems of ordinary situations in life. This was very different from the foreign scholar who comes in touch with the people more or less on the top and then tries to find out what is going on below.

Beginning of an Academic Career

My work provided a very strong modifying influence on my ideas about Chinese and white people in spite of my living in a concession as a privileged foreigner. I despised the white people in the European and American community in which I lived, considering them terribly philistine and unaesthetic. This prevented me from having the attitude that all white men were superior to all those yellow people.

In Tientsin, the young men of my age never bothered to learn Chinese. They would say "This chap Lattimore is a real queer one. He likes talking the language, and he likes traveling in the interior." This does not mean, however, that I kept away from others. I played rugby in the cold weather, rowed on the river in the warm season, and did a lot of riding. But this was not enough. Though I always wanted to write, I did not have a very clear idea of what to write. The Tientsin Club, exclusively for foreigners, had a very good library, and I read a great deal of poetry and a good deal in the way of novels and other literature. Then, having traveled a little in the interior areas accessible from Tientsin, I started reading books by travelers, botanists, ethnologists, and those who had traveled farther than I had. Geographically the farthest place I had actually reached was only the fringe of Inner Mongolia. I suppose I had a tendency to romanticize myself as a man who penetrated into this alien culture. Therefore my commercial negotiations in the interior were not entirely separated from my romanticism.

In the course of these negotiations, I discovered that one of our big exports from Tientsin, the main seaport for goods coming out of Mongolia and Sinkiang, was wool. The stuff came by caravans down to Changchiak'ou (Kalgan) or to Kueihua, the frontier cities from where goods could be transported to Tientsin by rail. The railhead was at the edge of Inner Mongolia. There the camel caravans bringing the wool from Mongolia and Sinkiang filed into the railway yard where the camels squatted while the bales of wool were lifted off their backs and loaded onto the freight cars—the age of Marco Polo meeting the age of steam. I decided that I just had to go up to where the caravans came from and see things for myself.

I met Chinese who had traveled through Inner Mongolia to Sinkiang, and even on to India. What impressed me was the fact that we dealt with Chinese agents who were really brokers. These agents got hold of their cargoes from caravan merchants. The caravan merchants in turn got their goods from far up in the interior from still other merchants. Even when I met a well-traveled caravan man, he did not know the exact details of the goods he had gathered from some other caravan merchants whom he met at the other end of the route. Here we were dealing with such things as camel wool, goat hair (cashmere), and so forth, which were going into the international market; but we never knew what, up in the distant interior, were the statistics of each year. How much of these goods was produced here and how much was produced there? What were the conditions this year? Was there an oversupply or undersupply? I got the idea that if I went up there I could find out something about the actual economic conditions in the places where the goods in which we dealt originated.

I did not want to go into the deep interior as a naturalist or military or political intelligence officer or anything like that. Nor was I equipped to go in any such capacity. So I went to the firm with a business proposition: "Let me go up there, to the ultimate regions from where our goods come, and get an idea of the conditions. If we have a better idea of the conditions, we can beat our competitors." The firm said: "That's a very good idea. But not in these times. The times are too uncertain, and you might be killed or captured by bandits, and we might have to pay a big ransom. So we can't do it." (This was in the mid 1920s. The first United Front between the Kuomintang [Nationalist Party] and the Chinese Communists was forming, and civil war was going on all over China.) Upon this, I said: "Then I resign, and I'll go on my own." While working for the firm, the farthest place I had been to was Kueihua; but I had made contacts with the merchants, and I knew that through them I could get camels and arrange a journey accompanying a caravan. I would follow the caravans to the end of the line, and see what there was to see.

Although the managers of the firm saw no business in paying me to wander in the deep interior and find things out, they suggested that before I left them I should spend a year in Peking in temporary charge of their "diplomatic" office, which dealt with government officials and contracts. I jumped at the offer, and it was lucky that I did, because it was in this year, 1925, that I met and married Eleanor Holgate, who was in Peking working as secretary to an international art association. Later she told me that she had written to her parents saying that she had met an interesting "Englishman."

For years, until I married Eleanor, I had always regretted that I had not got to Oxford. Only at this time did I begin to realize that I was capable of making a new kind of life of my own and a new kind of career for which at that time there was little competition. I had a field wide open to me and an opportunity which I could not have had if China had been as it is now after the Communist Revolution. Eleanor helped me a great deal to reach this changed outlook, though at the time we married, I had already planned my journey on the desert road to Turkestan. It was not a sudden beam of illumination to discover all this. I only slowly realized that by not going to Oxford, I had escaped from having an ordinary sort of career, all of which actually suited my qualifications and my intellectual cast of mind better than an Oxford education would have.

I left Peking for Kueihua in March 1926 to start my first long journey. Eleanor came with me to see me off. She had wanted to travel with me in a caravan, but I finally managed to persuade her to join me at the end of the desert road. Our plan was that when I got to Sinkiang, I would send a telegram to Eleanor in Peking. Then she would travel by the Trans-Siberian Railway to Semipalatinsk station, where I was to meet her. When we reached Kueihua, however, we were immediately cut off by a civil war which had a subordinate relationship to Chiang Kai-shek's Northern Expedition which started in June. For six months I could not get into Mongolia and she could not return to Peking.

While we were in Kueihua, the U.S. naval attaché in Peking asked me to write some reports for him, for which I was moderately paid. It was curious that in those days the U.S. Navy looked more deeply into inland China than the Army looked outward into the ocean. I wrote, of course, to a cover-address under a cover-name. After a few reports, however, I was asked to discontinue. Obviously, this was because my reports were too much like those I used to write for my commercial firm: civil war interference with transport, goods coming from Mongolia and Central Asia, misbehavior of troops, corruption among officers. On strictly military matters, I was incompetent. Still, I can say that I was once a paid spy—but for the Americans, and not for the Soviets as I was later accused of being.

I am not going into the details of our adventures that followed; my part of the story is written in my *The Desert Road to Turkestan* (1928), and Eleanor beautifully describes in her *Turkestan Reunion* (1934) how she, not finding me at the Semipalatinsk railway station, hired a sled and, driving through blizzards in February 1927, reached the border town of Chuguchak and found me, stuck there because of not being able to obtain a Soviet visa. The account of the subsequent journey together, in both the northern and southern parts of Sinkiang, is in *High Tartary*, published in 1930.

Nevertheless, perhaps it will be worth a few words of comment here on how extremely complicated the situation in China was, particularly in certain parts of China. When I was in Sinkiang, it was ruled—and had been ruled ever since 1911—by one warlord, Yang Tseng-hsin, who had always maintained his local power in that one province and had managed to avoid being controlled by the Peking government or any other government. This had some effect in limiting the trade of his province with the rest of China, which made it very difficult for him to obtain arms and ammunition to maintain himself in power. He therefore wanted to keep people prosperous and happy without using force and expending his ammunition. To compensate for the difficulty of his relation with his own country, he kept up a lively trade with the Soviet Union, even when successive governments in China refused to recognize it.

Here is an example of what contradictory things were possible in China in those days: Yang stationed at Semipalatinsk or somewhere in Siberia a man who was his consul general for the province of Sinkiang. Though China did not recognize the U.S.S.R., the Chinese Foreign Office recognized the appointment of this man who represented Yang, who had himself not been appointed by the central government. This went on hand in hand with the fact that Yang, while promoting external trade with the U.S.S.R. and allowing representatives of the Soviet State Trading Firm to reside and travel in Sinkiang, at the same time maintained his own secret service, which was extremely tough and efficient in suppressing any leftist movement in his own province.

When I reached the frontier of Sinkiang after traveling through Inner Mongolia, I was immediately arrested by a frontier patrol and accused of being a Japanese spy. I said that I did not look very Japanese: I had a large, red beard, blue eyes, and so forth. They thought a bit and then said: "Ah! We know what you are. You are a Soviet agent, working for Feng Yü-hsiang." Fortunately, the firm for which I had worked had had a contact in Sinkiang Province in the person of a young Chinese named P'an. He was a very interesting man whose father had been a high official in Sinkiang before the fall of the Manchu Empire. The father, a scholar very much interested in history, had helped Aurel Stein to organize his famous archeological expeditions, and Stein repeatedly refers to him. This young man spoke excellent English and very fluent Russian and was one of the very, very few Chinese officials who also spoke Uighur, the main Turkish language in Sinkiang.

He had had some business dealings with our firm, and the military border control who had arrested me allowed me to send a message to him at Urumchi, the capital of the province. On receiving my message, he went to the governor, stood personal guarantee for me, and said: "I know this man. He is all right." It was dead winter, and travel was very difficult; since it took a long time for the message to get through to Urumchi, and then for the message to come back, I was a prisoner for something like three weeks.

Afterward I met Yang, the old governor. He questioned me about my travels and what I was interested in. It would have been very easy to satisfy himself that I not only had no political connections, but was politically very ignorant. I did not know the intricacies of Chinese politics, or of Chinese relations with the Soviet Union. The provincial authorities found it difficult to believe that I was really a private person traveling at my own expense. They assumed that there must be somebody else behind. I was told much later by a Chinese that he had been in Sinkiang at the time of the collapse of Chiang Kai-shek's regime, and that he had the duty of going through the provincial archives to see what papers should be carried to Taiwan; among these archives he found a complete record of the police watch that had been kept on my wife and me all the time we were traveling in Sinkiang.

Eleanor and I reached Kashmir in October 1927. From India we went on to Europe. We had very little money left, and the cheapest place to stay was in Rome. We spent the winter of 1927-28 on the top floor of a house near the foot of the Spanish Steps. This house has since become the Keats and Shelley Museum, because John Keats lived and died there in 1821. While staying in Rome I wrote my first book, which was to be published as *The Desert Road to Turkestan*. Then we went to Paris. Within 45 hours after our arrival Eleanor came down with a lightning appendicitis, and I came down with badly ulcerated wisdom teeth. Fortunately we met a girl who was a childhood friend of Eleanor's, and she kindly lent us some money, about 200 dollars, just enough for us to get back to the United States.

In Paris, I met Paul Pelliot, the leading Sinologist and Mongolist of his time, but he simply did not want to be bothered by a youngster who had been roaming about in Central Asia. In contrast, in London Douglas Carruthers, the famous naturalist who had written *Unknown Mongolia* (1913), the two big volumes which I had taken with me on my long journey, received me very warmly and gave me advice. Remembering his kindness to an unknown youngster, I have always tried to be helpful to the young people who have come to me for assistance. It was the approval of Carruthers that in fact launched my academic career. It was therefore not only a great honor, but a joyful privilege when I was asked by the Royal Geographical Society to give the First Douglas Carruthers Memorial Lecture on 14 November 1977.

When we got back to the United States in 1928, at the age of twenty-eight I saw my native land for the first time since I had left it before I was one year old. We had spent all our money and had no clear idea of the future except that we wanted to go on traveling and writing. A chance conversation led me to apply to the Social Science Research Council for a fellowship to travel in Manchuria to study especially the settlement of Chinese colonists coming from inside the Great Wall. Although its fellowships were supposed to be granted only to advanced research workers, the council imaginatively ruled that a journey from China to India, resulting in a certain amount of new geographical and other information, and the publication of *The Desert Road to Turkestan* was "equivalent" to a Ph.D. The council again showed more imagination than can be expected from academic institutions by helping me to prepare for the year in Manchuria. As I had no university education, they made me a preliminary grant to spend the academic year 1928-29 as a graduate student in the Division of Anthropology at Harvard, where I worked principally under the late Alfred M. Tozzer and the late Roland B. Dixon.

While I was at Harvard, Dixon introduced me to Robert Barrett, who also gave me a valuable support to launch me on my new career. The son of a very rich family in Chicago, Barrett studied geology at Harvard, traveled to Norway and wrote a classic paper on the glaciation of the country, but subsequently took a dislike to universities and university life. Since he had money, he could do as he pleased. What pleased him most was unconventional travel. He first traveled in native fashion through the areas of present-day Sudan and Ethiopia. Then he went to Ladakh and became interested in the area that included the Karakoram, the Himalayas, and the Pamirs. Hiring a young Turkish-speaking American who had a degree in geography and a Uighur-speaking Ladakhi-Tibetan, who had traveled with several famous expeditions, such as Sir Francis Younghusband's and others, Barrett made a caravan crossover into

Sinkiang. The Ladakhi and the young American did not get on very well, and as Barrett found that the Ladakhi could speak broken English, he discharged the young American, who hastened back to the States, wrote a book called *The Pulse of Asia* (1907), and so became the famous Professor Elsworth Huntington of Yale.

With the Ladakhi caravan man, Barrett traveled to the Tibetan plateau and from the headwaters of the Yangtze went down the river to Hankow and Shanghai. Before being paid off, the caravan man said: "If I only could write, I could write a better book than any of the sahibs, because I had been with all of them." So Barrett taught him the English alphabet and the rudiments of writing more or less phonetically and presented him with the King James version of the Bible saying: "I'm giving you this to read. Don't believe any of it, but it is written very well. If you model your writing on this, you will write a good book." Long after returning to the United States, where he married, Barrett began to receive from Ladakh, once in every few months, a packet of a long strip of course mulberry paper rolled up like toilet paper. From these rolls his wife digested extracts that were published as an interesting book with the rather obnoxious title *A Servant of Sahib*. Barrett and his wife started to travel again and made a visit to Ladakh and found this old caravan man. They also did a lot of traveling in Patagonia.

It was this extraordinary Mr. Barrett that Dixon arranged for me to meet in a manner that was typically unconventional. Dixon was one of the few academic people Barrett had any use for. Dixon said to me: "Here's a man whom you really ought to meet. I think he will be interested in you, because he traveled in Sinkiang. The trouble is that he and his wife are very shy; and they don't like to meet strangers. But I have a plan. His aunt, the widow of Barrett Wendell (the famous professor of English literature at Harvard), is in Boston, and she is the only person in the world who can give him orders. I am going to arrange for you to be invited to give a lecture to a club in Boston, a typical club of women with jewels on their bosoms. You will give them a talk with lantern slides on Sinkiang. Mr. and Mrs. Barrett will receive a command from Mrs. Wendell, and they will have to attend the lecture." This was the late 1920s, a period when all kinds of young Americans were knocking round the world. They were writing fashionable books, talking about the hardships, fleas, the terrible food, not being able to communicate with the people because of not knowing the language, and that sort of blundering through everything, and all the rest of it. Eleanor and I had not traveled that way. We had had a very good time, and we liked the people, and got on fine. So, I lectured that way.

At the end of the lecture, when people were going out, an enormous man sitting at the back row got up and said in a very deep, resounding voice: "You two young people seem to have enjoyed yourselves." He was not fat but very big-boned and tall, with beard and bald head, and apparently in his sixties. Beside him was a woman dressed in a shawl-like gown. He said: "I would like to talk to you and ask you some questions. Are you too tired?" I said: "No." So we went to their hotel, which was an old-fashioned one with only three or four big rooms. We found that they had taken the whole top floor; they had thrown out all the hotel furniture and fixed up the apartment with their Patagonian camping equipment, living on the floor with camp chairs, etc. It turned out that they had been planning to go to Patagonia again; but Mrs. Barrett's arthritis got bad, and they were in Boston to consult a specialist.

We sat there and talked with them until the small hours of the morning. They sent us home by taxi; and the next day, when I came back from lectures and looked into the letterbox, there was a little note which was written on a page torn out of a notebook. Scrawled on it was: "We think you two young people are doing the right thing; but your caravan looks rather lean. We think you could do with an extra camel or two." And thrown in with this note, without even an envelope, was a check for one thousand dollars, which in 1929 was a very, very handsome sum. We were very grateful for that. It did make a difference when we got back to China.

In Manchuria and Mongolia

As a result of the nine months that my wife and I spent in Manchuria (the Northeast of China) in 1929-30, I became the only American to have traveled widely in Mongolia, Sinkiang, and Manchuria—the frontier zone between China and the Soviet Union, traveling always as an individual and speaking Chinese. It was also as a result of the time spent in the Mongol-inhabited regions of Manchuria that I developed an interest in the national minority political problems of the Mongols. My experience in Manchuria produced *Manchuria, Cradle of Conflict* (1932).

When the book was published, the Barretts wrote to me saying:

"You are becoming just another university footnote-lover." I wrote back a very polite letter, pointing out that there were actually fewer footnotes than there were in *The Desert Road*, which they liked so much, and I added: "I am very, very sorry that you are not pleased with what I am doing, but after all, research has been always a part of my life. Travel was in order to get materials for research, and I have to go on as I am doing now; but I do not like the idea of your being dissatisfied with us. So, please never make us any more gifts of money." They had been giving us money from time to time. After this, we lost all contact with them for many years.

In Manchuria I was shocked to see that while the Chinese could rightly claim that they suffered from foreign imperialism, there was also a second level of Chinese imperialism against the Mongols. The Chinese were encroaching on Mongol-inhabited territory, taking land from them, driving them out—a bit like Europeans in America driving out the Indians. Clearly, the military colonization by the Chinese was not strengthening the Chinese position, but instead was preparing the Mongols to accept (and in some cases to welcome) any Japanese aggression against the Chinese that would put an end to the Chinese aggression against the Mongols. At the same time, the Japanese military were deliberately practicing a policy of treating the Mongols more humanely than the Chinese did. Some of the Mongols, however, were beginning to realize that this meant, especially in northeast Inner Mongolia where the Japanese were already strong, the transformation of the Mongol economy so that the Mongols, instead of being independent owners of their own herds, were in danger of becoming just—to use an American expression—cowboys on ranches owned by the Japanese. Again at this time, because of the Revolution in Northern (Outer) Mongolia in 1921, there was already a very strong echo of Soviet influence. The Mongols were the object of Chinese propaganda, Japanese propaganda, Soviet propaganda, and Northern Mongol propaganda.

This, however, did not immediately lead me to spend a lot of time studying political theories. I was not concerned with who was right theoretically. Questions like: Is capitalism better than socialism? or Is socialism better than communism? did not concern me. My awakening to politics was in a different way. I saw that the people in whose lives the Japanese, Chinese, and new communist commissars of Northern Mongolia were interfering were not interested in what these overlords said in their respective propaganda but in what they did. At that stage, everybody was making promises, but they were doing things only to take power into their hands.

During the time of hasty collectivization in Northern Mongolia (1929-31), many Mongols, including poor herdsmen, were coming into Inner Mongolia. I began to find that quite a number of these refugees, after having been in Inner Mongolia for a while, were saying: "Oh, God! It's worse here than what we ran away from." And many of them were actually doing a reverse emigration, going back to where they had come from. On the other hand, I found that Inner Mongolian intellectuals were saying: "We must not just let the real power pass from Chinese hands into Japanese hands. We must organize an Inner Mongolian nationalism which will aim for independence, or at least autonomy."

The next three years (1930-33), we spent in Peking under a fellowship from the Harvard-Yenching Institute and two successive fellowships from the John Simon Guggenheim Jr. Foundation. It was in these years that the Japanese completely seized Manchuria and extended their encroachment into North China and Inner Mongolia. I began to study Mongol. After spending a winter studying written and spoken Mongol with a Chinese-speaking Mongol tutor, whom I had met through a Mongol nationalist, Merse, a Daghur from Hailar, I told him that I had become aware of the political importance of Inner Mongolia and that in order to understand the Mongol point of view I felt it necessary to learn Mongol. I needed to be able to talk with the common people, to those who were neither feudal nobles nor politicians, to Mongols who had been least affected by the Chinese culture and did not speak Chinese. On his next visit to Peking, Merse found me this good teacher. This was a few months before Merse was killed in a political murder.

In September 1931, a few days after the Mukden Incident, Merse suddenly appeared in Peking, very agitated, very nervous. It was obvious that he was getting in touch with other Inner Mongolian Mongols in Peking, though he would not tell me anything in detail.

They must have been discussing: "What do we do as Mongols? What will the Japanese intervention in Manchuria mean for the Mongols?" When he went back to Hailar, his hometown, he was arrested and shot. Hailar was still in the hands of one of Chang Hsueh-liang's generals who had not immediately surrendered to the Japanese but had kept on fighting for some time. (Chang Hsueh-liang was the son of Chang Tso-lin, the warlord of the Northeast who had been assassinated by the Japanese in June 1928.)

The general was afraid that Merse might bring some Mongols over to the Japanese side. Merse had been the head of a school for training Mongol interpreter-bureaucrats for Chang Hsueh-liang's administration of the eastern part of Inner Mongolia. Just as Indian nationalists flourished among the English-educated Indians, such educated Mongol nationalists were often produced in this kind of school under Chinese rule. The way in which Merse had been conducting his school seems to have invited the suspicion of the Chinese authorities. He had, moreover, a record of having collaborated, for a period, with Japanese policy at the time of the Russian and Mongolian Revolutions.

The next summer, I went up to Inner Mongolia, bought four camels, and traveled about with a Mongol companion who spoke no language but his own. He kept my camels for me when I went back to Peking, so I was able to travel with him again in later years whenever I could get away from Peking. (See *Mongol Journeys*, published in 1941.) My tutor, Bügegeseg, introduced me to Sain Bayar, who was an example of a type of aristocrat-radical that recurs in many periods of history. In the early 1920s, he was a founder of an Inner Mongolian Kuomintang, which got on well with the left wing of Sun Yat-sen's Kuomintang. Later, however, he could make no headway with Chiang Kai-shek, primarily because Chiang never really controlled the northern Chinese warlords whose provinces controlled and exploited the adjoining sectors of Inner Mongolia. He therefore joined the Inner Mongolian autonomy movement of De Wang (Prince Te in Chinese). For lack of Chinese support, this autonomous movement was to be taken over by the Japanese military during the period of their occupation of Inner Mongolia.

It was through Sain Bayar that I first met De Wang on one of his visits to Peking. His full name was Demchukdonggrob. As the ruling prince of the Banner of West Sunit, he was one of the top leaders of the Inner Mongolian autonomous movement. By that time, De Wang had undoubtedly been approached by the Japanese militarists. Certainly when I met him, De Wang had come to Peking for the purpose of trying to persuade the Chinese authorities to take a more intelligent line. I felt very frustrated about Inner Mongolia, because it seemed to me that this was not a question of De Wang being a traitor to China, a collaborater of the Japanese imperialists.

It was Chinese policy that pushed the Mongols into the arms of the Japanese. I thought that the Chinese could not demand that the Mongols be patriotic and support China, unless the Chinese gave the Mongols something to be patriotic about. When I expressed this view to De Wang, he, in a diplomatic and discreet way, encouraged me to pursue this line. There was a young man in De Wang's entourage who was his resident adviser in Peking. Shortly after, he was murdered in a dark alley by a man of the Blue Shirts, a Kuomintang secret service agency.

Nevertheless, it certainly was not entirely the fault of Chiang Kai-shek that De Wang was finally taken over by the Japanese militarists. On the actual frontier of Inner Mongolia, Chinese military power was represented in Jehol by one big Chinese military figure, in Chahar by another, and in Suiyuan by still another. The difficulty that made it impossible for De Wang to negotiate effectively was that each of these sectional political-military bigshots demanded that for his section of Inner Mongolia everything should be passed through him to Chiang Kai-shek in Nanking. What De Wang wanted was the recognition by China of a body representing the whole of Inner Mongolia, which would have a direct channel to Nanking without having to go through the local warlords. This he could not obtain because Chiang Kai-shek was not powerful enough to force a policy on these sectional warlords. Nominally he could give them orders; but he had to think very carefully beforehand: "Is this an order that A, or B, or C will obey?" Even if Chiang Kai-shek had thought that he could help De Wang to organize an Inner Mongolia that Chiang could use as a balancing element against the various local militarists, he was unable to bring this about. As a result, he was never able to negotiate with De Wang in a way that led anywhere.

In the 1930s, De Wang was remarkably frank with me, considering that I was a foreigner. I remember him once saying to me: "I could do business with Chiang Kai-shek, if I could only get to him." All these frontier people made it impossible, of course. De Wang made it clear that if the Japanese insisted on marching in, he could not stop them, not having the strength for armed resistance, since the Chinese would not give him arms. The man with whom he had to deal at that time was Fu Tso-yi, governor of Suiyuan Province, who was not only strongly against Mongol autonomy but also was extremely racist.

Fu Tso-yi was then in Suiyuan City (New City of Huhehot) to deal with De Wang, whose headquarters were in Pailing Miao, a famous temple site to the north of Suiyuan. While I was waiting in Suiyuan for a chance to go to Pailing Miao, my Swedish friend Torgny Öberg, with whom I made several journeys in Inner Mongolia, and who was also a friend of Fu Tso-yi, suggested that I should meet him and said that he thought he could arrange it. Torgny was a small businessman, and Fu was friendly to such people, recognizing that a man like Torg was helpful to the economy of Suiyuan. This was the liberal-progressive side of Fu Tso-yi. The meeting was arranged very discreetly. I did not call on him as governor, but the governor just happened to drop in for a friendly call at the house of his friend Öberg, and I happened to be there.

I very cautiously suggested that if the Chinese were afraid of Japanese penetration of Inner Mongolia, they could not expect the Mongols to resist Japan unless they were given something to fight for; in other words, autonomy, so that the Mongols would feel that they were defending Mongol interests and not just Chinese interests. Upon this, Fu Tso-yi burst out with: "Among the Mongols there are no civilized people like you and me. [He politely included me for the moment.] The Mongols are not human beings. They are *sheng-k'ou* [domestic animals]. If they do their work, you feed them [and he used the word for feeding animals, not human beings]. If they're not docile, you beat them."

It should be added that Fu Tso-yi was one of the most respected of the Chinese generals, and under him oppression of the Chinese peasants was very much lightened, but when it came to the Mongols and taking Mongol lands to give them to Chinese peasants, nobody was more relentless. It is super ironical that later in the civil war after Japan's surrender it was Fu who surrendered Peking to the Chinese Communists. With the civil war going badly in the North, the American military were worried because the Kuomintang side was fatally weakened by corruption, with the generals appropriating the money that should have been used to pay their troops. It was the Americans, and chiefly the military, who decided to force out the corrupt generals and put in command in Peking Fu Tso-yi, who was considered reliable because he was not corrupt and had never changed sides or betrayed a patron in China's endless civil wars. This trustworthy man, nevertheless, in the end surrendered Peking to the Communists, on the justifiable plea of "saving human lives" when further military resistance had become hopeless. The Communists appointed him to a high government position.

There were many other episodes concerning Mongol nationalism. I was invited once to a lunch in Peking given for De Wang by some Chinese university people who were supposed to be liberal and friendly to the Mongols. De Wang, of course, had an excellent old-fashioned Chinese education. He knew the Chinese classics and wrote a nice hand in Chinese, besides being able to speak it. There is a way of seeming to treat a man as an equal, while at the same time being condescending, and that was the way the hosts treated him. One of the Chinese said to him something like: "You stand for a progressive policy in education and enlightenment among the Mongols. Why do you continue to wear your hair in a braid?" This meant the hairstyle which Westerners contemptuously called a "pigtail."

De Wang very politely answered: "I do so many things already that offend the other princes that I do not want to cut off my braid and give them another offense from which I would gain nothing." The Chinese could never understand the difference between the Mongols wearing their hair in a braid and the Chinese, when under Manchu rule, wearing their hair in that style. The Chinese had been forced to do so, as a conquered people, while the Mongols, like the Manchus, had always worn their hair in a braid. Actually, with many Mongols it was an act of pride to keep their traditional hairstyle.

Shortly after the Sino-Japanese Agreement was signed by Ho Ying-ch'in and General Umezu Yoshijirō on 10 June 1935, calling for Chinese demilitarization of North China, the Peking corre-

spondent of *The Times* of London came to me and said: "I have
found that there are some Mongols in Japanese service in Peking,
on a temporary mission of some kind. I have arranged an interview
with them. Will you come with me as interpreter?" So we went to
see them. *The Times* correspondent spoke very poor Chinese, but he
could understand quite a bit. We talked with them in Chinese and
got exactly the standard answers you would expect in such a situation, namely that the Japanese were true friends of the Mongols
and so on.

After the questions which an ordinary newspaper correspondent
would ask, I spoke to the Mongols in Mongol. They were astonished and asked: "How do you know Mongol?" I said: "I was a
friend of Merse. I have traveled in Inner Mongolia and I wanted to
learn more about Mongolia. So Merse helped me to get started in
the Mongol language." Then the senior of these Mongols in Japanese uniform said to me: "If you speak Mongol, and if you were a
friend of Merse, then we speak to you not as a foreigner but as a fellow Mongol. You must know this: Do not look at our uniforms.
When the day comes, we will act as Mongols and not as paid soldiers of the Japanese." A remarkable statement to be made in 1935.

I refer those readers who are interested in the details of Inner
Mongolian nationalism to the Introduction to *The Diluv Khutagt,
Memoirs and Autobiography of a Mongol Buddhist Reincarnation in Religion and Revolution* (1982), which I translated with Fujiko Isono. The
Diluv Khutagt (Dilowa Hutukutu, in the Chinese transcription,
which has passed into international usage) whom I met, as in the
case of De Wang through Sain Bayar, became a lifelong friend.

Chapter Two

■

FACTS, NOT THEORIES

The Institute of Pacific Relations

My earliest connection with the Institute of Pacific Relations was in 1933, when I went to their international conference held at Banff in Canada. Just at that time I had finished my series of foundation grants and was going back to the United States, wondering what kind of job I might find. Somebody heard that I was returning, and I got an invitation to attend the conference. To give some idea of the atmosphere through which I was feeling my way during these first days of contact with the IPR, I quote the following from the notes which I wrote each evening:

> Very stiff at first. Both Japanese and Chinese wary and unwilling to be the first to come out in the open. . . . A crude man, American but attached to the Philippine delegation, made a clumsily bluff suggestion that none of us was going to say anything of value anyhow except about the Sino-Japanese antagonism, so why not set about it right away and "settle" it! He got no response. As a matter of fact I think the Japanese delegation is going to be hard to budge. They don't want to spar with the Chinese or anybody: they fall into a clinch right away and hang on, smothering everything they can.

While the conference was going on, the editor of *Pacific Affairs*, the quarterly of the IPR, resigned, and there was a question of appointing a new editor. A committee was set up; and H.G.W. Woodhead, editor of the *Peking and Tientsin Times*, with whom I had

33

worked in the early 1920s, put up my name. Woodhead was attending the conference as a British delegate. Many of the British at that time were feeling a little uncomfortable about the IPR; they thought it was too anti-colonial. A very conservative man, Woodhead was suspicious of Japanese ambitions in Manchuria and elsewhere in China, which he felt were a threat to British commercial interests, but he was also deeply anti-communist. He thought that the IPR was too goody-goody, trying to please everybody, and that a reasonably conservative and well-informed person like me would make a good editor of *Pacific Affairs*. At that time he knew me chiefly from my attitude toward Manchuria and Inner Mongolia. He considered that this was a good conservative attitude and thought it would do more to restrain Japan than would the romantic type of American anti-colonialism. He also knew that through the Royal Geographical Society and the Royal Central Asian Society I had a good standing in Britain.

I accepted the appointment on condition that I could edit *Pacific Affairs* from Peking by correspondence. For the winter of 1933–34, however, Eleanor and I moved to New York to work at the American headquarters of the IPR to learn something of the organization and what was required for the editorship. In late 1934, we returned to Peking and stayed there, as it turned out, until 1937.

Many people thought, and still think, that the IPR was an American organization. It is true that it first started in Hawaii and originally had a strong Y.M.C.A. background. Wealthy philanthropists in Hawaii did not want the good relations between the Japanese and Chinese that existed in Hawaii to become worse as the result of the tensions growing between their ancestral countries. Hawaii, they reasoned, was the one place where a large Japanese population and a large Chinese population got on together perfectly well. If, therefore, a conference could be held about the problems of the Far East, participated in by Japanese-American and Chinese-American delegates who were able to talk reasonably, perhaps some constructive ideas might be reflected back to their ancestral countries, because they had an American outlook as well as a Japanese or Chinese outlook. I think that was the basis of the first conference. Then there was another conference to which Japanese from Japan and Chinese from China were invited.

The organizers went on to invite people from other countries:

British, French, Dutch, and so on; and after two or three congresses, it became an international organization with an international coordination center, namely, the Pacific Council. Each country had its own council; but as most of the money came from the United States, the secretary-general was always American, though he was elected by the Pacific Council.

Though the IPR was supposed to be a place to express private, individual opinions and to be independent of governmental directives, one could frequently detect the shadow of an establishment hovering over people's shoulders. In Britian, the Royal Institute of International Affairs, known as Chatham House from the name of the building where it had its office, appointed within itself a sort of committee which became the British Council of the IPR. I think there were similar arrangements in France and Holland. I do not remember exactly what the status of each IPR council was in China and in Japan. From the beginning, the American Council was independent of any official connections.

As soon as the thing started, Edward C. Carter came on board. A long time Y.M.C.A. representative in India, he had learned there the knack of being on good terms with both the British Raj and the Indian nationalists. He had a belief, indeed a faith, that if you could only gather together the spokesmen of warring ideas with their knees under the same table, a way out could be reached by consensus. In 1926, Carter became the secretary-general of the IPR, the main driving force of the organization.

The chief goal of the IPR was to try to find points of agreement between the various powers in the Pacific. At that point, however, in the mid 1930s, the possible points of agreement were not as many as the points on which nations were quarreling. From the beginning of my editorship, I tried to learn as much as I could about the areas and subjects of controversy. There were questions not only of Japanese expansion, but of the Tripartite (Britain, the United States, and Japan) Naval Agreement on parity, as decided at the Washington Conference of 1921. Questions of the imperial colonial countries like Britain, France, and Holland, and many other problems were also involved, and of course there were the growing importance of the Soviet Union in Eastern Siberia and the much-disputed questions of the connection between the Soviet Union and the Chinese Communists.

In these circumstances, one of my guiding principles as editor was: When there was a controversial question on which I was not well informed and would like to learn something, I would make inquiries to find out who did know about that question and then ask him or her to write an article; or when I came across the name of somebody who had written something interesting, I would write to him directly, asking him to contribute an article. Copies of such articles were circulated in advance to the various national councils to give time for the preparation of rebuttals. Then if there were protests, I would publish the criticisms.

Because of my attempts to find controversial material for *Pacific Affairs*, the question of my editing of the journal came up from time to time. I think it was at the 1936 Yosemite Conference that the Dutch first raised objections to the way in which I edited the journal. There were also quite strong criticisms from some of the British delegates. To the committee which considered the complaints, I replied that this was a controversial period, and we had to face these controversies. As long as I was the editor, I should certainly go on publishing controversial articles and replies to them in which people could criticize each other toughly. If they thought I was too controversial, they had my resignation there and then. Carter was always my strong backer; and he also discreetly lobbied for me among the national delegates, and I stayed on with a renewed mandate.

Carter, as secretary-general of the International Council, wanted to draw the Soviet Union into the general international group of the IPR. In 1936 he arranged to visit Moscow to have consultations with the Soviet Far Eastern experts, and he invited me, then in Peking, to join him in Moscow. There may have been preliminary steps in which the Soviet people set up a research unit of their own, which was called Tikhii Okeanskii Kabinet, or something like that. Then in 1936, when I was there with Carter, the negotiations sought to arrange for this already existing Soviet research unit to effect a liaison with the International IPR. The Soviets objected that our institute took no clear stand against Japanese imperialism, and they could not join such an institute. Carter's reply was that we provided a forum for international discussion, in which we took up the trouble between Japan and China with both Chinese and Japanese taking part. All this is amusing in view of the fact that later, at the

McCarran Committee Hearings, it was charged that the IPR had been infiltrated and taken over by the Russians and Communists in general. The truth was comically and exactly the opposite. Here was Carter working away trying to infiltrate the Soviets.

The result of Carter's visit was that the Soviets sent a delegation to the IPR Conference held in that year in Yosemite, California, and published for a year or two a journal called *Tikhii Okean* (Pacific Ocean). Among the Soviet delegation at Yosemite there was a young man named Konstantin Umanskii. I do not know what his job was at that time; but one of the organizers of the Soviet Council, whom I had met in Moscow, said to me: "There is a rising young man. Keep your eye on him." In two or three years, this young man was the Soviet ambassador to the United States. Within the Soviet system, people pop around from diplomatic jobs to journalistic jobs and to academic jobs and so on even more than we do. This was the only IPR Conference which the Soviet delegation attended. Very soon after, the Soviet IPR simply faded out of the scene.

In editing *Pacific Affairs*, I tried to get spokesmen from all the countries that were members of the IPR to contribute. My greatest difficulties were to get articles from the Soviets and the Japanese. The Soviets objected to every mention of Soviet policy. You could not say that their policies had strong points here but weak points there. They were objecting to my publishing articles which were not 100 percent pro-Soviet, and they threatened to withdraw from the IPR. Once I even published an article by an American Trotskyist, Harold Isaacs (September 1935), for which the Soviets gave me the rough side of their tongue.

It is amusing that the Japanese behaved exactly in the same way as the Soviets. I remember having received a very good article from Matsukata Saburō on the history of capitalism in Japan. Nevertheless, when, for example, I would send an advance copy of an article on Japan written by somebody to the Japan office of the IPR, inviting criticisms and comments, they would come back with: "The article is absolutely unsuitable, ill-informed, etc." Upon this, I wrote: "Please put your objections in the form of a reply to be printed in the same number; or if you want to do it at a greater length, do a longer article which I will print in the next number." No, no, no, they would not do it. I would get an answer: "We do not have anybody available for the moment," and so on.

From the Japanese IPR members, those I remember are Matsu-kata Saburō, Matsumoto Shigeharu, and Uramatsu Samitarō. They were nicknamed by the IPR people as the "Three Musketeers." Matsukata had already been interested in journalism. At the Yosemite Conference, there was nothing like debate in strong words between the Japanese representatives and those of any other country. They would not get up in a conference of mixed nation-alities and make a speech criticizing their own country. My general impression was that the Japanese delegation wanted to keep out of difficult debates, maintaining a low profile, so to speak, though they might in private conversation say: "I have some doubt about the present Japanese policy," and so on. Even from Matsukata and Matsumoto, to whom I wrote personally, asking them to contribute to *Pacific Affairs*, I would get a personal reply saying: "In view of the other work I am doing at the present time...." Again evasive.

I knew that Matsukata, like Ch'en Han-seng (Ch'en Han-sheng) and Chi Ch'ao-ting from China, was well informed about Marxist theory and that he considered Marxism one of the important intel-lectual factors in the contemporary world. My impression was that the Japanese delegates to an international IPR conference would have the feeling: "As liberal Japanese intellectuals ourselves, we have a certain limited influence in Japan. If we express our opinions too openly in an international environment, that would diminish whatever influence we still have inside Japan, instead of increasing it."

I am sure that the Chinese and Japanese delegates had some direct contact with each other; but I never sat down with a small group of Chinese, Japanese, and American members to exchange private opinions. It was all off stage where you would be talking today with a Chinese and tomorrow with a Japanese. The principal Chinese spokesman would go only so far, and the principal Japa-nese only so far. At least in public discussions, they avoided contro-versy too much, all of them. This was something comparatively difficult for Americans to understand. My personal reaction was: "We are living in a very controversial period, and unless these con-troversies are pulled out into the open where everybody can see them and discuss them, you won't get anywhere."

My closest friends among the Chinese members were Ch'en Han-seng and Chi Ch'ao-ting. Ch'en Han-seng was a member of the secretariat of the Chinese IPR group: I met him first in 1933, at the IPR Conference in Banff. We immediately found each other mutually sympathetic. He was a most interesting and intelligent man. While still very young, he had studied, or at least traveled, in France and Germany, and used all kinds of languages in his research. He had never told me, but I heard many years later, only recently in England, that his Russian was so good that he could act as a simultaneous translator. I have just read in a book written by Wang Fan-hsi, a Chinese Trotskyist, and translated into English as *Chinese Revolutionary* (1980), that Ch'en Han-seng was also in Moscow while he was there in the late 1920s.

Ch'en, as well as Chi Ch'ao-ting, thought that the agrarian problems of China had an importance that had not been properly recognized. Ch'en conducted a rural survey, not for the IPR, but for an institute of economic research at Nankai University in Tientsin, which had a number of distinguished people in it. One of the things Ch'en had investigated was the growth of tobacco production in Shantung Province, which had the result of shifting peasants from paying rent with a percentage of their harvest to having a commodity to sell, which removed them from the old Chinese production basis to a new money economy.

Chi Ch'ao-ting was another interesting man. I knew that he was influenced by Marxism; but I had no reason to believe that he was a member of the Chinese Communist Party. After the war, I have been told that in fact he was a member. I did not know at that time that members of the Chinese Communist Party going to the United States were told not to become too closely involved with American Communists, because the American Party was regarded by the Chinese as too leaky. People were always joining and leaving so that you were not safe in associating with them. But I will tell more about Chi later, because, though I met him at a number of IPR conferences, it was only in Chungking in 1941 and 1942 that I came to have more personal contact with him.

Both Ch'en and Chi were among those Chinese who thought that the Kuomintang ought to take a much more combative line in resisting the growing Japanese aggression; and they were both in favor of the United Front between the Kuomintang and the Chinese Communist Party. But we talked more on general questions than on current issues. I was not posing as an expert on international situations, and my relation with them was much more one of my asking questions in order to acquire information and educate myself than of putting myself in a position of debating with them.

Carter stayed almost to the end as the secretary-general, until he was succeeded by William L. Holland for the last few years of the IPR. Carter was regarded as naive, in an innocent sort of way, and on the other hand as a skillful lobbyist for progressive ideas. Holland was a New Zealander who was by then an American citizen. He had studied in England under Richard H. Tawney, the economist and sociologist who wrote *Religion and the Rise of Capitalism* (1926), and had accompanied Tawney on his visit to China. From there he entered the secretariat of the IPR and was originally more or less in charge of their economic research. After I went to China in 1941 to work for Chiang Kai-shek and had to resign as editor of *Pacific Affairs*, he succeeded me. I should describe him in general as a social democrat.

As for F.V. Field, his full name Frederic Vanderbilt came from the famous Vanderbilt millionaire family on his mother's side. In the 1930s, when it was fashionable to talk about millionaire Bolsheviks, he was the richest example of the Parlor Pink. In his autobiography, *From Right to Left* (1983), he describes himself as a communist and tells how he became one. In fact, I was not at all concerned about whether someone was a communist or any other thing. I was only interested in what he or she said or did. My own opinion, when I knew him, was that he was a radical but independent man. I knew, for example, that he was friendly with Earl Browder, who was at that time the head of the American Communist Party. I do not think, however, that he took orders or directives from Browder. Fortified by his wealth, he could say: "I can go as far as I like. I can also stop as I like."

I have been told, though I have to check, that at Harvard he was a student of Professor Joseph A. Schumpeter, who was a very conservative anti-Marxist; but unlike many anti-Marxists, he knew his Marx very well and actually quoted Marx in his attacks on Marxism. He made Marx and Marxism so interesting that some of his students became more Marxist than anti-Marxist. As for my personal feelings about Holland and Field, I liked them both and got on well with them both. They were people with whom you could discuss real problems in real language, instead of just exchanging jargon.

Some people have asked me about my relations with *Amerasia*. The *Amerasia* people, it is true, were more left wing because while the IPR was an international organization, *Amerasia* was purely American. They could be freer to express American views, and they were very anti-colonial. As far as I know, however, this group was not founded by dissatisfied members of the IPR. I do not remember any case of somebody saying: "I am fed up with the IPR. I am going to resign and join the *Amerasia* group."

People in the New York secretariat of the IPR were very good friends with people writing for *Amerasia*. I allowed my name to be put on its editorial board in order to show that as editor of *Pacific Affairs*, an international magazine, I was not jealous of a new publication which dealt primarily with the United States and Asia. On the contrary, I thought this was a time when the wider the discussion and the more people involved, the better. Though I wrote one or two articles for *Amerasia* and was on its editorial board, I did not actually take part in its editing, and I do not think I was ever in their office. Later there was the famous business of the F.B.I. raiding the *Amerasia* office.

I know that there was a division of opinion within the U.S. IPR about *Amerasia*, because Carter was the kind of man who wanted to be the spider at the center of the web of all U.S.-Asia relations. Nevertheless, I do not remember that Carter said anything stronger than: "Do you think it is wise for you, as the editor of *Pacific Affairs*, to be also on the editorial board of *Amerasia*?" My answer was: "This is a widening of the field and not the beginning of a destructive rivalry." In any case, Carter's objection, if there was one, was not serious enough to remember, or I would have remembered it.

The driving force in the *Amerasia* group was a man named Philip Jaffe. I do not remember whether he belonged to the IPR or not. A son of an American Jewish family of fairly recent immigrant origin, he had become rich by founding and running his own company selling greeting cards. Having taken an interest in international affairs and also in the history of radicalism in the United States, he knew about many subdivisions among the Marxists in the United States and had a great comparative knowledge of the extent to which these American splinter groups were of American origin and how many had been transplanted from European radical movements. He set up an organization for Latin-American studies, and also one for African studies. It was only later on, in 1937, when he asked me

to accompany him to Yenan that I had any real connection with
him.

Peking People

In the first half of the 1930s when I was studying Mongol and
traveling repeatedly in Inner Mongolia, I had practically no contact
with the Peking University Chinese intelligentsia, either the profes-
sors or the students, and relatively few friends among the foreigners teaching at the Chinese universities. I was interested in the back
country and traveling in the interior meeting people who were not
in political power but were trying to get rich or trying to stop being
poor by playing through the cracks of power structure and all the
rest of it. I was interested much more in China as China than in
individual politicians. Moreover, by then I was regarded as that
man who was the friend of the Mongols; and the Kuomintang
people did not like my support for Inner Mongolian nationalism.
Those foreigners who had Chinese friends of this kind just stopped
coming round; but most of them did not know anything about
Mongolia.

On the other hand, I knew practically all the foreign correspondents in Peking. These were the men I usually met in the bar of the
club and asked what was going on. I had been prepared, during my
business years, for digesting all they were talking about, because in
working with merchants I had learned that under various combina-
tions of circumstances, people who theoretically ought to be totally
opposed to each other might in fact cooperate with each other, and
in other circumstances, people who theoretically ought to be natural allies might actually become rivals. The debates among the Chinese intelligentsia, especially Peking university professors and
students, were forming a new kind of Chinese public opinion; but
this I was badly prepared to understand.

I had not, for example, fully understood the significance of some
of the earlier events at the time that they occurred. I had not
returned to China until several months after the May Fourth
Movement of 1919. At the time of the May 30th Incident of 1925
in Shanghai, I was visiting Peking. An ironical thing about that
incident was that though it first started with a labor quarrel in Japa-

nese-owned factories, the workers and their supporters then spread into the International Settlement in Shanghai, and the police fired on them. The policemen are frequently referred to as if they were British police, but they were mainly Sikhs and Chinese serving under British officers. The Chinese at that time regarded the British as the principal imperialists, and most of the anger over this shooting was therefore directed against the British. During my visit to Peking I found that instead of demonstrating imperialist unity against the revolutionary students, many Americans were putting little American flags on their rickshaws as if to say "I am not British."

The *Peking and Tientsin Times*, for which I was no longer working, was taking the attitude that the demonstrators were "ignorant workers, organized by immature students who thought they were revolutionaries." My own reaction to this was: "That is what one would expect the British to say." I thought it was natural for young Chinese intellectuals to be furiously indignant about this shooting; nevertheless, from my boyhood in China and from my years of business experience, my underlying attitude, I suppose, was that they were not politically competent but were rushing around shouting about things they did not understand. On 18 March 1926, when there was a large demonstration and police shooting in Peking, I had just left for Kueihua to start on my long journey on the desert road to Turkestan; and again, when Chiang Kai-shek cracked down on the Communists in Shanghai in April 1927, I was far, far away in Sinkiang.

Traveling in Inner Mongolia, I was not dealing with the students' protest against this or that. There were hardly any students in Inner Mongolia, and the kinds of reality I was dealing with were the military factor, like the power of the warlords, and the economic factor, like the Chinese policy of taking Mongol land and creating on this appropriated land new rich landlords who invariably affiliated themselves with the nearest powerful warlord and exploited Chinese peasants who had taken up the land, not really as pioneers but as refugees. These things could be seen as realities; that was what preoccupied my mind, not book theories.

In Peking, Eleanor and I had remarkably little contact with Western Sinologues or professional Sinophiles. There were a lot of younger people, mostly Americans, who were attached to various universities. They were filled with enthusiasm for the student movements in China and were, of course, in close touch with Chinese students. I was not avoiding them, but I just had too much else to do. I was concentrating in the first years on studying Mongol and learning about Mongolia. I also had a private teacher for Chinese, with whom I was reading the official Chinese sources on the history of the Northeast. Moreover, I was working on the first draft of what was eventually to be *Inner Asian Frontiers of China*, published in 1940.

Various young American scholars arriving in Peking would already have read something of what I had published and would come to look me up. I was always glad to see them, but very soon I discovered that I did not have the kind of sources, or the kind of guidance, for which they were looking. John Fairbank, for example, had become interested in the history of the Chinese foreign treaties and the customs and that kind of thing. About this I knew absolutely nothing. In his memoirs, *Chinabound* (1982), he himself writes that he knew Chinese scholars and intellectuals, but did not know anything about the peasants, the real people. And *that* was all I *did* know. These Sinologues had been equipped with something which was entirely different from my background.

Judging from my later career, people may think that I was one of the "progressive" Americans in China; but I was, in fact, well apart from them. I was, so to speak, apolitical except for the politics between the Chinese and the Mongols. In Chinese things, I was decidedly conservative, still sharing in large part the attitude of the Treaty Port foreigners, especially the British. It seems that John S. Service, in his memoirs ("Some Personal Reminiscences," *China Quarterly*, January-March 1972), mentions me as a regular member of a group of foreign intellectuals living in Peking; but I was never a member nor did I attend their meetings as far as I can remember, though I may have dropped in once or twice. It was not because I was against their views or the way they conducted their meetings. I was just too preoccupied with the Mongols, while at the same time editing *Pacific Affairs* as a part-time job. Eleanor and I met John Carter Vincent in the early years of our marriage and became friends in a social way. At that time he was a secretary in the U.S. Legation. I never had any special contact with him until I met him again in

Chungking, where he was the first secretary in the U.S. Embassy.

Edgar Snow came later. Eleanor and I liked him very much. I do not think Snow belonged to the IPR. Later he helped me to arrange a trip to Yenan; but it was in his last years, when he was living in Switzerland with his second wife, that I came to know him well. The longer I knew him, and the better I knew him, the more respect I had for Ed Snow.

Snow was living in Peking, but Anna Louise Strong and Agnes Smedley operated mainly from the International Settlement in Shanghai. I do not think I ever met Strong in Peking. Eleanor had known Anna Louise at the end of the First World War in Seattle, where she was a social worker and Eleanor was also working as a counselor in a girls' camp (to keep them away from soldiers in the training camps). Anna Louise's father was a Protestant clergyman. As a pacifist, he announced, after the United States got into the war, that if he were conscripted, he would refuse to fight. In any case, he would never have been conscripted, for he was already more than sixty years old; but in the wartime mood in the United States, even this was considered scandalous and Anna Louise lost her job.

At this point, the Russian Revolution had broken out and Hearst, the owner of the Hearst newspapers, was interested in the revolution, which was still in the Kerensky stage. Hearst was of Irish origin and was very anti-British in an Irish way. This made him also anti-monarchist. He therefore rejoiced in the fall of the Tsar and picked up Strong and sent her to the new revolutionary Russia as a correspondent. This is rather ironical, considering how Hearst later became one of the loudest-voiced opponents of Bolshevik Russia. In Russia, Strong became more and more radicalized. She soon lost her Hearst job, and in the early 1920s, in the period of the first United Front, she came to China. Eleanor was then waiting in Peking for a message from me to come round by Siberia to join me in Sinkiang. Having been acquainted years before, they became quite good friends.

Agnes Smedley I met first on the Canadian Pacific steamer in which Eleanor and I came back from the United States to China in October 1934. She was fascinated by our baby boy, David, and made friends with him. In this way we became friends with Agnes through David, and she visited us once in Peking. She was a typical

Western American radical. I said to her at the time: "You are against the government, against those who are governing. Now you and your friends are for those Chinese who are against the present government. If they ever come to govern China, you will be against them too." In fact, however, she later followed every twist and turn of the Chinese Revolution until her death in 1951.

Occasionally I met visiting scholars like Paul Pelliot. Unlike many "experts" who depended essentially on Chinese materials translated for them by Chinese who knew a foreign language, he really worked his own material and knew it well. There was another man, Herrlee Glessner Creel, who was interested in Chinese archaeology and early history. At a relatively young age, he published an excellent book called *The Birth of China* (1936). His interest touched mine in the field of archaeology and early Chinese origins; from studying the Chinese frontiers I was turning my attention to the question of why the Chinese and the frontier peoples were so different from each other and what were their respective origins.

Another archaeologist, an American and a very good friend of mine in Peking, was Carl Whiting Bishop. He knew a little Chinese and worked closely with Chinese archaeologists. Through them he became familiar with the progress of the famous pioneering work in Anyang on the Shang Dynasty. The fashionable attitude among the European and American professional sinologues was to claim, or sometimes to pretend, that they were so good in written classical Chinese that they did all their work by themselves. As a matter of fact, most of them depended on Chinese who knew English or French to do the main work of gathering materials for them, which they just polished up. Bishop was the first one I knew who mentioned by name the Chinese who had supplied him with his source materials, and he made it clear where he adopted their opinions and where he used their materials but formed his own opinions.

I was very much influenced by Bishop's work and theories. He was primarily a field archaeologist rather than a social theorist working from other people's findings. He worked in the way in which I myself was trying to work: observe the facts and see if from these facts you can derive a theory. I showed Bishop the typescript of my first draft of *Inner Asian Frontiers of China*, and when I would enter into speculation, trying to identify this or that primitive tribe in the earliest Chinese references, Bishop would send my draft back, saying: "This is complete nonsense and must be thoroughly rewritten." Later he became the curator of one of the art galleries of the Smithsonian Institution in Washington.

It was in this period in 1935 that a man named Karl Wittfogel turned up in China. By the way, though John Fairbank writes that I had helped Wittfogel to come to the United States, the fact was that he had already emigrated to the United States. Wittfogel had shown so much interest in my work that I was letting him read the draft. He would come to me and say: "Now, on this point, could you add the following quotation from me?" I did refer very favorably to Wittfogel in my Introduction to *Inner Asian Frontiers of China*, thinking that this might help him to get established in the United States. It was over Wittfogel that I had my only real quarrel with my wife. Eleanor was always a much better judge of people than I was. She said: "Look, be careful! This man is flattering you in order to get started in the United States. He is the kind of man who is always either licking your boots or jumping on you with his own boots. He could turn against you at any time." But I refused to listen to her.

I can say that of all the Marxists I have known, Harold Isaacs, a Trotskyist, was the only one who made a serious effort to convert me to his particular form of Marxism, though I knew him only slightly. After the break between Chiang Kai-shek and the Communists in 1927, there was a split within the Chinese Communist Party between Trotskyists and Stalinists. In the early 1930s, there was a peculiar situation. While Chiang, for example, was hunting down the Communists of every kind, the foreign Marxists, protected by the laws of extraterritoriality, could live quite freely in a place like Peking and talk all they liked and with whom they liked. Anyway, Isaacs tried to convert me to Trotskyism, and when he found that I did not convert, he became disgusted. I was not interested in the niceties of these theoretical controversies. It is true that I published the Trotskyist article by Isaacs in *Pacific Affairs*, in spite of furious Soviet opposition, but it was because I thought he had something to say.

At the IPR Conference in Canada in 1933, I ran into several people who were debating in Marxist terms. While I had absolutely no grounding in the classics of Marxism, I could see that a great deal of what these IPR people were saying about current international affairs corresponded with a class analysis of what was going on in Inner Mongolia. When I went back to China as editor of *Pacific Affairs*, however, I was too busy and could not spare the time to settle down and become a student of Marxism, though in a time of controversy like that I gave space in *Pacific Affairs* to people who were Marxists or Marxist-influenced contributors as well as to other people.

Like many other foreigners living in Peking at that time, I became increasingly depressed. I thought that the few Chinese intellectuals whom we knew in Peking seemed to be quite ineffective. All that they could think of was: "Why can't Americans do something to stop this?" or "Why can't the British?" and so on. They had no confidence in themselves. As for the military and political people, those whom Chiang Kai-shek had in Peking acting for him, they gave first priority to crushing the Chinese Communists, believing that only then could they resist the Japanese. The reaction of many foreigners, including ourselves, was: "Why can't the Kuomintang and the Communists bury their differences and join together to defend their country? Once they have a country of their own, they can settle their own political differences; but why fight a civil war when your country is being invaded?"

Of course, not everybody saw it that way. I remember that about this time, John Foster Dulles appeared in Peking. He was touring all over Asia on behalf of some kind of council of American Missionary Societies. I met him at a lunch at the U.S. embassy. He was quite firm in his opinion that certainly it was ridiculous for the Chinese to resist the Japanese invasion until they had settled the Communist question in China. Only then could they turn to other business. Dulles's opinion and Chiang Kai-shek's opinion at that time were quite the same.

I had practically no contact with the Japanese. I was frankly very anti-Japanese in a general way. In Japan itself, when I met people like Matsumoto and Matsukata, I knew I was talking to reasonable people, and I could talk with a certain freedom; but my feeling in Peking was that I did not know who was who, and I might be talking to an agent provocateur. I suppose the most important Japanese I met in the 1930s was General Dohihara Kenji. He held a sort of informal press conference; and I went along with one of my newspaper friends. Military propaganda at that time presented him as a kind of Japanese Lawrence of Arabia, a man who could melt into the Chinese mass and so forth. This one press conference made it clear to me that he could never pass as a Chinese.

An Awakening of Political Consciousness

As I paid little attention to Chinese internal politics, I did not have any connection with important political people. Except for Chang Tso-lin, whom I met as an interpreter, and Fu Tso-yi in Suiyuan, the only Chinese high political figure I met was Chang Hsueh-liang. I met him through his Australian adviser, William H. Donald, on the latter's suggestion. Donald knew that I had been in Sinkiang, a frontier where the Soviets were in the background. He thought that Chang Hsueh-liang, then the most important figure in the Northeast, would be interested in meeting me and asking me questions about Sinkiang. I had one meeting with him in Mukden (present Shenyang). It was a very pleasant talk. I soon saw that he had a general idea of Japanese and Soviet problems, but had no comprehension whatever of the political nature or the political importance of the non-Chinese ethnic peoples of the frontiers. He did not know and he did not understand anything about the Mongols or Uighurs or other non-Chinese peoples. At that time the term "Uighur" had not yet come into fashion, and Western travelers called the Uighurs (who in fact are largely of Indo-European descent) Turki. When this name came into the conversation, Chang Hsueh-liang assumed that they were "Turks."

There are some comical anecdotes which show how ignorant I was about the political world in general. I have already mentioned that in 1936 I visited Moscow with Carter. The Soviets knew about me as a man who had written many articles about China, Japan, Inner Mongolia, and other areas. They therefore assumed that I also knew their people, but actually I did not know how important the people to whom I was talking were. During this visit to Moscow, I was asked to give a semi-official public lecture. A good deal of what I said was contrary to Soviet doctrine of the time. I was very critical of the Chinese policy in various frontier regions of Inner Mongolia, whereas the Soviets avoided saying anything against it, not wanting to stir up Chinese political trouble. They had criticized a lot of the stuff I had published on Inner Mongolia, saying that I was supporting bourgeois nationalism, which was not really good for the Mongolian people. While talking, I noticed that there was a man at the back of the hall who, every once in a while when he could see an opening, would get into the aisle and come down to a seat nearer to me. By the end of the lecture, he was sitting right in front of me.

Afterward I asked: "Who was that man who kept pushing down to the front?" They looked at me, surprised, and said: "Borodin, of course!" They assumed that I knew Michael Borodin, a very important person in the history of the Chinese revolutionary movement. They must have thought: "Here is this man Lattimore. He was living in China all the time Borodin was there. If he hadn't met him, he would at least know his face from photographs or something." I had certainly read the name Borodin in newspapers and knew that he was the man who finally left Hankow after the Kuomintang-Communist split and returned to the Soviet Union. He had returned through Mongolia, and Anna Louise Strong traveled in his company. That much I knew; but what they were assuming was that I also knew where Borodin belonged in the complicated maneuvers among the Canton group, the Hankow group, the Shanghai group, and other factions, of which I actually knew absolutely nothing. I learned later that Borodin was then, it seems, already under a cloud, being partly blamed for the failure of the United Front to hold together after Chiang Kai-shek's attack on the Communists in 1927.

Again, I did not know that the man who was conducting a discussion at one of our meetings was Gregory Voitinskii, and all I knew was that I had heard, and read in the papers, that he was a Soviet agent who had worked with the Chinese Communists. There is something ludicrous about my qualification at that time. The Soviet experts, especially the Russians, were assuming that I was an American intelligence agent of some kind. They therefore found it difficult to understand that I had to have various political personages—like Voitinskii—explained to me.

Once we were at an opera together. In Russia in the entr'acte you come out and walk in the foyer in a circle, round and round, having a smoke before you go in for the next act. I was walking with Voitinskii. He was correcting me on everything I said on China. So I said to him with a perfectly straight face: "It must be wonderful to be a Marxist, a Communist, because you have this Marxist, scientific approach to politics and history. And that is why you are always right." He did not see that I was teasing him. His answer was: "Yes, if you are a Marxist you can always be right. But," he added, "difficulties remain. Sometimes it is a question of *when* to be right." I always remember this remark when I think of those poor Russians who were right at the wrong time and were liquidated by Stalin, to be rehabilitated later on (even if, all too often, posthumously).

At one of the meetings there was a man named Sergei Stepanovich Borisov. He was introduced merely as one of their Mongolian experts, but I had never heard the name before. They again took it for granted that Lattimore, a specialist on Mongolia, must know all about Borisov and that there was no need to explain who he was. It was years before I found out that Borisov was the first official Comintern representative sent to Outer Mongolia in 1920. Thus I missed a marvelous opportunity to talk with a man from whom I could have learned a great deal. One thing I did learn at that time was that Borisov was a Russian whose mother was an Altaika (a woman of a tribe living in the Altai, a range that begins in Siberia and runs on into Western Mongolia. Their language is a variable of Turkish, not Mongol). But we did not talk about Mongolia at all. The importance of being able to have a serious talk with a man like that is that later on I might have remembered: "Yes, it was important that Borisov said this and that in 1936, but never mentioned certain other things."

By this time, I was already convinced that if I wanted to understand the general picture of the frontier regions, it was absolutely necessary to have the Russian language. So I arranged with the Institute of Pacific Relations that in the winter of 1936–37 I should spend several months in London, working intensively to study Russian with a private tutor, and then go back to China. After the IPR Conference in Yosemite, I went straight to London with my family. While in London I became aware of what the Spanish Civil War meant. That war was coming to a crisis with the increasing importance of Mussolini and Hitler in European politics.

In China I had a rather cynical, disbelieving attitude toward politics. There was nothing in Chinese politics to engage my interest. I might have become political if I had been an undergraduate either in England or in the United States, but such politicizing influences did not exist in the European community in the North China in which I was living as a man in my twenties. I just took for granted the semi-colonial system in China. In the early 1930s when I was traveling in Manchuria and Inner Mongolia, I was always an onlooker and also overheard what the Mongols were talking about among themselves. What they were saying led me to think not in terms of who was being *democratic*, but simply: "Here the Soviets have power, here the Japanese have power, here the Chinese have power. How well are they treating the people who are not Russians, not Japanese, not Chinese?" I did not think: "Are they treating them *democratically*?" That is to say, my question was: "Are they treating them in a way that makes them want to rebel? Or are they treating them in a way that makes them accept a new form of rule?"

At that time I had not lived in the Western culture except for my school years in Switzerland and England, and there had been no occasion for me to think about these things theoretically. I had gone only so far as to see the difference between a government which had been elected by votes and a government which was being imposed with the bayonet. With the situation in China, I did not think that in these respects the Chinese were *less democratic*, but that they were *less modern*. I thought in terms of development. The Spanish Civil War politicized me in a way quite different from any political interest in the internal affairs of China and Mongolia. What particularly agitated me in the Spanish case was the policies of Britain, France, and the United States. These three most powerful democracies in the world officially deplored fascism, in either its Italian or German form; yet they were favoring the expansion of Fascism into Spain. This was democracy being betrayed by democracy.

It had a peculiar effect on me, as it was different from being a spectator of Japanese imperialism. Japanese and Chinese were not my people; but Western democracy *was* my affair. I realized that I was disgusted by the way the Spanish Republic was being called "Communist-controlled" and thus an instrument of Soviet policy, thus justifying the "democracies" in being "neutral" in the Spanish Civil War—neutral in a way that favored the fascists. The Spanish Civil War was a sort of bridge between two periods of my own thinking. It was perhaps not a revelation, but it was certainly an eye-opener. I had it rubbed into me that "democracy is not what you say but what you do." This experience helped me to analyze the situation in China. For example, it greatly widened the field of my interest and study; and now being able to read Russian as well as Mongol, I got a wider view of the minority politics of different countries.

My personal ideas of democracy date perhaps from an incident in 1937, about January, when my wife and I were on our way back from London to China via Suez. We traveled from Greece to Egypt on an Italian ship which was carrying as deck passengers a large number of Muslim pilgrims of the Chinese province of Sinkiang. This was the first time in many years that pilgrims had been allowed by the Sinkiang authorities to go to Mecca. Of course, they had to pass through Soviet territory. They were supposed to cross the Black Sea to Turkey and then go on by rail to eventually reach Mecca.

Because of a plague alarm, however, they had been diverted to Greece and then were put on this Italian steamer. They did not know where they were and what was going to happen to them, which made them very nervous. We went down and talked to them. Although they were Turkish-speaking Uighur Muslims, there were a number of them who spoke very good Chinese. I asked about the journey and how they were treated in the Soviet Union. They said: "Oh, that was wonderful! We traveled by train, and we were well received everywhere. When we got to Odessa, we were driven about in big, shiny cars, and we were shown everything." So, I said: "How did you pay for a journey like this? What do you do for money for your expenses?"

They looked around to see if anybody was watching, and then one of the men reached into his gown and pulled out a little bag of gold dust and said: "When necessary, we change this or sell some of this." I said: "But how do you do that? Under the Soviet regulations foreign currencies have to be surrendered as you enter Soviet territory, and I should think that gold would be still more controlled." They said: "Oh, no problem at all. The Russians are democratic." Upon this I asked again: "What does *democratic* mean?" The answer was: "Democratic means friendly to Muslims." From that time I understood that when people of different cultures and different situations talk about ideas like democracy, you have to try to find out what it means in *their* ideas, instead of trying to fit it into *your own* previously conceived idea of what democracy is; and I have always emphasized this to students.

I have to mention here that while I was in London, the famous Sian Incident occurred. In December 1936, Chiang Kai-shek flew to Sian to deal with the troops of Chang Hsueh-liang, whom he had appointed to step up the campaign against the Communists; but these troops, being from the Northeast, in concert with the troops of provincial ruler Yang Hu-ch'eng mutinied and made Chiang prisoner, demanding resistance against Japanese aggression, not renewed civil war against the Communists. Yang, on his part, did not want his province to be tightly controlled by Chiang Kai-shek, as it would have been if made the base of a fresh campaign against the Communists. Chou En-lai flew from Yenan to negotiate the liberation of Chiang in exchange for forming a united front.

As soon as the news of the kidnapping of the Generalissimo came in, I got a telephone call from *The Times* and another from the London Communist paper, the *Daily Worker*. Both of them asked the same thing: "Could you come round to the office and tell us what is happening in China and what it means?" I had to give both of them the same answer: "There is no use in my coming to your office, for I can't tell you anything. I don't know any more than anybody else does." I have a peculiar feeling when I remember this: the only time in my life when I have been asked simultaneously by both the top local Establishment paper and the local Communist paper to "enlighten" them.

Later, I heard the Chinese Communist analysis of the incident, which I think is quite reliable. They consider that among the various people in Chiang Kai-shek's group there were those who were unwilling to make a united resistance against the Japanese and those who were willing to do so. Chiang personally was the most important of those who were willing to make a stand, but on his own conditions, namely, that he should be "commander-in-chief" of the united resistance. The Communists considered that the moment he decided would be when the balance among his own followers, loyal or disloyal, would permit him to make a stand.

Accordingly, when Chiang Kai-shek was arrested by the troops of Chang Hsueh-liang and Yang Hu-ch'eng, the Communists obviously came to the conclusion that this was the moment. Up to this time, Chiang had maintained Chang Hsueh-liang's army at Sian for the purpose of blockading the Communists at Yenan. The Yenan people had used on Chang's troops such propaganda as: "You people are from the Northeast. Your homeland is occupied by the Japanese. What are you doing here, getting ready to fight your fellow Chinese? Why don't you join us? Then we can all fight together to recover the Northeast." This had led to informal fraternization, and people were coming and going between Chiang Kai-shek's lines and the Communist lines. Some of Chiang Kai-shek's officers were saying to Chiang: "Look, we are going to lose control of our own troops unless we do something." This was the background of the arrest of Chiang Kai-shek.

I went back to China in the spring of 1937. When we got back to Peking, everybody was talking about restoring the United Front. At the same time, in Peking there was an immense sensation, because Edgar Snow had succeeded in getting into the Red territory and came out to write newspaper articles, which became the foundation of his *Red Star Over China* (1938). As a part of the new agreement between Chiang and Chou, the Kuomintang barricade on Yenan was at least nominally lifted. Everybody was trying to get there: not simply inquisitive foreigners, but hundreds of Chinese intellectuals, university professors, and students. Nevertheless, though the cordon around Yenan no longer existed theoretically, in fact, the Kuomintang authorities did their best to slow down these pilgrimages. The reconstructed United Front against Japan did not frighten us—we felt that real politics was at last beginning in China—and we extended this to a general sympathy for United Front resistance to the Rome-Berlin-Tokyo aggression.

Visit to Yenan

Just at this moment, two Americans, Philip J. Jaffe and Arthur Bisson, turned up in Peking. I do not think I had met either of them before. Bisson had a connection with the IPR, and it had given him a letter of introduction addressed to me. As has been mentioned before, Jaffe was the driving force in the *Amerasia* group. Bisson had formerly been teaching at an American missionary college somewhere in the Yangtze valley. There he became interested in the Chinese student movement and came to know various Chinese student leftists. Though I was never really close to him, I would say that my overall impression was that he was the type of man of whom there were quite a few in China, namely, those with a semi-missionary, Christian-influenced background, who were against Japanese aggression and in favor of the United Front. He was the kind of open-minded liberal whom Marxists later would call a progressive, and people who did not like that kind of movement would call him a fellow traveler. Bisson had gone back to the United States, where he got into touch with Jaffe, and the two of them, together with Jaffe's wife, came to Peking.

When they came to me and asked if I would travel with them to Yenan, I was, of course, enormously interested. Jaffe had never been in China before; and Bisson, in spite of his period in China as a teacher, spoke only a very limited amount of Chinese. Neither of them knew anything about traveling in the interior of China, and they wanted me to come as their guide and interpreter. They would pay all my expenses. Having had to say to *The Times* and the *Daily Worker* that I could not explain the Sian Incident to them, I wanted to find out what was happening; again, not what people were saying, but what they were doing. Therefore, I replied that I would gladly go along with them. As both Jaffe and Bisson were connected with *Amerasia*, and I was at that time already on the editorial board, we might be called an "Amerasia group," though it certainly was not such a formal mission as the name might suggest. I first went to Edgar Snow, whom I already knew, though rather slightly. He gave me the address in Yenan to which I should write. At that time the Kuomintang blockade of Yenan was loose enough so that the letter went by ordinary post, and I got an answer saying: "You will be welcome."

We started off from Peking early in June 1937. As a precaution against being targeted as people trying to get to Yenan, we pretended to be traveling as tourists. Instead of getting on a train and going straight to Sian, we first went up to Shansi Province, to Taiyuan, and did some touring in the region. Then we came down on another railway and eventually ended up in Sian, thus establishing ourselves as tourists. In Sian we put up at a hotel, and every day Jaffe and Bisson played tennis. We also talked about going to see some antiquities outside Sian.

In the meantime, I found a young Swede, Effie Hill. He was the son of missionaries, had never been out of China, and spoke very fluent Chinese. He was also a good motor mechanic. Because of his abilities he had been employed by the Sven Hedin Expeditions through Inner Mongolia to Sinkiang. By this time the Hedin Expeditions had been completed, and he was running a private business in Sian with a car of his own, an American car, for hire, while also making a bit of money repairing cars for Chinese car owners. We hired him with his car to take us to Yenan. Because of all this semi-civil war atmosphere, he was not doing much business and jumped at the chance.

One fine day, we all piled into his car. We did not give up our rooms at the hotel, saying we were just going out to see some tombs. When we got out of the city, we just kept going and reached a border post between the Sian troops and the Red Army. The Swede, being a local man, knew where the warlord troops were fraternizing with the Communists, so we passed through without any trouble. As soon as we reached the Communist side, everything was fine. They were very hospitable, there was no trouble at all, and we got up to Yenan all right.

In my *Manchuria, Cradle of Conflict*, you will find that at the beginning of the 1930s I thought that the Chinese Communists were simply a twentieth-century form of the peasant rebels who had appeared over and over again in the history of China. Neither did I think, however, that they were tools and puppets of the Soviet Union. As I had no affiliations, I had not been influenced by any particular persons on this question; but from what I saw and heard around Peking, while the Communists had been in the southwest, I thought that the Chinese Communists were not in a geographical position to have close contact with the Soviet Union, though there were returned students from Russia among them. Such were my ideas about the Chinese Communists when I actually arrived in Yenan.

We were received in a very friendly way. Jaffe and Bisson had taken me on not only as a travel guide—without me they would never have found this young Swede, for example—but also as their interpreter. Once in Yenan, however, I was very much relieved to find that for interviews with important Chinese Communists, the Chinese naturally preferred their own interpreters, and they had a number who spoke excellent English. In fact, I had been apprehensive about these interviews, because my Chinese vocabulary was not a political one, least of all the vocabulary that distinguished the Marxist terminology from that of the Kuomintang. I had no experience in that.

Those who have ever had the experience of interpreting a serious discussion will know that the interpreter must concentrate so closely on using exactly the right word in each language in translating back and forth that his mind does not retain what went before and does not properly look forward to what is coming next. At the end of the interview, he finds it hard to tell what it was all about. There are all the details, but not the general picture. In Yenan, I had the great advantage of being present when these Americans were questioning such important Chinese Communist leaders as Mao Tse-tung, Chou En-lai, Chu Teh, and others, and getting their answers. Here I was sitting at the side listening, and I could come away with a much clearer impression than if I had had to serve as interpreter.

I was amazed that Mao should be willing to spend hours and hours with a couple of previously unknown Americans. They had said that they wanted to write about the Chinese Communists, but he did not know how competent they were. They were asking rather simple-minded questions, but Mao was willing to come right down to earth, talking in A B C terms with them. It was not that I was listening to their interviews as if I were the judge of a political debate and deciding which debater had a better argument. Having once been a newspaperman, I had an impression that these spokesmen of the Chinese Communist Party certainly understood how to talk in a way that would get them favorably quoted in an American newspaper. They were extremely intelligent and realized that their stories would appeal to anti-imperialists all over the world. They would do their best to get out a good story by making it simple, by trying to keep the interviewers from making mistakes or exaggerations. They knew that even if some mistakes were made, any story about the Chinese Communists was bound to do them more good than harm. In other words, it was a situation in which any publicity was good publicity. They therefore showed endless patience.

You could tell that Chou En-lai was a university-educated intellectual who had been abroad and knew something about the outside world as well as China, while Chu Teh was a military man who had become political. Mao Tse-tung was a man of the people—a man of very powerful mentality, but clearly a man of peasant origin. Quite recently, the small notebook in which I scribbled down in pencil the record of these interviews turned up among my old papers. As I could follow the questions and answers twice, in English and in Chinese as interpreted by the Chinese interpreters, I can say with confidence that these records are fairly accurate. There are no new "revelations," but it is important as a record of what these leaders actually said to foreigners at that time in Yenan.

We stayed in Yenan for four days. Already many leading Communist members had been distributed to the countryside around the city, where they were training cadres and so on, although top men like Mao Tse-tung himself, Chou En-lai, and Chu Teh had quarters of their own in the city. Yenan itself, being a small place, was filled to the brim with some rank-and-file Communists and with United Front Chinese, who had come from all over China to see what Yenan was like. Agnes Smedley and Nym Wales, the first wife of Edgar Snow, were also there. During our stay, I was asked to give a speech in an open-air place in the city. The audience was primarily United Front sympathizers rather than what is now called hard-core Communists.

I spoke simply about the general American sympathy for a United Front Chinese resistance against imperialist invasion and aggression, and hoped that it would become stronger. I do not remember whether there was any discussion—certainly not much—following my lecture. Somebody must have been translating my speech, which was given in Chinese, to Agnes, because she did not know Chinese. At the end of the meeting, she came up to me and said: "Well, Owen! You are not such a ~~son of a bitch~~ after all!" Agnes had visited us in Peking, where she had found that I did not have any Chinese left-wing friends (Ch'en Han-seng and Chi Ch'ao-ting were both in the United States), while I had some missionary friends, most of them working in the frontier regions. As Agnes had the left-wing attitude that the missionaries were a part of the imperialistic mechanism, and that all of them were imperialists, her attitude to me was: "This is one of these comfortably well-off bourgeois intellectual types who is not actively imperialist and is never going to take any risks."

At the end of our visit, they said to us: "If each of you has any particular and specialized interest, tell us about it. We will arrange a special interview on that subject." Of course, my interest was the frontier question; and I knew that on the Long March the Chinese Communists, who had passed through the Tibetan grasslands, had brought to Yenan tribesmen from Kueichou and some Tibetans both from Sinkiang and Ch'inghai Provinces. They had also Huimin (Chinese-speaking Muslims) from Kansu and Ninghsia, one or two Uighurs, and some Mongols. The Communists had set up a center for minority peoples. When I indicated that I would like to go there, they said: "That's easy," and sent a cadre to take me to the center. The people there were mostly teenage boys who had tagged along with the Red Army, not so much because they were radicals, but just out of youthful curiosity. Of course, conversation with them had to be in Chinese, interpreted by cadres, for I could not speak Tibetan or any of the southwest tribal languages, or any Turkish. With the Huimin I could talk directly in Chinese.

Suddenly two young Mongols appeared. When I was duly introduced to them, I brightened up and started to talk to them in Mongol. Up to this point everything had gone along fine. The moment I started to talk to them in Mongol, however, the cadres looked at one another and at their watches, and said: "Oh! It is getting late. We are sorry, but we have to go back to Yenan and run to the next appointment." You can understand that they, as cadres, did not want to be questioned afterward about what Lattimore was talking with the Mongols. So the interview was cut short. It was very ironical, for these were Mongols from the nearby Ordos region, where the Mongols were very badly treated by Chinese warlords; and what they were saying was: "Of course, all Chinese have been oppressers of the Mongols; but these are different Chinese, the first Chinese we have met who treated us like human beings." If I had been allowed to continue, the conversation would have made a wonderful article for publicity favorable to the Chinese Communists.

I had one private talk, without the other Americans attending, with a man who was in charge of their minority policy. I was rather disappointed at this time, because there was nothing original in it. The Chinese Communists were then repeating completely the Stalinist doctrine as far as minorities were concerned. It was not that I was criticizing Stalin's minority doctrine, but that I was wondering why the Chinese, under quite different historical conditions, should mold themselves so closely on Soviet practices.

There was a rather amusing episode about this journey to Yenan. Mao Tse-tung was very eager to persuade our driver, the Swede, to stay in Yenan. Effie was born and brought up in a district of the Inner Mongolian frontier a bit east of Kueihua. I never visited the place myself, but all along the Chahar, Suiyuan, Ninghsia, and Kansu borders of Inner Mongolia, the number of Chinese dialects is astonishing. They are mutually understandable; but they are very, very different. This is probably related historically to different periods when the Hsiung-nu, and later the Turks, surrendered to the Chinese dynasties and settled there. The way they learned Chinese must have affected the Chinese dialects of the region. Now, the dialect of the place where this young Swede came from was considered by everybody else to be in itself extremely comic, and the moment you heard a man talking in that dialect, everybody would start to laugh. The Swede, while he knew standard Chinese, could speak that dialect perfectly.

In the evening in Yenan, they had entertainment gatherings. The big men, Mao, Chou, Chu Teh, and other top leaders would all be there, sitting in the audience, without any privileged seats, just mingling with the crowd. This was one of their very important ways of getting the feel of how people thought about things. On these occasions people from different parts of China would get up on the stage and sing folk songs from their regions or tell stories. This young Swede, one evening, pushed his way up and got onto the platform. There he put on a stunt, telling stories in this comic dialect. He could also sing very well. The whole theater was rocking with laughter. Mao was particularly impressed and wanted to meet this young man; and the young Swede was brought to be presented to him. It then turned out that not only had he worked for the Sven Hedin Expeditions, but he had hired out his lorries to different warlords and had had encounters with bandits, and all that kind of thing. In the course of these adventures, he had become a very good motor mechanic.

In all newly industrialized countries, when new equipment, such as motor cars, is introduced, the critical problem is that it is much easier to learn how to drive a motor vehicle than to keep that vehicle in good condition. Even before he made this sensational appearance on the stage, the young Swede, having nothing to do, went round to see things. The Chinese did not have much motor equipment, but they did have some, and a lot of it was in bad condition. The Swede would say: "Here, let me take a hand. I will show you how to fix this." In this way, he was getting a local reputation as a motor vehicle fixer, and this immediately struck Mao Tse-tung. He must have thought: "Here is a young man, a different type of foreigner, who speaks more than one dialect of the common people and gets on well with ordinary mechanics. He can explain things to a peasant who had never handled machinery and teach him how to become a mechanic. If I can persuade him to stay with us, he will be extremely valuable in a practical way. I don't give a damn about his politics." Mao Tse-tung spent a lot of time trying to persuade Hill to stay with him in Yenan.

Everybody knows the expression "lumpen proletariat." This man Hill was a "lumpen bourgeois," if there is such a thing. He was a type of missionary son who had reacted against his pious upbringing. He drank, he gambled, and he went to the houses of prostitution, not as a foreigner but along with whatever Chinese he was working with. He took all kinds of jobs and had spent his life knocking around the interior with all kinds of Chinese; but he still retained a sort of white man's contempt for the natives and basically looked down on the Chinese. He was very poorly educated. He had heard little about the Communists and thought that they were a disreputable bunch. There was no danger that he would ever become sympathetic to Marxism. If he thought that the Chinese Communists were nothing but a gang of bandits, he would say: "Well, that's all right. I've dealt with bandits. On a man-to-man basis, I can always get along." Nevertheless, he did not want to stay in Yenan. By this time, he had quite a thriving little business in Sian, and he wanted to get back and go on with it. So he resisted all Mao Tse-tung's blandishments and went back with our party.

One day on our way back to Sian, while we were waiting for the engine of the car to cool off, I asked Hill: "Effie, you have seen all kinds of Chinese. What do you think of this lot?" As he had been wandering about Yenan, talking to people, I wanted to get his reaction. He said: "I tell you what. I've met a lot of these Kuomintang intellectuals. I have dealt with warlords. There is hardly any kind of Chinese I've not dealt with. But in Yenan, I have seen for the first time a man who could become the new emperor of China." (That was Mao Tse-tung.)

Chinese Peasants and the Japanese Invasion

I had no theoretical comprehension of what was behind the United Front; but I had the impression, passing through Communist-held territory between Sian and Yenan, that these Communists knew what they were doing. They were successful in winning the confidence of the peasants. As my former contact with Chinese merchants involved traveling in rural areas and staying in villages, I knew something about Chinese peasants. During my stay in Manchuria also, I became familiar with peasant villages. In February 1933 I had made a trip into Jehol (the southwest part of Manchuria) that further revealed to me what Chinese peasants were like.

The Jehol trip came about thanks to a strange English adventurer named Sutton. He was known as One-Armed Sutton because he had lost an arm in the First World War at Gallipoli in Turkey. He had been an oil engineer in Mexico before the war and had learned how to handle the first primitive trench mortars during the war, and after the war he came to China. Later, he went to Manchuria and persuaded Chang Tso-lin that he could get the upper hand over his warlord rivals by using this new weapon. After Chang's death he came to Peking. In spite of his living in China for a good many years, he did not know a word of Chinese. One day he came to me and said: "I got an offer from the Hearst newspapers to go up to Jehol to report the Japanese invasion that is about to begin there. I never worked for a newspaper before, and I may not be able to get an interpreter up there. Will you come along?" So I went up with him, thinking that it would be a valuable experience. We were traveling in company with some American military attachés.

As soon as the Japanese invasion began, we hired a car and went up toward the front, which we found to be crumbling very fast. The Japanese had always been able to cut through the Chinese lines; but this time, instead of breaking through and then waiting for support, they "leap-frogged." Using armored cars, followed by lorries, they broke through the Chinese lines. Troops were then unloaded from the lorries and ordered to march ahead. The lorries went back, loaded more troops, overtook the marching troops, and drove on a few more miles, unloaded the new troops, under orders to march ahead, and repeated the maneuver by driving back to pick up still more troops. In this way they took thousands of square miles in two days.

We made haste to drive back to Jehol City, because we did not want to be in a village overrun by the Japanese, who might hold us and prevent us from seeing any more action. We were always only a few miles ahead of them. I remember that at one village, the villagers had received orders to block the road to stop the Japanese motor transport. As in many villages of China at that time, there were huge willow trees planted along the road. Instead of just cutting down and throwing the trees across the road, which would have been enough to delay motor transport, the villagers were cutting the trees into sections so that the sections fitted nicely into the road which had been worn down by long years of carts and people going back and forth. This made it much easier for the Japanese to remove the sections one by one than if they had had to lift up the heavy tree trunks thrown across the road. The villagers were not intentionally sabotaging the orders to hold up the Japanese; they were simply ignorant of modern warfare.

This province had been run for many years by an old friend of Chang Tso-lin, a former bandit named T'ang Yu-lin, who was one of the most corrupt and cruel of the warlord governors. He was anticipating that the Japanese would come in. To get ready for that he was robbing right and left and moving his wealth down to the safety of the foreign concessions in Tientsin. The treasures from the old Manchu palaces in Jehol were all being sent down to Tientsin to be sold by T'ang and his son. The people of the province called him T'ang Lao Hu (T'ang the Tiger).

We would stop in a village for a meal and a drink of tea. Knowing that in a few hours the Japanese would be there, villagers were sitting around looking glum. Their own troops had run away, and they did not know what was coming. I talked with them and asked: "When the Japanese come in, what are you going to do? Are you going to the hills and become guerrillas?" They would say: "We don't know the Japanese. We don't know how they are going to behave. We will wait and see. In the meantime, we know our governor. We know what a wild beast he is. As long as we can drink his blood and eat his liver we'll be satisfied." This was exactly the expression they used. There absolutely was no disposition to oppose the Japanese. The Japanese had not yet arrived, and the resistance had not yet begun.

By the end of the war, however, the Communist-led partisan movement in Jehol was among the most bitter and effective. I do not think it was entirely due to Communist indoctrination that these people, who had formerly been so apathetic, became so politically active. They had realized that the Japanese were even worse than the Tiger. There were many Mongols in the province of Jehol, and many of the Mongol aristocrats went over to the Japanese side; but the ordinary herdsmen very quickly saw nothing in this for them. Before that they were at the bottom of the heap with the Mongol prince on top; now they were still at the bottom with the Japanese officers on the top.

The old Western idea that the Chinese peasant had no knowledge of politics or was not interested in politics is complete nonsense. Peasants had a very sensitive political feeling; but this does not mean that they would act politically in a rash manner, which would only get them killed off. They would wait and see if there would be an opportunity for resistance. This materialized through the interaction of Japanese imperial rule and the appearance of the Communists. The first Jehol partisans started spontaneously; then the Communists came in and said: "We will show you how to do it," and the whole thing developed. The first coordinator of the Jehol guerrillas was a French-educated Communist.

With my past experience of direct contact with Chinese peasants, I knew the kind of material with which the Communists were working. Even before going to Yenan, in Peking itself, especially through talking with foreign correspondents who were trying to keep track of military moves and defense preparations on both sides, I knew that the mood of the ordinary soldiers of the Kuomintang's own army in and around Peking was: "Our own generals cannot be trusted. The next time the Japanese are going to attack, we are not going to obey orders to retreat, but will stand and fight." My impression in Peking had been that there was a changing mood among the people as well as among the rank-and-file of the army; and the political higher-ups of the Kuomintang did not seem to know what to do about it. Then I visited Yenan and talked with people who gave me the impression: "Aha! They do know what to do about it!"

The Marco Polo Bridge Incident (7 July 1937) broke out soon

after we got back to Peking from Yenan. The future was not at all clear. One did not know yet whether the Japanese militarists were going to try to go deeper into China, and I was in no position to predict the future except for being sure that the Japanese military certainly would not cease being active. Nevertheless, I think I probably appreciated already what has since become my basic analysis of the difference between the Kuomintang version and the Communist version of the United Front.

Chiang Kai-shek, I know, always regarded himself as a revolutionary; he wanted to destroy the old structure of foreign privileges in China and to create a completely independent China. His idea of how to reach this objective was to train a young elite of his own, his own Youth Corps, who would understand his objective and, having understood it, would go among the people, the city people and the peasants, and tell them what to do. The people would respond to the ancient Chinese belief that the scholars knew all about it and would follow the orders as everyone was supposed to do.

On the other hand, the Communist theory was that this was now a form of invasion that affected the whole people and affected them directly. It was not just the Japanese military dictating to the Chinese government and the Chinese government obeying their orders. It was now the question of a direct Japanese invasion, in which the people, even in villages, could see Japanese troops and see how they behaved. They would like to resist. If they were going to resist, it would not be just because they got orders. They would resist effectively only if they got something out of it. This meant agrarian reforms and lower taxes and a voice in their own future.

Chiang's major effort was to assert and expand his own authority, while the Communists' major effort was to say to the people, especially to the peasantry: "You have something to defend!" I had not known any Chinese Marxists in Peking, but when I got to Yenan and listened to the Chinese Communist leaders, my impression was: "These people are undoubtedly Marxists, theoretically and ideologically; but the human material with which they are dealing is a non-Marxist peasantry, and they know how to use it." They had their own ideas about the material on which to build their version of the United Front. They were able to combine peasant unrest with political organization better than Chiang, who was hampered by the fact that so many of his officers were the sons of landlord families.

When I got back to Peking with Bisson and Jaffe, I thought that since these chaps were going to write articles on Yenan, I would try my hand too. So, I sent an article to *The Times* of London, and a long article to the *Saturday Evening Post*. Both of them were received with joy and appreciation. I was even paid for them. I received the galley proofs, corrected them, and readied them for publication, but just as they were about to be published, the Marco Polo Bridge Incident occurred.

In my articles, I emphasized that the Japanese would come to the limit of getting concessions from China by threat of a second aggression, and then would begin another military invasion of China, but this time it would not be the same as the lightning job in Manchuria. The Chinese army would fight even if some of the generals should sell out and go over to the Japanese. The United Front would hold, and the Chinese would continue their resistance. Here I was a bit ahead of times, but I said that if resisitance actually materialized, the Japanese, because of the enormous size of China, would not be able to win a lightning war. The longer the war went on, the worse the situation would be for Japan. Also, on the Chinese side, the longer the war went on, the stronger the Communists would get.

I did not prophesize that there would be a civil war if Japan should be defeated. All I said was that at the end of the war, the Communists would be likely to wind up holding large areas in which they would control the taxes and revenue; they would have their own base and would be able to maintain their own army. They would therefore be a permanent major factor in China's politics. The trouble was that until the Marco Polo Bridge Incident, all kinds of speculations were being made and were published. But the moment the incident occurred and the Japanese troops began marching, then all the old clichés came up: "The Chinese do not understand modern warfare. Trained Japanese armies would cut their way through the Chinese like a knife through butter. All would be over in a matter of weeks."

The Times did not, perhaps, care about *my* reputation, but they did not want to print an article which they thought would make them look foolish in a few weeks. So they simply killed the article. The foreign editor of the *Saturday Evening Post* was a man whom I had known when he was its correspondent in Peking, and he was editing my article. He wrote to me saying: "Dear Owen, you sure are lucky! I was just in time to save your hide. Your article was in the press when we got the flash about the Marco Polo Bridge Incident; and I just got down there in time to have it clipped off the plate and put something else as a substitute."

I never recovered the carbon copy of my article for the *Saturday Evening Post*, but I did find a copy of the corrected proofs of my article for *The Times*. In about 1964 or 1965, a memorial volume was being published for the late Victor Purcell of Cambridge, and I was asked for a contribution. As I was very busy and did not have time to write a new article, I sent the article with a little explanatory note; and it was finally printed under the title of "Unpublished Report from Yenan 1937" in *Studies in the Social History of China and South-East Asia*, edited by J. Ch'en and N. Tarling (1970).

My Yenan visit was in June 1937, and almost immediately after my return to Peking, I went to Peitaiho with my family. When fighting started near Marco Polo Bridge on 7 July, it was very dramatic to be at this summer seaside resort situated not far away from Shanhaikuan, the most important passage between Manchuria and North China, where the eastern end of the Great Wall comes down to the sea. All night long we could hear the Japanese military trains coming through Shanhaikuan. It created an impression of endless numbers of Japanese troops pouring into China.

Everybody had thought that it was coming, sooner or later, but I do not think anybody had been able to pinpoint that it would come that July. Everybody knew that there were Japanese detachments all around Peking, and it was a sort of powder-barrel situation, in which there might be a spark that at any moment would ignite an explosion. Radio was not very general at that time, and we did not have one ourselves, but a few of the neighbors did; and it must have been through the radio that the news came through. Immediately everybody was rushing to get hold of a radio. The Chinese news was mainly coming out of Shanghai. When the word came that resistance was also beginning at Shanghai, the local Chinese were tremendously cheered up because they thought that the United Front was really working, and China was fighting. Even the ordinary Chinese were somehow already confident that this time they would fight, and if they really fought they could win. Chiang Kai-shek's stock was, of course, enormously high.

One thing I remember is that after we got back to Peking when troop movements had stopped enough so that we could get a train back to Peking, somebody, a Westerner, came to see me. This happened as usual in those days, through a friend of a friend of a friend. What he wanted to know was whether I had a copy of the *Seven Pillars of Wisdom* (1926) by Lawrence of Arabia. I said: "Yes, but what for?" He said: "There are some Chinese starting guerrilla resistance in the Western Hills, and there are some university intellectuals with them. They have heard about Lawrence of Arabia and his theory of relying on the people: that if the people are with you, then the people themselves will be your eyes and your ears, and you get better intelligence than the enemy. They want to get hold of what Lawrence himself wrote so that they can use it in organizing the guerrilla resistance." So I gave them my copy of the book.

At the very first, life did not change a great deal after the Japanese occupation. You saw Japanese patrols, and the Japanese took over the local Chinese police organization, and that was that. There was no trouble and no resistance in Peking. No sabotage. A major part of the Japanese military propaganda was that Japan stood for law and order and that foreigners were safer under the Japanese occupation than they had been under the independent Chinese. Of course, the real danger to foreigners in China was the danger to the big business enterprises, which would be crowded out by the Japanese as they had already been crowded out in Mukden, Kirin, Harbin, and other places in Manchuria. Peking, however, was not a business center, and the Japanese could easily put on a show to "just continue life as before. It's all right." Even the universities were no great problem to the Japanese, because academics whom the Japanese would regard as subversive had already run to the hills and become guerrillas, and only collaborationists, or at least outwardly submissive types, were still sitting there.

It was obvious that we would not be able to stay on in Peking. I had two jobs. One was my research work, largely on Inner Mongolia, and the other was editing *Pacific Affairs*, which I did by mail. *Pacific Affairs* carried far more anti-Japanese than pro-Japanese material. With a Japanese-controlled regime in Peking, it was obvious that I would not be able to do that editing work very long. So I wrote to the United States to a man named Isaiah Bowman, whom I had known when he was director of the American Geographical Society in New York. He had since become president of Johns Hopkins University. I wrote to tell him that I had to give up Peking and asked if he knew of any university where I might get a job, that I would be very grateful if he would let me know, and still more grateful if he would act as a reference if I applied for an appointment. I got a prompt letter back saying that he would not give names of any universities and would not write any letters of recommendation for me, because he intended to give me a job right there at the Hopkins.

We finally left Peking toward the end of December. On the way back from China, we stopped over in Tokyo for a few days. There we stayed with the famous Japanologist George Sansom, who later became Sir George Sansom. At that time he was commercial consul at the British Embassy. He had a long experience in the Far East, having been a young consular officer in Korea, before the Japanese takeover in 1910; and he was the author of a widely admired *Japan, a Short Cultural History* (1931). The beginning of our friendship with Sansom was when he and his wife came to Peking sometime in the 1930s, and he took the initiative of calling on me.

I had never heard of him at that time. But we instantly understood each other and started to talk about all kinds of things, with comparisons of the Japanese and Chinese societies. Sansom was one of the few Westerners who knew that among the Japanese intelligentsia there were many important and influential thinkers who were not Marxists but knew a great deal about Marxism and were influenced by what they considered the importance of certain aspects of Marxist theory in understanding Japan. It was from Sansom, and later from E. Herbert Norman, that I came to know the existence of non-Communist-Marxist influence among the Japanese intelligentsia.

I have already mentioned how the Japanese members of the IPR all complained whenever I published something on Japan in *Pacific Affairs*. They said: "In the present circumstances, it is difficult for us to write an article; but these people whom you get to write articles on Japan just make things worse. There aren't any Westerners who really understand Japan." Now, one night during my stay in Tokyo, I went out to dinner with two or three IPR people. I think one of them was Matsukata. We were walking back from the restaurant to the Sansom's, and they were reciting the same old complaint that nobody understood Japan. I put in a word and said: "Well, what about George Sansom?" There was a silence, and then one of them spoke up: "Yes, Sansom does understand Japan; but being a consular officer he could not write an article for *Pacific Affairs*, you know." The other one added: "Well, but he learned it all from the Japanese." When I got back to the Sansom's, I immediately told this story. He roared with laughter and said: "That is the best compliment I ever had!"

Probably through Matsukata, I was taken to see Prince Konoe Fumimaro. He had become prime minister just before the Marco Polo Incident and was already regarded at that time as the most hopeful influence for restraining the hotheaded militarists. (He held the office of prime minister three times: June 1937–January 1939, July 1940–July 1941, July 1941–October 1941. He was finally replaced by General Tōjō Hideki.) While I was with Konoe, Kishi Nobusuke was announced to have come to see him. Prince Konoe asked me: "Oh, excuse me. Is it all right to receive him?" Of course, I had no objection, and Kishi came in. His name was already known to me. In Peking he was considered to be one of the most active civilian supporters of the Japanese militarists. (He was then an important member of the Manchukuo government.)

Kishi started talking about the importance of developing more railway communication between the Peking part of North China and Manchuria. What he said was interpreted to me. Konoe then said: "Mr. Lattimore has just come from Peking. So he will be interested." Being asked my opinion, I replied: "For this you will be using large quantities of conscripted Chinese labor, doing pick and shovel work laying tracks and making new roads. This will, instead of increasing the Greater East Asia Co-prosperity Sphere, increase and intensify the Chinese feeling that Japanese presence is not a co-operative but an imperialistic presence. You will increase anti-Japanese feeling in China." When Kishi left, Konoe turned to me and said: "Thank you!"

Though a conversation of this kind with Konoe was necessarily very roundabout and very discreet, Konoe as well as the Three Musketeers of the Japanese IPR allowed me to have the impression that they were deeply worried. I felt they were afraid that this inter-vention in China would lead to a larger scale intervention—probably to a big war and great danger for Japan, but there was not anything they could do about it. Of course, they could not say so outright, or give me any inside information such as the names of the people who were behind this drive.

From Japan we went to California and spent six months or so at Berkeley, as Johns Hopkins would not start until September. I was writing *Inner Asian Frontiers of China*, which I had started in Peking. I wanted to get the work done before taking up my university work. This university work was rather unusual. Johns Hopkins had a small institute called the Page School of International Relations, which had been founded after the First World War by friends of Walter Hines Page, who had been American Ambassador to Great Britain during the First World War. He was a friend of President Wilson's and of men who believed in the United States taking a full part in international affairs.

Nevertheless, the funds gathered for this institute had turned out to be rather limited, and all they really had was enough for my sal-ary plus two very modest postgraduate student grants; namely, it was a three-man institute, and I was the only permanent member, because the other two would get grants for one or two years and then move on somewhere else. When I got there, the other profes-sors looked upon me as a bit of a curiosity, because I had not been to a university myself, but finally both the History Department and the Political Science Department invited me to give lectures in their departments. The Page School itself was not a teaching department but a research unit.

Franz Michael held the first research fellowship at the Page School, and then there was John DeFrancis who translated Ma Ho-tien's *Chinese Agent in Mongolia* (1949). We had a couple of Indians at different times, and one of them published a book on Sir Francis E. Younghusband. For an year or two I had Ch'en Han-seng and another Chinese. There was also a young American, Shuyler Cam-mann, who had done some travel on the edge of Tibet and was in China during the war. He later became a museum curator and worked on art history. Another man who worked with me was Daniel Thorner, who later held important appointments in India and Paris. I got some extra money to do a volume of research on

Sinkiang, which came out under the title of *Pivot of Asia: Sinkiang and the Inner Asian Frontiers of China and Russia* in 1950. Having a school made it possible to go to foundations for grants for some specific research projects.

As the Page School was very small, I was appointed on a half-salary and remained editor of *Pacific Affairs*, which provided me with the other half. Of course, as usual in a situation like that, I was paid for two half-time jobs, but was really doing two full-time jobs. This made it impossible for me to launch a full academic career and left me only limited time for writing articles and giving occasional paid lectures, through which I could pursue my campaign in support of China. I did not belong to any seminars or groups which discussed the technical aspects of politics in China, Kuomintang or Marxist. I just stuck to the general proposition that China was in a situation in which it could survive only under a United Front: if there were simultaneously a civil war and an attempt to keep up national resistance, then the civil war would kill the national resistance.

At this time I was thirty-eight years old and had not spent more than two years in the United States. My idea about my native country was that it was a good place to live and that I could easily make a living there; but I felt that in dealing with conflicting propagandas of imperialist powers in Asia, of Chinese Nationalists, and of the Marxist revolutionaries, my countrymen were extraordinarily naive and provincial, as I could see from the articles submitted to me for *Pacific Affairs*. Already at that time, there was a kind of American oversimplification that has since become even more prominent. When I gave a lecture, people wanted to know: "Is there really a Red menace?" "Haven't we got to concentrate everything on stopping the spread of communism?" A few idealists, on the other hand, thinking especially of the years of Lenin and the early years of Stalin, hoped that the Russians had found a better, more humanitarian road ahead for all humanity. In this atmosphere, I became more and more committed to my own "bottom line" thinking: "It is not what they *say*, but what they *do* that matters."

I had seen imperialism at work in China and in Mongolia; and I had had the experience of watching the Spanish Civil War from London, noting that all the young idealistic British intellectuals were flocking to Spain as volunteers on the Republican side. Also, having returned from Yenan, I had the impression that the Communist leaders were seriously for the United Front with the Nationalists of Chiang Kai-shek. Roosevelt also wanted a united resistance in China, with no civil war. It was already becoming clear that while Roosevelt approved of arrangements like the United Front, he was more and more convinced that after the war the main decisions about China would not be made in China, but in the United States and the Soviet Union, in which case a good understanding between the United States and the U.S.S.R. was essential.

Chapter Three

■

NOMINATION BY PRESIDENT ROOSEVELT

A Telephone Call from the White House

When I went into the university one morning in June 1941, everybody was buzzing. "There's a call for you from the White House.
They want you to call back immediately." The telephone message
transmitted to me was just: "This is Lauchlin Currie, assistant to the
President, calling from the White House. Will you please call back?"
So I telephoned to the White House, and Currie said: "Will you
come over to see me?" We made an appointment for the next day,
and as soon as I could I went home to talk to Eleanor.

What could it all mean? It must have something to do with
China, but why the White House? Could it be that the Department
of State was arranging for someone on the White House staff to
rap my knuckles, to warn me to stop rocking the boat? At that time
I was criticizing U.S. policy as being too soft on Japanese imperialism and not strong enough in support of China. I had no friends
among the top men in the department. Most of the Japan-trained
men accepted the Japanese militarists' propaganda that Japan was
the "only bulwark against Bolshevism in Asia" and that this justified its creation of the bogus state of "Manchukuo." Some of the
China-trained men also accepted this view and therefore disliked
my continuing criticism. I had friends among some of the China-
trained men, but they were not senior enough to shape policy; and
in any case they respected my knowledge of Inner Mongolia and
frontier questions but did not rate me as an expert on international
matters or as an expert on Chinese politics in questions like the
relation between the Kuomintang and the Communists.

Or could the call mean that I was going to be offered a consultancy of some kind? That is one of the classical ways to shut the mouth of a critic—offer him a "confidential" status that will allow him to be a critic in private debate (always on a carefully prepared agenda) but that will also debar him, because of the "confidential" relationship, from public comment. I have seen that work, many a time.

The next day I went to Washington to meet Lauchlin Currie in his office in the administrative wing of the White House. I had never met him before, and I think I had never heard his name. When I went in he said something like: "I would like to talk to you about the possibility of your going to China for a job." His attitude was businesslike, but it did not make me feel that I was being examined. It was like meeting somebody who wanted to make my acquaintance. He had obviously already had some kind of preliminary check made, so he knew what kind of career I had had and that I knew and had published a good deal about China.

I cannot remember in detail, but he was a very direct person. He must have been in his middle thirties, a little younger than myself. When we talked generalities for long enough to let him make up his mind that I was a man to whom he could say the things that needed to be said, it soon emerged that he wanted to talk to me confidentially about the possibility of an assignment in China, and the name of Chiang Kai-shek came out very soon. Currie had been to Chungking two or three times as Roosevelt's personal envoy, outside of ordinary diplomatic channels. These visits went so well that Chiang wanted to establish a permanent link—something like what we would today call a "hot line"—personally between himself and Roosevelt. The link would be a man nominated by Roosevelt but appointed and paid by Chiang Kai-shek.

Of course, I had not expected that kind of proposal. If the State Department was mixed up with it, I could not have imagined how I could be nominated. I cannot remember how long the interview lasted. It may have been ten minutes, or it could have been an hour; but I do know that it included asking me to give the names of people who could be asked for references. Apparently at this first meeting, Currie decided that I would fit the job. Of the names I gave, I can remember only two: Admiral Harry E. Yarnell and Isaiah Bowman. Yarnell had been commander of the China Squadron of the U.S. Navy in the Pacific, and I had met him when he visited Peking a couple of times in the 1930s. He had asked me shrewd questions about what was going on in North China, Manchuria, and Inner Mongolia and seemed to take seriously what I had to say. Now in retirement, he was an adviser to T.V. Soong (as he spelled his name Sung Tzu-wen in English), Madame Chiang's brother, who was the head of the Chinese Purchasing Office in Washington.

As for Isaiah Bowman, the president of Johns Hopkins University, I was at this time his white-haired boy (though he later turned against me), and he rated me highly as a geopolitical expert on the Far East. Lauchlin told me later, when my appointment went through, that when Roosevelt was told that I had Bowman's endorsement, he said: "If Isaiah Bowman says he's all right, then he's all right," and wanted no further reference. This was because Bowman, America's best-known geopolitician, was a well-known conservative and no supporter of Roosevelt's New Deal. Thus Bowman's approval would mean that Roosevelt would have no serious trouble from the Right for nominating me.

In a week or ten days after this first meeting with Currie, the telephone rang again, and I went to see him. He said: "It all seems to be clear. You can have the job; but I would like you to meet a group of the Treasury people who are concerned with financial and economic policy toward China." Lauch Currie, not wanting to carry the sole responsibility for my appointment, had in fact decided to have me vetted; therefore he took me not to the Department of State but to the Treasury. Here I met with a group of four or five senior members, too informal to be called a committee. The informal chairman of that informal committee was a man named Harry Dexter White. Though I had never heard of him before, he was a brilliant financial economist and was very influential with the secretary of the Treasury. It is said that he was able to hold his own in debate with John Maynard Keynes at financial conferences after the war. In fact, he forced Keynes to modify his position to accommodate U.S. policy.

(Harry Dexter White, seven years later, was summoned before the House Un-American Activities Committee. At the hearing of August 1948, he asked for a suspension of the hearing because he was extremely tired; but his plea was not granted. When the questioning was finally ended, he thought that he would walk home to have some fresh air, and on his way home he just dropped dead of a heart attack.)

The Treasury people simply wanted to know a few general things. Among these there was whether I had any conception of the importance of economic and financial factors in the U.S. policy toward China. They also mentioned that they had to be on guard against corrupt people in the Chinese government who would divert some of the money. One important thing which Currie and the Treasury people wanted to know was my attitude toward the United Front in China. They said that U.S. aid to China in whatever form should not be used in a way that would encourage Chiang Kai-shek to give priority to his quarrel with the Chinese Communists over his resistance to Japan. In other words, the United Front, even if it was only nominal, should be continued, and there should not be a civil war in China, weakening the national resistance to the Japanese invasion.

On the whole, the meeting was more like getting acquainted and exchanging views than an interrogation. They quickly understood that I was not emotionally committed either to Chiang or to the Chinese Communists and that while not a Marxist, I considered the Soviet Union to be a kind of ally-in-waiting. (Remember, this was just before the Nazi attack on the Soviet Union.) Once it was found that our views were in general accord, the rest was a briefing, though not in detail, for they obviously understood that it was a situation in which I would have to find out the details only after arriving in China.

After this interview with the Treasury group it was agreed that a dispatch would be sent to Chiang Kai-shek nominating me; and if and when Chiang accepted the nomination, I had next to be received by T.V. Soong, who would then send his corroboration to Chiang, and then the appointment would be made. T.V. Soong was the head of the Chinese Purchasing Office in Washington, which at that time, six months before Pearl Harbor, was still very important, because U.S. material could be shipped to French Indochina and then taken by rail to Yunnan Province. This gave Soong a position from which he could press on Chiang Kai-shek the importance of his views as an expert resident in the U.S. capital. The Treasury already had a representative in Chungking; but I do not know whether the nomination went through him or through the Department of State.

When I paid my formal call on T.V. Soong, I went alone. As I entered his office, he was sitting behind a big desk, behaving like his idea of an American big boss. Just after I came in a buzzer went off on his desk, and he spoke into a kind of communicator. A moment later, one of his Chinese assistants came in and spoke to Soong deferentially, in such a low voice that I could not hear, and offered him a paper. Soong did not ask him to sit down. He took the paper, glanced at it, scribbled on it, and handed it back. The young man left without another word. The whole scene gave me an impression that Soong was trying to show that he was an important man, who bossed his staff rather than consulted with them.

Soong then turned to me. He was brisk and brief. No oriental courtesies here. He spoke only in English, making no attempt to test my Chinese. English was good enough for foreigners. I was an outsider, not an insider. He congratulated me on my nomination and said that he would report accordingly to the Generalissimo. He knew that this interview was a matter of formality, because he had not been consulted. His manner was as distant as it could be without being rude. In Washington and in New York, T.V. Soong wanted to give the impression that he was not only Chiang's brother-in-law, but his confidential man in the United States, and anything important should go through him rather than the Chinese ambassador. In fact, T.V. Soong did not want to endorse me at all. He would have preferred to strengthen his position within the "family" by having a hand in the selection of Chiang Kai-shek's adviser. I think the only real question he asked me was what my address in Chungking would be (thus inadvertently revealing his own lack of inside knowledge). I told him it would be "care of the Generalissimo's Headquarters."

After this interview with Soong, I had a short talk with Ludvik Rajchman, a Pole who was T.V. Soong's personal consultant. It is more likely that this interview had been arranged by T.V. Soong than by Currie. Rajchman was a medical doctor who had worked with WHO, the World Health Organization, which had already existed under the League of Nations. He had been in Shanghai on a public health mission for consultation with Chinese medical authorities when the Mukden Incident occurred in September 1931. He immediately got in touch with T.V. Soong, who at that time was the minister of finance, and strongly urged that instead of launching an all-out military resistance, China should bring the whole affair before the League of Nations.

This resulted in the Lytton Mission which went to Manchuria and, upon consulting with both the Chinese and the Japanese, came up with some kind of a compromise formula that in fact was an appeasement and allowed the Japanese to strengthen their position in Manchuria, without any international sanctions against them. Though the Japanese may have thought this Lytton Report entirely pro-Chinese, it had a lot of pro-Chinese verbiage but absolutely no anti-Japanese action.

Before I saw Rajchman, Currie had warned me that this Pole was extremely anti-Soviet and anti-communist. Working for T.V. Soong and for the Chinese government, he would accept the United Front pro forma, but would by no means support it in reality. In my conversation with him, Rajchman made it clear to me that while the Soviet military aid to China was necessary in the present circumstances, one thing of which I had to be aware was that the aid might be converted into Soviet intervention in China, the implication being that I should advise Chiang Kai-shek accordingly. I suppose he did not anticipate a direct Soviet military intervention, but an infiltration. Perhaps he was thinking back to the Canton days and the Soviet influence represented by Borodin and others.

My meeting with Rajchman was a brief, rather formal interview. He did not hide the fact that for him the most important thing was to find out whether my mission was to be as a middleman for Roosevelt, Chiang, and the Chinese Communists. I made it clear that I had no directives from Roosevelt and that I was to be under the orders of Chiang Kai-shek. Rajchman was a shadowy figure who evidently thought of himself as an *éminence grise*.

Then a confirmation came from Chungking, making my appointment definite though not yet public. After this confirmation and before the Nazi invasion of the Soviet Union, which came very soon after, E.C. Carter arranged a meeting over lunch between Soviet Ambassador Konstantin Umanskii and myself. I cannot say for sure how Carter already knew about my appointment. Probably when my appointment became definite, I wrote or telephoned to him from Baltimore to New York, because with this new job I would have to resign as editor of *Pacific Affairs*. As Carter was the international secretary of the IPR, and also the American secretary, he had a legitimate right to know about the change in my situation. Carter had also been working very hard first to get the Soviet Union to set up their unit of the IPR, and later to keep them in it.

At that time, Roosevelt's personal relations with the Soviet Union were not bad at all. Because of the Japanese naval "envelopment" of China, U.S. supplies by sea were almost totally cut off, and the principal source of military supply for Chiang Kai-shek, including airplanes and artillery, was the Soviet Union. Therefore perhaps one could legitimately say that it was not only useful, but also important, that the Soviet Union should know about a new U.S. adviser to Chiang Kai-shek.

It was for these reasons that Carter immediately stepped in to see that I had an interview with Umanskii, whom I had met as one of the Soviet delegates to the international conference of the IPR at Yosemite in 1936. I have already mentioned that at that meeting the head of the Soviet delegation had told me to keep an eye on Umanskii's career, because he was a "coming man." Umanskii spoke English very well. He was also a very cynical man. He certainly believed in the Soviet policy of supplying arms to Chiang, and to Chiang only, not diverting any to the Chinese Communists so as not to stimulate any split within China.

I can remember very clearly, however, that in the course of the conversation, he said: "I suppose you know what kind of a ~~son of a bitch~~ you are going to be working for." In other words, while supporting Chiang Kai-shek's government, he had no personal illusions about Chiang himself. At the same time, it is possible that he was one of the Soviet experts who were already wary of the Chinese Communists. Li Li-san, who had been their man, had fallen from power in 1930, and they had no reason to count on Mao Tsetung as "their man."

Later, at the McCarran hearings, when I was asked a question on this meeting, I said, by a slip of memory, that it took place *after* the Nazi invasion of the Soviet Union. As they knew, of course, that it was shortly *before* the invasion, my answer was made one of the indictments for purgery against me. According to the point of view of the McCarran Committee, after the Nazi attack on the Soviet Union, the United States and the Soviet Union automatically became Allies, and therefore such a meeting was permissible; but if

I had met Umanskii *before* the attack, this could only have been because I was personally pro-Soviet and was revealing to the Soviet ambassador things that had not been announced in the United States.

Well, in the meantime, the Nazi invasion started, and there came the great moment of my being introduced to the President. The Nazi invasion was perhaps already a week old; and the sensational news was coming in about the speed of the Nazi penetration. When I went into the President's room, Roosevelt was already there. Though he had never set eyes on me before, he breezily greeted me by my first name, in the familiar Roosevelt manner. (To use the first name was a fashion started by Roosevelt and was not yet common in those days.) I think I can remember the exact words he pronounced. He said: "Come in, Owen. Sit down. Tell me what you think of this Hitler invasion. Are the Russians going to hold?" This was the first thing he said, without any reference to my going to China at all. Although surprised by this question, I answered promptly: "Yes, Sir, I think so. The Russians will have to make a deep retreat, and it will be a long war; but in the end, the Russians will come out on the winning side."

"Good!" said Roosevelt. "All my generals tell me that the Russians will be washed up in two or three weeks. ["All my generals" would include the famous General Marshall who was the chief of staff.] But I agree with you. Now, when you get to *Chun kin* [his American way of pronouncing Chungking], you tell *Chang* [Chiang] that the Russians are going to hold." Obviously, his meaning was to let Chiang know that he, Roosevelt, thought that the Germans would not succeed in defeating the Russians, and therefore Chiang should not be panicked into thinking that with the collapse of the Soviet Union, which was providing so much military aid, he would have to make some kind of surrender or semi-surrender to the Japanese.

This was about the whole of the interview. Roosevelt did not say anything about U.S. policy toward China, and the interview could not have lasted more than eight or ten minutes. When I took leave, he said: "Good luck!" or something like that. This kind of interview was totally unexpected, for I had naturally expected him to say something about China; but seeing me off to China, the only thing he talked about was the Soviet Union.

Now, I have to explain why I disagreed with the opinion of the

President's generals. Though Roosevelt's question was quite unexpected, my answer was not given on the spur of the moment. It went back to 1936 when I had been in Moscow with E.C. Carter for the setting up of the Soviet branch of the IPR. We had a round of social engagements along with the Soviet negotiations; and naturally the Americans and British were interested in what was going on. At that time, there was already a great deal of discussion regarding the Hitler-Mussolini Axis and the Berlin-Rome-Tokyo Axis. The general opinion was that the Soviet Union had the kind of army that had been brought into being by the revolutionaries but was professionally absolutely incompetent to face anything as well equipped and well trained as the German Reichswehr.

On two separate occasions, however, one at the British embassy and one at the U.S. embassy, I met the assistant military attaché of each embassy. Because of the increasing Japanese pressure on China, and because everybody was aware of the Japanese threat to Siberia as well as to China, I asked each assistant military attaché (quite separately) what he thought of the Red Army and its capacity for a major war. The answers in both cases were so identical that I can quote them in the same words. Both men had taken the trouble to go on maneuvers with the Red Army and had made a serious study of it—not simply an ideological study. Both said that the Soviet Army would present no threat either to Japan or to Germany. It was not capable of carrying out a major invasion or attack; on the other hand, it was a very strong defensive army. All Soviet equipment and training were based on defense and not on offense. If anybody should attack them, the attacker would have a rough time of it. Remembering these conversations, I gave Roosevelt the answer that the Russians would hold.

It will be worthwhile to say a few more words about these two military attachés. The Englishman had been an officer in a Welsh regiment. He was an open-minded fellow who, instead of being a cut-and-dried officer, had taken the trouble to learn Welsh in order to have better rapport with the Welsh-speaking soldiers in his regiment. In the 1914 war, he had been captured by the Germans and had been put into a prisoner camp for officers. There he had met captured Russian officers and occupied his time learning Russian. So as a military attaché in Moscow he was able to talk with Soviet officers in their language, as a fellow professional.

The American was also an interesting character, Lt. Colonel Philip Faymonville. He had been sent to Japan to learn Japanese in order to become a military intelligence expert on Japan. At the time of the Russian Revolution, when Japan intervened in Siberia in 1918, he was sent from Japan to Vladivostok. As the United States was very much worried that Japan might try to occupy the Maritime Province, he was sent there to keep an eye on the Japanese. In Vladivostok he proceeded to learn Russian and became a great lover of Russian opera and ballet and the whole of Russian culture. Eventually, he too ended up in Moscow. Before World War II, senior military attachés of the Great Powers were high-ranking men, whose previous experience would give them no knowledge of the Russian language. They would, however, have under them assistant attachés who knew that language, such as the two men I have described.

These men were both lieutenant-colonels. I do not know what has become of the British one. As for the American, by 1941, when the United States became an ally of the Soviet Union, he, as an engineer, had been assigned to some military arsenal. A high opinion of the Soviet Red Army was not popular in the U.S. service, so he was still a lieutenant-colonel; but when Hitler actually invaded the Soviet Union, Roosevelt looked around and said: "Haven't we got somebody with first-hand knowledge of these Russians?" In the course of scratching around they found the name of this man. Roosevelt immediately lifted him up to the rank of brigadier general and put him in charge of lend-lease supplies to the Soviet Union.

Now coming back to my interview with Roosevelt, since it was often insinuated later that I belonged to the F.D.R. inner circle and had an influence on him, it is appropriate to emphasize that this interview with him, which lasted barely ten minutes, was the only time I ever met him. It was he who did most of the talking, and I do not think I ever met him again. On coming back from Chungking on leave in February 1942, I may have been received by the President as a matter of formality; but if I really was, I do not remember anything about it.

I want to make it very clear here that I was *nominated* (not *appointed*) by Roosevelt. I was *appointed* by Chiang and all my correspondence was to go through Lauchlin Currie, using a code, and not directly to the President. Nevertheless, brief though it was, the meeting with the President was an important tip-off (which I did not properly appreciate at the time) on the relative importance of China and the Soviet Union in Roosevelt's thinking.

How the Choice Fell on Me

Before going on with my story about what I did in Chungking, I must deal with the situation and atmosphere in which I came to be selected to be personal adviser to Chiang Kai-shek. Roosevelt's chief interest was in helping Churchill save Britain from following France into defeat. China had a low priority with him, such a low priority that he used China as a dumping ground for getting rid of ambitious people to whom he did not want to give jobs that would help them build up their personal political influence. This was something I, not being an experienced prowler in the corridors of power then or later, did not understand until I was told about it, many years afterward.

Thus when Roosevelt appointed the noisy retired general, Patrick Hurley, as ambassador to China, after Hurley had left the room Roosevelt turned to his entourage and is reported to have said: "Well, there goes Pat. Now the next thing will be his book, the title of which will be *Alone in China*." This does not mean, of course, that Hurley would be isolated in China; on the contrary, Roosevelt's reference was to Hurley's overbearing self-confidence. The President expected Hurley to come on as the master of military policy, political policy, and everything else. In general, there were all kinds of missions being sent out to China to discuss transport on the Burma Road, economic problems, and that kind of thing. I can remember one man, whose name was Donald Nelson, and who had at one time been considered a top figure in economic policy in the United States; but I was told later that when he was sent to China, knowing people said: "Aha! That means that Donald is starting to go downhill!"

Moreover, even though Hitler had not yet attacked the Soviet Union, Roosevelt already believed, as is confirmed by the later course of his policy, that at the end of the war the European colonial empires in Asia would be weakened and the United States and the Soviet Union would be the Great Powers of the Pacific. For that reason he thought, quite mistakenly, that if he and Stalin could agree, they would together be able to make the major decisions about the future of China and Japan. His order of priority was therefore: Stalin first, then Chiang Kai-shek.

I think that Roosevelt was prepared to accept China nominally as one of the world's Big Four. But he assumed that with the Allies' victory over Hitler, there would be three Big Powers—the United States, Britain, and the Soviet Union—and that the main decisions in Western Europe would be made by the United States and Britain, and the main decisions for the Pacific, and particularly for the position of China, would be made by Roosevelt and Stalin. To Chiang, this meant the possibility that nominally there would be Four Big Powers, but that in fact China would be squeezed into a corner and have to accept the decisions made by the Big Three. Evidently Chiang's asking Roosevelt to send a personal adviser to him was a part of an attempt to make Roosevelt more committed to China.

Politically, the relationship between the United States and China was good. At that time, the principal form of aid used was financial, and it was carried out through the Treasury rather than the Department of State. There may have been some jealousy on the part of the State Department that this policy should be handled directly through the Treasury without going through the State Department and diplomatic channels. Roosevelt's top priority was to send as much military aid as possible to Churchill, and this very heavily diminished the amount of such things as airplanes and artillery that Roosevelt could send to China. As a result, the principal military aid for China was coming from the Soviet Union—from Siberia to Sinkiang, then to Kansu, and on to Chungking.

Though the relations between the United States and the Soviet Union were very bad, especially after the Soviet attack on Finland, Washington and Moscow had a common interest in countering the Japanese invasion of China; and some people may have thought that the more guns and airplanes the Soviet Union sent to China, the better, because Russia would not make so much trouble in Europe.

The U.S. policy was to try to stabilize the Chinese economy and currency to prevent a runaway inflation. I think there had already been formed something called the ABC (America, Britain, and China) Financial Committee to consult about exchange rates and such things. As Currie would be classed as an economist of the Keynesian school, in Washington he would be a link between Roosevelt and the Treasury. In other words, he was a man for exercising White House influence in the middle levels of the Treasury. In those days, it was frequently mentioned in the newspapers that the President had around him a group of personal advisers, consultants, and experts who were paid out of White House funds and did not belong to any department. They were quite often referred to in the press as Roosevelt's Bright Young Men, and Currie was one of them. With a strong isolationist mood in Congress and in the country as a whole, Roosevelt needed these personal intimates who enabled him to keep his New Deal going in the United States and to pursue his own foreign policy, which was interventionist, where the official policy was one of neutrality.

Currie had had no particular connection with China, but because of his relation with the Treasury, he had been to Chungking two or three times, and on these visits his principal interpreter in talking to the Generalissimo had been Madame Chiang. The visits went so well that Chiang wanted to establish a permanent link. On the ·other hand, Roosevelt also obviously did not trust the State Department too much for handling China affairs and wanted to establish a more direct personal contact with Chiang Kai-shek. That was why he had sent Currie as the primary contact between himself and Chiang. But Chiang thought: "Now, I am talking to a junior intimate of Roosevelt, but he is kept too busy working for the President. How can I find somebody who has the same kind of confidence as Currie, but who can work exclusively for me?"

Another reason for Chiang to want to have this kind of channel was that he deeply distrusted the Department of State, being convinced its policy for the Pacific and Asia (and the Soviet Union, too, as I learned later) was influenced by too many Japan-appeasers. In fact, Joseph Grew and his young Japan experts were too much in sympathy with the Japanese militarist propaganda that Japan was the only barrier against the Red Flood. The State Department had a strong element which thought that Japanese militarists could establish law and order in China; and the senior people dealing with China lacked confidence in the solidity of China, in China's ability to resist.

Consequently, journalists and academic people going to talk

with the people of the State Department about the situation in the Far East were more likely to encounter and be influenced by those who thought that they could do business with Japan than by those who thought that China could be succesfully supported. The former group thought that they could do business with a dictator, and that those who supported anti-dictators were too ideological and were in danger of being influenced by Soviet propaganda.

One more reason for Chiang's suspicion of the State Department was that he personally disliked the then U.S. ambassador in Chungking, Clarence E. Gauss (a dislike which Gauss cordially returned). This was not entirely the ambassador's fault. He had previouly been U.S. consul general in Shanghai for a good many years, a post very different from that of ambassador. In the China of the 1930s every consul general in Shanghai had been his country's principal protester against the efforts of Chinese merchants, bankers, and industrialists, backed by the local and national Chinese authorities (whose most effective tactic was bureaucratic delay, passing complaints from department to department), to erode the privileges of foreigners under the Unequal Treaties imposed on China in the nineteenth-century age of imperialism.

This kind of experience predisposed Gauss to look for the catch, the hidden trap, in every Chinese initiative. He was in fact an orderly minded conservative, who wanted everything to be done in proper sequence. He could not even be stampeded into the kind of anti-communist policy that Chiang wanted, because he did not want the United States to be wheedled into taking a stance that would apparently increase Chiang's personal power in the short run but in reality weaken China in the long struggle against the Japanese invasion.

As far as I know, it was entirely Chiang's initiative, and not Currie inviting Chiang's request, that led Chiang to ask Currie to send an adviser. Chiang most likely wanted to have someone like the famous Harry Hopkins who, without holding any position like that of ambassador, was running about as a personal go-between for Roosevelt and Churchill. This was not acceptable to Roosevelt. A Harry Hopkins between himself and Churchill, yes, but not between him and Chiang Kai-shek. Chiang would have accepted Currie himself as adviser; but Currie did not want to do that, because going out to Chungking would take him out of the inside circle around Roosevelt. Neither did Roosevelt want to send one of his inside men to Chiang, because he did not want Chiang to be able to ask: "Who is on the way up and who is on the way down in Washington?" He was not prepared to grant Chiang that kind of foothold in the White House. So Roosevelt's way out was not to send an expert on Washington, but to send an expert on China. The less that man knew about Washington, the better.

Up to that time and in all my years in China, I had met practically no high-up Chinese politicians or government people. This, from the White House point of view, or at least from Currie's point of view, was a good qualification, for it meant that I was not previously identified with any of the cliques in Chungking. In editing *Pacific Affairs*, I had had contacts with and had published articles by various Chinese authors, some of whom were orthodox Kuomintang, and others who were more or less left-wing progressive Kuomintang; but they did not give me any idea of the inside stories within that party.

Currie gave me a rather strong hint about this gap between Chiang's request and Roosevelt's reaction to it. He said to me something like: "The President doesn't want to send one of the White House crowd" to suggest what Chiang really wanted. Nevertheless, the difference between the expectations of Chiang and Roosevelt did not worry me; for I knew by then that in my job in Chungking, I would have the strong backing of Currie, who said; "Your line of communication will not be directly to the President, but to me."

In fact, whatever Currie told me was on a "need to know" basis. About the background of the financial aid to China, I knew in general, as everybody did. With the Japanese cutting the oceanic lines of communication, the supply of munitions to China came more and more from the Soviet Union, and the U.S. support for China became more and more financial in form. Therefore, one of the areas of maneuver was to see that the money made available to China was not gobbled up by Chinese generals and politicians, but was used to try to hold down inflation in China and help the economy. But it was only step by step, partly in Chungking and partly in Washington after the war, that I learned a great deal about the underlying pattern of bureaucratic civil war among Washington departments and vendettas among the individuals concerned.

Here I have to tell you how Currie came to know my name. I had always assumed that he had simply asked somebody to make a list of people who were publishing, writing, and lecturing on Japan, China, and the United States and that in time my name had come up. I never asked Currie about it. Much later, in the late 1940s, between the end of the war and the McCarthy-McCarran period, on an occasion when Eleanor and I were dining in Washington with friends, somebody asked me: "How did your name come to be selected to be recommended to Chiang Kai-shek?" I had to say (as so often before): "As a matter of fact, I have never known in detail."

At that moment, someone sitting two or three places away at the table, whom I had never met before, spoke up and said: "I can tell you. I was responsible." The speaker was a man named John M. Gaus who had been a professor of economics at Harvard; one of his prize Ph.D. students was Currie. When I met him at this dinner, he was a professor of political science at the University of Wisconsin. He was a rather anonymous man, one of those people who, in those Roosevelt years, circulated in areas where such things as personal appointments were made. In other words, he had been a talent-spotter, finding bright young men for Roosevelt's brain trust and for various New Deal agencies. He had recruited Currie for Roosevelt's service. From time to time he would visit Washington to see how his protégés were getting along.

One day in June 1941, Gaus had been on such a trip to Washington to see some of his "boys," as he called them. When he went into Currie's office, Currie greeted him by saying: "Ah, John, this time I've got a job for *you*. You've got to go to Chungking to be adviser to Chiang Kai-shek." Gaus said: "Oh, no! I don't know enough about China and Japan and all the rest of it. But I've got the name of a man who may be the person you want. On the train from Wisconsin to Washington, I was reading an article in the *Atlantic Monthly* about the U.S., China, and Japan by a man named Lattimore. Never heard of him before. But he makes more sense than anybody I've been reading for a long time. Just check up on it."

At that time the Treasury had its own representative in Chungking and, from Currie's point of view as an economist, possessed all the technical economic information. What he needed, he thought, was somebody whose general economic ideas would be friendly to the Treasury attitude. Such a man would, however, have to operate in a very political context. He had therefore found it very difficult to locate a man who would know his way around the politics of China and at the same time *not* be a Roosevelt intimate and *not* be tied up with any particular faction either in China or in Washington. Then I fell out of the sky.

Of course, there were other specialists on China, but some of them would have been regarded by a person like Currie as appeasing Japanese imperialism and vulnerable to Japanese propaganda. These were the kind he wanted to displace. Others would be pro-China people whom he would regard as too Left. Suddenly he was recommended a man who was neither Left nor Right, not even, in a political sense, a centralist belonging to some centralist group, but merely an individual who had sensible economic and political ideas and knew China. Currie had told me that when my name came up, he went over to the Treasury and asked if any of the people there had ever heard of Lattimore. Several of them had and had even read things written by me and thought well of me, though they did not know me personally. Upon this, he said to himself: "Okay. He might do!" So the telephone call for me from the White House.

I did not know whether there were other candidates, but now I know that there was a volunteer for this post as Chiang Kai-shek's adviser. He was William Bullit, a wealthy man from Philadelphia, one of those who were known in those days as "parlor pinks" or more recently "radical chic," very left-wing. He had married the widow of John Reed, the author of *Ten Days That Shook the World* (1919). I had met him in Moscow in 1936, when he was Roosevelt's first ambassador to Moscow, after Roosevelt recognized the Soviet Union in November 1933. Roosevelt made the mistake of thinking that a left-wing ambassador would be welcome in the Soviet Union; but Bullit was not a success with the Soviets.

Roosevelt then withdrew Bullit and replaced him with a millionaire, who had made his own money and married a woman who had inherited money. The Soviets said: "Aha! Here is a man who has made money and married money. These are the men who really run the United States, not the radical chic." This man, Joseph Davies, was a very successful ambassador in Moscow. One of my correspondent friends in Moscow once told me that it was not the U.S. leftists who impressed the Soviets, but the rightists.

Bullit now wanted to have this job in Chungking. Where you

have a confidential structure, you have always leaks; and the very fact that Currie had already started looking for somebody would get talk going around. I did not know about Bullit's candidature until the McCarran hearings, when Bullit testified very bitterly against me. After this failure to get the job in Chungking, his last official appointment was as U.S. ambassador or whatever in Vichy France, where he became a supporter of Marshal Phillippe Pétain. It happens often that upper middle-class rich intellectuals, starting out as young flaming radicals, as they grow older, move farther and farther to the Right, winding up as extreme right-wingers.

So this is the story of how I was nominated by Roosevelt. To sum up, it seems to have been one of these cases that happen in politics a great deal. You appoint somebody not because you think he is really the right person, but because otherwise you have to appoint someone who definitely would be the wrong person. I suppose that Chiang Kai-shek, before he agreed to the nomination made by Roosevelt, must have been informed about me and found out that I was not the kind of person he preferred. Nevertheless, he accepted the nomination, because this man proposed by the President stood totally outside the State Department (in fact, the State Department thought him a nuisance because he was too pro-Chinese). If Chiang could not get someone who would be able to tell him the inside secrets of the White House, then maybe the thing for him to do would be to accept this man whom Roosevelt was accepting as an expert on China, to influence him in Chungking so that through his dispatches to Washington he would in turn influence Roosevelt's thinking on China.

Why I Accepted the Job in Chungking

When I returned from the White House after my first interview with Currie, I discussed the matter with Eleanor. Of course, she was much surprised, but she said: "You have to go." Actually, we did not really have anything to discuss, for I was going out to an unknown kind of job. Though it would mean separation from Eleanor, she was enthusiastic about my going. Ever since the military element in Japan had moved from the invasion of Manchuria in 1931 to an all-out attempt, beginning in 1937, to break the will of China, Eleanor and I had been campaigning for a tougher U.S. policy in Asia. We wanted an embargo on the shipment to Japan of scrap iron and other materials to feed the Japanese war industry. We also knew that since the fall of France and the battle of Britain in 1940, Europe had held the top priority in Roosevelt's foreign policy. It seemed, therefore, that the Department of State and the White House had agreed to keep as quiet as possible about Japan's aggression in China until things could be straightened out in Europe. We had already been deeply committed to U.S. support for China.

During the 1930s, I quite frequently wrote articles in the press criticizing the U.S. policy of supporting the Japanese militarists with the materials of war. I cannot swear that I never submitted a memorandum to the State Department, but the only official approach I can remember in these years was through a small Baltimore committee, a part of a general national committee, trying to stop the export of war materials to Japan. On one occasion I, with two or three other people, made up a deputation which requested an appointment with Cordell Hull, a celebrated Tennessee politician, who was at that time the secretary of state. I think several of us went over to Washington together to present our view to Hull, though I may have been the only one representing the group.

Quite likely, I was brought to the meeting with Cordell Hull by Stanley Hornbeck, who was the head of the China Desk of the State Department. When I was admitted and received by the secretary of state, I made a little statement objecting to the U.S. policy. I do not even remember whether it was read out or spoken. At any rate the reply was: "In the State Department we are professionals and know what we are doing. You amateurs should stay away." One thing I remember is that when I was waiting to go in to see Hornbeck, his secretary sat there and chatted with me until I was invited to enter his office. This was Alger Hiss. Later when Hiss was accused of being a Soviet spy in 1948 (The Hiss Case), it was entirely unexpected to me, because my firm impression of him was that he was a very conservative young man, a solid member of the "Establishment." I never have believed, and still don't believe, that Hiss was guilty.

My foray was one of the usual petitions which U.S. citizens often undertake when they hope to change the official policies of the government. Later, however, even that sort of thing might have been interpreted as my having a special connection with the State

Department and as evidence of an attempt to exercise my personal influence over the department. On the contrary, except for a few, quite uninfluential people, the State Department thought of me as a bit of a nuisance, an uncontrollable outsider who had a crazy notion that the Mongols were important. Yet I felt very strongly that I had to do something to change the official policy toward Japan, and on two or three occasions, I went to see Stanley Hornbeck on my personal initiative, not as a representative of any group or organization.

I think Hornbeck went to China first as an attaché to some kind of U.S. financial mission and stayed on as an adviser to the Chinese. Like so many such advisers, he thought that his mission was to tell the Chinese what they must do, rather than suggest to them options on what they might do. He was also one of those people who had spent a long time in China, twenty years or so, but did not know enough Chinese to ask for a cup of tea. This meant that his connections in China were only with, or at least through, American-educated Chinese. The higher the position people like Hornbeck held, the more likely they were to know no Chinese at all. The China-born, or the people who had grown up in China, were regarded as too limited and too provincial in their knowledge, knowing only China and not understanding the world situation.

I had met Hornbeck at several IPR conferences, at which he was a State Department observer, and had been able to listen to him while he was exchanging views with other people. I think he was an honest, upright man, but of limited mentality. I remember that there was one occasion in connection with the IPR in which I made a flippant remark that was meant to be an oblique criticism of the Department of State. I wish I could remember what I said and what it was about, but all I can remember is that Hornbeck was very indignant. He thought that it was not something to try to be funny about.

He was in favor of a "softly, softly" policy toward Japan and largely accepted the idea that Japan was an essential barrier against the Soviet Union. He thought that my idea of trying to restrain Japan with sanctions or similar actions was ridiculous. At the same time, he was very pro-Chiang Kai-shek in Chinese domestic policies. I think it would be fair to use a phrase that my wife and I wrote in our joint book, *China, a Short History* (1947): "America and other imperial powers always wanted in China somebody who would be strong enough to carry out the orders issued to them by the international powers, but not strong enough to resist the orders." Hornbeck, and a lot of Americans, thought of Chiang Kai-shek as the kind of man who, with enough support, would be able to control China, but would be dependent on that support and would therefore never be able to become really independent of the United States and the other Great Powers.

Though I had agreed to go out to work for Chiang Kai-shek, I did not really have any special idea about him as a person. Indeed, right up to that day my personal knowledge of China had been heavily concentrated on the North, Northeast, and Northwest of China. As a consequence of Chiang Kai-shek's coup d'état in 1927, which broke up the First United Front with the Chinese Communists, the Kuomintang elements located along the Yangtze and to the south came to be dominant.

This involved local and regional conditions with which I was not at all acquainted. If you had asked me at that time what part did Canton, Kuangsi, or Kueichou play in Chinese national politics, I could not have given you an answer. I had not traveled there, I did not know economic conditions there, and I had not done business there, as I had in North China. The influence of the North, the part of China I knew well, was decidedly limited in national politics. When I was asked whether I would accept a position as adviser to Chiang Kai-shek, I felt enthusiastic about the job because of the international situation and the national unity of China. I knew also, however, that, having to work with all these unfamiliar personalities in the Kuomintang, I would be up against very difficult problems.

One of the great problems of China, I knew, was that although there was already a widespread and growing feeling of China as a nation which ought to be united, regionalism was still very strong. In 1927, Chiang Kai-shek had made a big mistake in the way he broke the United Front and turned against the Communists. The defeat of the Chinese warlords had by no means been completed, and the moment the United Front was broken in this way, it left a number of warlords in different parts of China independent or semi-independent of Chiang Kai-shek. For this reason, there was not in fact a united China to resist Japanese aggression when the invasion of Manchuria came in 1931. I accepted the appointment because I totally agreed with Roosevelt's policy that while the Japanese invasion was going on, for the Chinese to start fighting a civil war against each other again was all wrong. The Second United Front, formed as the result of the Sian Incident in December 1936, was essential for the survival of China.

Unfortunately, the tendency in the United States was, and still is today, to treat Chiang Kai-shek primarily as the ideological symbol of anti-Communism. People forget that during that period, especially with Wang Ching-wei having gone over to the Japanese (December 1938) and having set up a collaborationist government in Nanking (March 1940), Chiang was the symbol of something else. Even though the United Front was pretty nominal, and even though there were incidents like the attack by Kuomintang forces on the New Fourth Army (originally Communist forces in Central China, but placed under the command of Chiang Kai-shek) in January 1941, the Chungking-Yenan United Front did exist, and Chou En-lai was in Chungking as the representative of the Communist Party. Chiang was actually the symbol of the Kuomintang higher-ups who would not go over to the Japanese. Therefore, the thing to do, as I saw it, was always to talk about China, rather than about the Kuomintang and the Communists. My visit to Yenan in 1937 had convinced me that the United Front against the Japanese was not only important, but also possible.

In my previous experience as a commercial agent, I had become familiar with the phenomenon of Chinese merchants who, like all Chinese of the time, were in general anti-imperial nationalists. But in certain circumstances, merchants who contracted with foreign firms, such as mine, would lose their money if the firm lost money, and in such cases they would act with the imperialist foreign merchants against the warlords of their own provinces. This prepared me for the phenomenon that in the United Front—I think this is probably true in all united fronts and in all revolutions—a person like Chiang Kai-shek would feel: "If I get the right kind of foreign aid in sufficient quantity and can be successful enough in leading the resistance, there will be certain elements in the Communist part of the United Front who, for the sake of their own interests, will come over to my side of the United Front." I was proved correct when I got to Chungking, and undoubtedly, as the evidence that came out later shows, the Communists in exactly the same way were thinking: "If we conduct our part of the anti-Japanese resistance successfully, there will be elements in the Kuomintang who will come over to us."

Most of the U.S. IPR members were in favor of the United Front in China and were more afraid that Chiang Kai-shek would wreck the Front than they were that the Chinese Communists would wreck it, though this cannot be said for the whole of the IPR. I would say, for example, that the British Committee representing the IPR was probably more pro-Chiang than the Americans. It is true that many of the U.S. IPR members were critical of Chiang for being oppressive and not democratic; but this does not mean that they were entirely pro-Chinese Communists, because at that time in the Chinese United Front, there were National Salvationists and others who were somewhere in the middle. They included many business and professional people who formed a political movement rather than a political party. In the U.S. IPR in general, it was felt that a united China was essential not only for anti-Japanese imperialist resistance, but also for opposition to the Berlin-Tokyo Axis.

Japan had come over my horizon early in the 1920s when I was working for the *Peking and Tientsin Times* in Tientsin. This was the period of broadened international intervention in Eastern Siberia, followed by the Washington Conference for Disarmament; and even a very conservative Englishman like Woodhead felt that the Japanese were really destroying the Anglo-Japanese Alliance (1902-21), because by their increasing aggressiveness they were not only encroaching on China, but were also encroaching on British interests in China. It was then that I became aware of the difference between Japanese commercial and economic enterprise and expansion into the China market on one hand, and the militaristic, territorial, geopolitical expansion and strategic control in China on the other hand. Therefore, with the invasion of 1931, my instant reaction was that now the Japanese military were embarking on a course of action which would create more international problems than it would solve.

When I accepted the job in Chungking, I certainly did not feel myself sufficiently well informed, and at that stage I had no theoretical conviction that would give me some idea of what I would think or do about the United Front. I did approve in general of Roosevelt's conviction that the United Front was essential, a conviction that was not a question of political theory but was based simply on his understanding of the obvious fact that if China was being invaded and the Chinese divided their own strength by fighting each other instead of fighting the Japanese, then everything would be lost. With that I cordially agreed, and as for any theories about exactly how it would be done, that would have to wait until I got to Chungking. In the letter of introduction Roosevelt gave me to present to Chiang Kai-shek, he said: "Lattimore understands my policy and thoroughly supports it."

I thought that the crisis in China between the Kuomintang and the Communist Party was between two kinds of authority rather than between democracy and non-democracy, and I was ready to cooperate with Chiang Kai-shek primarily because of the United Front. Even if the United Front had not existed, however, I would still have gone. I thought that certainly one of the things I would like to try to do, if I could, was to get Chungking to adopt a more intelligent policy toward the Mongols. If they had had a better understanding of the situation in Mongolia, De Wang would not have been driven into the arms of the Japanese.

Moreover, my job was to serve the common interest of democratic Europe and North America against fascism and nazism and Japanese militarism. In that cause, I thought, China would have a more important part to play than most people thought. Most people thought that we would settle the big question by defeating Hitler and Mussolini; and then when that had been done we would turn round and shake our fingers at the Japanese and the Chinese to tell them what to do. This was before Pearl Harbor, of course.

One obvious thing to be said is that I was not thinking of myself as a policymaker who could shape the destiny of China, a sort of Lawrence of Arabia figure or anything like that. I thought of myself in two ways: the first was that I would be a channel between Chungking and Washington; the second was that I would have a chance not to teach but to learn things about China that I could never learn in any other way. I had not quite a sense of mission, but I wanted to go and witness a very important chapter of history.

I was to be on leave from the university. Naturally, Isaiah Bowman, the president, was pleased that a member of his university should be getting such a confidential post. Though he disliked Roosevelt, he loved being on the doorstep of men who wield power. He wondered whether I was going to be used by Roosevelt to manipulate Chiang Kai-shek, or by Chiang Kai-shek to manipulate Roosevelt. He asked me a direct question: "In this job, is your loyalty going to be primarily to Roosevelt or to Chiang?" I answered with a story about T.E. Lawrence.

In 1919, Lawrence, then still holding the rank of colonel in the British Army, accompanied his comrade in arms Prince Faisal of the Hejaz to the Versailles Peace Conference, acting as his interpreter and confidential adviser. (Later, in 1921, as a move in British Middle East policy, Faisal was promoted to be King of Iraq.) As part of these goings on, Prince Faisal was received in state at Buckingham Palace by King George V with Colonel Lawrence at his side. Horrors! Lawrence was wearing Arab costume. There was no time to order him to go home and change, so he went in with the Prince. When they came out, a court official hissed in Lawrence's ear: "How dare you, sir, holding His Majesty's commission, appear before your monarch in fancy dress?" "When a man serves two masters," Lawrence replied, "and must offend one, he should offend the greater."

Bowman seemed to have accepted the formula. I myself think it was a good formula to guide me during my service with Chiang Kai-shek. After all, though I was nominated by Roosevelt, I was appointed by Chiang and I drew my pay from the headquarters of the Generalissimo. I was a kind of mercenary, and an honest mercenary is one who is loyal to his pay.

Chapter Four

■

CHUNGKING

What Chungking Was Like

I arrived in Hong Kong on the 15th of July and left for Chungking on the 19th. Flying between Hong Kong and Chungking in the summer of 1941 was hazardous. No American, British, or French passenger planes had been shot down or forced to land, but the Japanese navy controlled the coast and the Japanese army and air force held bases as far inland as Hankow on the middle Yangtze. Chungking was being frequently bombed. There was always the fear that if some important Chinese politicians were on the plane it might be shot down. Therefore the general rule was that planes would take off only when the weather was officially too bad for flying. It certainly looked unflyable when my plane took off.

The most notable passenger on the plane was Colonel Claire Chennault of the "Flying Tigers," the "volunteer" U.S. air force that had already made a name for itself fighting in the service of Chiang Kai-shek. Tactically, Chennault was perhaps the most brilliant trainer of fighter pilots of his day. His "tigers" were not, as most people still think, named after the jungle beast, but after the tiger shark. Each plane had a shark's head painted on the two sides of its nose, with gaping jaws and huge teeth. I met only a few of the pilots, but they all seemed to have the simple-minded conviction that when the Japanese pilot saw a winged shark's mask approaching him, he would be so distraught with terror that he would be easy to shoot down.

Chennault himself was a simple-minded man. Strategically, he had a blind spot in thinking that when the war with Japan was over, it would be easy for Chiang to "clean up" (that was the phrase) the Chinese Communists from the air with the air force trained in battle against the Japanese. This was the political-military line that he was trying to sell to Chiang—never with quite complete success—throughout the time that I had anything to do with such affairs. We all know that in the civil war with the Chinese Communists, Chiang Kai-shek's air force, with U.S. planes available to back them up, had complete control of the air but was unable to cope with the loose, flexible Communist style of campaigning on the ground. It is true that his pilots were good—there is no doubt about that. When on leave in 1942, I visited the main Chinese training base in the United States, where both fighter and bomber pilots were being trained. Their American instructors thought well of them.

Incidentally, I remember a talk with one of Chiang's most trained secretaries, who had been engaged in negotiations about Soviet aid. He was an unshakable right-winger, but he was openly bitter in saying that Soviet pilots in China slept on the flying field, instantly ready to man their planes in case of an alarm, while American flyers kept a high morale only if they had comfortable quarters and a plentiful supply of women.

After a flight through rain and cloud, but with no alarm, we landed at Chungking on a flat, gravelly island in the river. After landing, we were supposed to cross a channel and then be carried in sedan chairs up a steep, zigzag path to the top of the Chungking bank of the river. Not being warned of this, I gave way to an instinctive unwillingness to be carried by human beast of burden and insisted on walking. This was impolitic of me not only because protocol required that nice people from Chiang's entourage who had come to meet me had to walk with me, but also because in the Chungking of that time it was beneath the dignity of any "upperclass" person, especially a scholar or any official, to get from one place to another on his own feet. At the top, we got into cars, and I was driven to my residence, one look at which assured me that I was going to be treated as a person of consequence. (It later was assigned as the headquarters residence of General Joseph Stilwell.)

The next day, a car came to take me to my first meeting with the Generalissimo in his official residence. The man who accompanied me was Hollington K. Tong (his own way of rendering his name,

Tung Hsien-kuang, in an English spelling). Hollington was Chiang Kai-shek's most confidential interpreter. He came from the same village as Chiang in Chekiang, not very far away from the city of Ningpo. He had studied in the very famous American School of Journalism at the University of Missouri and came out of it as a newspaperman trained in the U.S. techniques and speaking completely fluent English. He was a man who was essential in handling relations with the foreign press corps.

When I was ushered into the Generalissimo's presence, he greeted me very courteously. Quite obviously, the first thing he wanted to satisfy himself about was whether I could really speak Chinese. As Hollington Tong had come in with me, there was an interpreter available; but Chiang immediately spoke to me with the usual polite phrases, in Northern Chinese (the official or standard Chinese), with a strong accent of his native province, and I gave him the proper answers in Chinese. From then on Chiang never had an interpreter, and we communicated with each other entirely in Chinese, which made possible a genuinely confidential relationship.

Now, it was well known in China that Chiang Kai-shek never learned to speak standard Chinese and had such a strong Chekiang accent that many Northern Chinese found it difficult to understand him. If you were a high official or a general, and there you were in front of the Great Man, it was essential to understand him completely. I more than once saw a Northern high official or general tremble for fear that they might get things wrong when the Great Man was laying down the law on a difficult subject. Here a very curious factor came into play—a phenomenon familiar to linguists. When I was taken to China as a baby, my nurse was a woman from the very same district as Chiang. Even before I spoke English, I spoke a bit of that particular Chinese dialect; but having moved to North China I had promptly forgotten it completely.

Nevertheless, it seems that I still had some ear memory of the sounds of that dialect. When Chiang Kai-shek was speaking bad standard Chinese, I had no difficulty in understanding him, though when he was talking to someone who was from his native district I could not make anything out of their dialect. Of course, I did not tell Chiang why I could understand him easily. It would have been most discourteous to put him on the same level as my Chinese nurse.

Chiang Kai-shek then wasted no time in getting down to business. On this day in early July 1941, with the Nazi Blitzkrieg roaring toward Moscow, still unstopped, the very first thing Chiang Kai-shek asked me was: "What does President Roosevelt think of the German invasion of the Soviet Union?" To this I answered: "The President thinks that the Germans will make a very deep penetration, but the Soviet Union will rally and in the end it will be the Germans who will be defeated, and the Soviets will be on the winning side." Chiang said, in exactly the same words that Roosevelt had used: "Good! I agree with the President. All my generals tell me that the Germans will win, but I think the Soviets will hold out."

In Chungking, I was provided with servants and a car with chauffeur. I also had a man assigned to live in the same house with me and be, so to speak, my secretary-companion. His name was Hsieh Pao-chao. As I heard later, when my name was first announced, people in Chungking began to ask: "Who is this man? What do we do with him?" The political people did not know me, but they quickly identified the fact that I came from Johns Hopkins University. It was Kuo T'ai-ch'i, a former ambassador in London, who nominated Hsieh Pao-chao to work for me. Kuo (who always wrote his name as "Quo," rather than Kuo) seems to have said: "You should give this man Lattimore somebody who is well informed about the Chinese system and also knows something about the United States. Now we have this man Hsieh, who holds a rather unimportant job in the Foreign Office. He is a Johns Hopkins Ph.D. with a thesis on the government of China." Hsieh was Cantonese and was extremely fluent in English. We became very fond of each other.

It turned out that Hsieh, before going to the United States, had graduated from Peiyang University, where he had studied English (which he learned very well) under my father and German (which he learned badly) under my uncle, Alec. My uncle failed him in his final examination paper. Thinking, however, that it would not be fair to fail him without talking to him, Uncle Alec had called him in. Hsieh had explained that he had taken German as a supplementary subject, imagining that German was close enough to English, but German grammar had defeated him. Uncle Alec (who, though fluent in several languages, was a bit shaky on the grammar of all of them, including English) had given him a mark that would put him above the average of his class, but not high enough to make some member of a busy committee suggest a second reading. It was thanks to my uncle's discretion that Hsieh managed to get his degree.

He was perhaps the most completely cynical man I have ever met. He was cynical also about his own Ph.D. He said: "There are two universities in the United States which are a soft touch for Chinese students: Johns Hopkins and Columbia. A Ph.D. there is a lazy man's job. As a matter of fact, my degree has been more of a handicap to me in my Foreign Office career than a help because everybody knows: 'A Johns Hopkins degree for a Chinese? He doesn't have to work for it. He just gets it.'"! He was an old Kuomintang member and he loved to talk. So I did not have to make any remarks myself which could be misconstrued. All I had to do was to sit and listen to him. He was an incurable gossip, and he would always have some gossip about anybody I met. For example, he would say that Minister so-and-so's wife's American lover was so-and-so; and through her lover she was able to exercise this particular line of American influence on this particular minister.

I would classify him as a totally untrustworthy man, whom in a way you could trust completely. I am sure that in his position he was required to turn in reports on me, and I am also sure that though these reports must have been written in a way to indicate that he was closely spying on me, they would not contain anything really important that would do me any harm. After the war, he got his payoff. He became the first Chinese ambassador to Thailand, and then he retired. The last time I heard of him was in Paris in the 1950s. Some Chinese told me that Hsieh had gone to Paris and opened a restaurant and done rather well, but he had already died when I was in Paris to lecture at l'École Pratique des Hautes Études in 1958 and 1959.

There has been some confusion about my real position in Chungking. The role of an adviser to Chiang Kai-shek was often interpreted as an adviser to his government. The official American advisers were not actually advisers in the technical sense of being paid by the Chinese government. For example, the Treasury had its advisers in the Chinese Treasury, but they were sent by the Treasury to set up a sort of branch office of the U.S. Treasury in Chungking to negotiate with the Chinese Treasury. Being appointed by their department, they always remained responsible to it. Their contacts with Chiang were only through the government, and each Chinese clique tried to influence them in its own way. In Chinese these people were called *taipiao* (representative), while my official title was *kuwen*. There was a Chinese joke in Chungking: "*Kuwen taoti shi shemma tunghsi?* (What are advisers anyway?)." The answer was: "*Ku, erh pu wen.* (We hire them and don't ask questions)." This was a pun on *ku*, meaning "to give consideration to," and the word with the same sound meaning "to hire"; *wen* in both cases means "to ask."

Though there were separate private U.S. advisers to high Chinese officials, I was the only foreign private adviser to Chiang Kai-shek. While I was in Chungking, my salary was paid by Chiang's "Headquarters of the Generalissimo," and I had no liaison with the Chinese Ministry of Foreign Affairs, only occasional conversations with individuals on a personal level without an agenda. In my work in Chungking I had no office of my own to which I went every day, nor did I see Chiang at any regular intervals. I read and received visitors at home and could make my own appointments to go to see other people as I wished. From time to time Chiang would send one of his confidential secretaries to me with some such request as "Can you come to see me tomorrow at such and such time?" Sometimes it was Madame Chiang who sent me a handwritten note to ask me to come.

In several meetings following the first one, Chiang Kai-shek gave me some work to do. It was obvious at once that he did not want "advice" on what was actually going on in Chinese politics or between the Chinese armies (including the Eighth Route Army of the Chinese Communists) and the Japanese invaders. From the beginning, what he wanted was ideas about what China would do after the war, and from the beginning he assumed that the United States would be in the war before very long. I never went on my own initiative to Chiang Kai-shek to propose something, because it always seems to me—and I think people who know China and other countries as well would agree—that in a situation like that the more you volunteer advice and try to look for influence, the less influence you have. If you reply straightforwardly, giving your opinion when a question is asked you, then you are much more likely to be influential.

If Chiang wanted to send a personal message to President Roosevelt, he would discuss with me what was to be said. I drafted a text according to what he wanted to say. My draft was then translated into Chinese at the Generalissimo's headquarters to be shown to Chiang Kai-shek. When necessary corrections were made, the English text was sent in code to Washington, not to the President directly, but to Currie. Therefore, even though the communication was sent under my name to Currie, it did not mean that this was my personal opinion addressed to "my friend" Currie. There were only two copies of the code, and one was in the hands of Madame Chiang while the other was in the hands of Currie at the White House, though Chiang's official representative in Washington was T.V. Soong

At our first meeting, Chiang Kai-shek discussed the question of my contacts in Chungking. In Chinese domestic matters, I was to consider that my primary contact was to be H.H. Kung. I might interject at this point that he also ordered me to establish contact with the Chinese Communists, who were officially represented by Chou En-lai. As far as the embassies were concerned, of course I had to call on them. I was to make the appointments for these calls myself, not through the U.S. embassy. Chiang was rather particular that I should call on the U.S. embassy only after having called on several other embassies, so as to emphasize that I was an adviser recommended to him directly by President Roosevelt. That is to say, I was not to give the impression around Chungking by too frequently visiting the U.S. embassy that I was part of the regular U.S. diplomatic apparatus.

As a cautious first step, I called the British ambassador, Archibald (later Sir Archibald) Clark Kerr, partly because of President Roosevelt's known support of Britain and partly because Chiang Kai-shek had already spoken to me admiringly of Churchill. I cannot think of anyone who could have represented Britain better in China at that time. He was not at all what we nowadays call "soft" on either the Soviet Union or the Chinese Communists, but he was a conservative, not a reactionary in the style of either a program-bound bureaucrat or a purblind academic.

I am sure he anticipated the future growth of the power of the Chinese Communists, though I am not sure he foresaw their total victory. What he said on this topic was carefully guarded, but he

certainly understood that if there was a base for the rise of the
Communists, that base was being laid not by Mao Tse-tung, but by
Chiang Kai-shek's appalling generals (rather than by Chiang himself, who was never as stupid as all that). I became quite friendly
with him. Clark Kerr was later a successful ambassador in Moscow.
His final ambassadorial post was in Washington after the war, but
he never really hit it off with the American establishment, which
was acquiring power more rapidly than it could put together an
understanding of what was really going on in the world.

At the French embassy, all callers were wary. I think the French
ambassador and most of the staff had been there at the time of the
fall of France in June 1940. Nobody really knew whether they
represented France nominally but Vichy really, or Vichy nominally
but France really; and nobody knew who was a Vichy man and
who, in his heart, was a supporter of De Gaulle. Still the French
embassy was important because even though the Japanese already
controlled Indochina, the French connection could not be ignored
as the Chinese government was certainly in touch in Yunnan with
the resistance elements in Indochina.

One man I did respect for his competence was the military
attaché who was then colonel and later became general. I met him
again in Paris in 1954 when he had just returned from Taiwan. His
mission had included a visit to the offshore islands from which the
Nationalists now and then exchanged artillery fire with the Communists on the mainland. On one occasion, he said, the local
Nationalist commander had entertained him at dinner on a terrace
outside instead of taking refuge in a dugout, saying that the
Communists were so incompetent that they had never yet hit his
headquarters. When I suggested, diffidently, that perhaps the Communists were merely sending a warning that they had the guns and
the correct range and could blast the headquarters if they saw any
threatening development there, the French general smiled gently
and replied, "I told you what the man said. I am not saying whether
it was true or not."

The Soviet ambassador was Ivan Luganets-Orel'skii, and Vasilii
Chuikov, who later became the hero of Stalingrad, was the military
attaché. The Soviet ambassador had a secretary who spoke very
good English and very good Chinese. While I could understand

Russian fairly well, my spoken Russian was not good enough to carry on a discussion. When I asked what language we should use, the ambassador said, again putting me to the test: "Since we are in China, let us speak in Chinese," which we did and which gave me the advantage of understanding most of what he said, before it was translated into Chinese by the secretary. I do not think I went to the Soviet embassy more than two or three times all during my stay in Chungking. Chiang Kai-shek must have had a channel of his own to Stalin, but I don't even know whether it was through the Soviet embassy or through someone—not necessarily the ambassador—in his own embassy in Moscow.

When I went round to the U.S. embassy (I think it was before I went to the Soviet embassy), I more or less drew a blank. I had known the ambassador, Clarence E. Gauss, when he was consul general in Shanghai, a post which, as has been mentioned before, prepared him badly for wartime Chungking. He and Chiang Kai-shek were totally incapable of understanding each other, though Gauss was as anti-communist as Chiang. Anxious as I was not to be taken as an emissary of the Department of State, Gauss was even more anxious to make it clear that I had nothing to do with his embassy. It was quite apparent that the official representatives did not like having somebody like me planted next to Chiang Kai-shek.

The U.S. embassy quickly realized what the game was and played it in the same way. They showed it by never asking me questions about anything and never taking me into their confidence, an attitude that clearly suggested that I was not a person through whom they could learn anything important. It was very hard for the State Department to swallow the fact that they had had no influence whatever in appointing the U.S. adviser to Chiang Kai-shek. Therefore why should they treat this unwanted American adviser as an intimate?

On the personal level, however, the ambassador was perfectly friendly, even cordial, but at arm's length. He never asked me for an opinion, and to have shown me even the rough draft of a dispatch to Washington would have been unthinkable. I was good friends with two of his secretaries whom I had known in the 1930s when they were young diplomats in Peking. One of them was John Carter Vincent. He would pass in general among Americans as a liberal in the sense that he did not believe in all-out support of Chiang and believed in the U.S. policy of maintaining the United Front; but I would say that in his personal politics he was more conservative than liberal.

John Service was also there, but I did not have much contact with him. Both of these young men were already skilled diplomats, never saying a word which, if I had repeated it to a Chinese friend, might have sounded like even a faint echo of "official" embassy thinking. My relations with the embassy were purely social, and I do not think I was ever invited to an embassy dinner given for Chinese officials. In this way, I was politely but firmly kept away from the official channels of U.S. diplomacy.

In September, around the time of the anniversary of the Japanese invasion of the Northeast (18 September 1931), I was to make a speech to a small group, which was to be reported to the press. The Chinese officials thought that they should do some publicity about my arrival, to add importance to the fact that the Generalissimo had an adviser nominated by President Roosevelt himself. The general theme of my speech was that the Northeast was an integral part of China. This was publicized by having an immense parade in Chungking, which filled the streets with people carrying banners saying: "We will fight to the end for a complete victory, including the recovery of the Northeast." Several Chinese said to me: "You know, this is an important development, because even Chiang Kai-shek, as head of the Chinese resistance against Japanese invasion, has up to this point never made it a specific war aim that the Northeast should be recovered."

This was considered politically rather important. By the time Chiang Kai-shek retreated from Nanking to Chungking, the influential people who remained around him were overwhelmingly from Central and Southern China, to the south of the Yangtze Valley. There were no Northerners left among Chiang's political intimates nor any Chinese from the Northeast in the military force commanding Northeastern troops. As a result, there were no Northeast voices in Chiang's immediate circle. I do not think that Chiang had forgotten the Northeast, but there was simply nobody to remind him of it: no Northerner with a regional power base of his own. Nevertheless, the moment I brought up this reminder, everybody was very enthusiastic about it, especially, of course, Chinese from the North who had been feeling that their influence had diminished. They were glad to have the North and the Northeast brought into the foreground again.

Chiang Kai-shek was very pleased with the effect of my speech. If he had not been, he would not have permitted the demonstrations. It was an expression of the hard line that China would never negotiate a peace treaty which would allow Manchukuo to survive in any form—and it was taken as an intimation of Roosevelt backing.

The first assignment Chiang gave me was to write three memoranda, on the Northeast, Mongolia, and Sinkiang. Of course, the Northeast was easy. All I had to say was that the Northeast was completely Chinese and that after the war no echo should be left of the bogus "Manchukuo," which the Japanese had proclaimed under the pathetic "boy Emperor," the last of the imperial Manchu house.

Mongolia was delicate. "Inner" Mongolia was under Chinese sovereignty, though the eastern half of it was under Japanese occupation. "Outer" Mongolia, after a genuine nationalist revolution backed by Soviet Russia, proclaimed an independent republic (the first to call itself "People's Republic") since the early 1920s. With strong Soviet backing, they had crushingly defeated Japanese troops in a series of border conflicts in 1939. But China had never recognized its independence and never did until it had to accept the result of a plebiscite in Outer Mongolia (October 1945). Roosevelt, at the Yalta Conference, had promised Stalin that he would persuade Chiang to agree to the arrangement in exchange for the Soviet entrance into the war against Japan.

To this day, however, most Chinese think that all Mongols are one of "China's minorities." A Mongol friend of mine told me that when attached to the Mongol embassy in Peking, he had gone into one of the shops reserved for foreigners. They refused to serve him saying that if he was a Mongol, he "belonged" to China. It took a lot of argument, backed by his passport, before they would allow him, as a "foreigner," to buy what he wanted. I had to circle cautiously around that subject, knowing the deep commitment of both Mongols and Chinese.

In the same way, in my memorandum on Sinkiang (where, under the Chinese government of today, there has been a continuing settlement by Chinese colonists that have drastically changed the demography of the province), I had to be sensitively aware of the fact that it is unreasonable to expect any Chinese to accept the historical truth that the Turkish-speaking peoples of Central Asia always have had more apprehension for being swamped by Chinese colonization than for the extension into their territories of the power of the Russians as a people—not the state power of Tsarist Russia or the Soviet Union. It was so in the old days of Manchu and Tsarist Empires—and it is still the same under today's firm Communist rule on both sides of the frontier.

On the subject of Tibet I did not write a memorandum, explaining to Chiang Kai-shek that I had never traveled in the country and did not know the language. I could tell that my frank declaration of my own limitations gave him confidence in me.

I remember one amusing incident involving a famous American correspondent, James Vincent Sheean, who turned up in Chungking. As a young reporter, he first made a name for himself by sending dispatches about the Riff Moroccans fighting the Spanish. Then he went to China in the early 1920s and met Madame Sun Yat-sen, Borodin, who was the Soviet adviser to Sun, and all those people and accompanied them to Hankow. He writes about this in his autobiography, *Personal History* (1935). He was very proud of knowing inside people and having important channels. He was also very vain, always wanting to show off. When he asked to see me, I did not want to have a tête-à-tête interview with him, because I thought he simply could not be trusted.

Therefore, I asked Hsieh to be with us all the time. Sheean came to lunch and we talked about this and that. Afterward, sure enough, on getting back to the United States, Sheean spread the word that Lattimore was isolated and constantly under the eye of a Chiang Kai-shek watchdog, so that he could not really talk to people freely. He was so vain and so stupid that it never entered his mind that I wanted to have Hsieh with me as a witness for what I actually said or did not say if Sheean should write up the interview.

This does not mean that I was not spied on. Undoubtedly I was being spied on, as was everybody else in Chungking. Chiang Kai-shek had at least three separate spy services, which were rivals of each other and hated each other. This made a very leaky security situation because one spy service might leak something to embarrass the other spy services. Sometimes I am asked whether I have any written record of my stay in Chungking. My answer used to be:

"No, nothing left." In fact, I have never had a habit of keeping a diary. Moreover, it was not safe, as I had no secure place to lock my things in. If I had asked for a safe, that would have raised suspicion. I am pretty sure that when I left the house, somebody came in to have a look round to see if I had been writing anything.

Yet a few years ago, I suddenly discovered a thick pile of onion-skin papers which turned out to be the carbon copies of my correspondence in Chungking. They are almost entirely letters or telegrams that passed back and forth between me, under my code name OMITA, and Lauchlin Currie at his office in the White House. In fact, however, these were messages which Chiang Kai-shek wanted to send personally to President Roosevelt through the procedure described above. I have no idea how I got these copies of confidential material from Chungking to the United States, where they had been stored all these years. The best explanation I can give now is that since it was all sent in the secret code which was in the hands of Madame Chiang, even if the material had been "discovered" by Chiang's spies, it would have been known to Chiang Kai-shek already, and so there was no reason for me not to keep a carbon copy. What it was impossible to keep was things like notes of conversations with Chou En-lai or with Soviet, British, or French diplomats.

Some Chungking People

Chiang said I should meet all the Chinese who wanted to see me, including newspapermen, but I should always remember what things were confidential and should talk about such things only with Chinese who were at the same level of confidentiality. Then he gave me a list of people to call on, such as heads of various departments. He also told me that I should not take the initiative in meeting people. Therefore, at receptions and on similar occasions, I never approached people. Simply because I was an adviser to Chiang Kai-shek, many people supposed that I might have more influence on Chiang than I really had. All kinds of people would say: "Ah, here is Lattimore! Let's go up to him and have a talk. Maybe he would put a favorable word to Chiang." This guaranteed that one person after another would be coming up to *me*.

Only one person whom I approached on my own was Feng Yü-hsiang, the once powerful but relatively democratic warlord, who had occupied Peking in October 1924 and obliged the last Ch'ing emperor to leave the Imperial Palace. My seeking him out was not particularly because of my interest in Mongolia (he had visited Ulan Bator on his way to Moscow in 1926) but because when I saw him he had almost no political influence, being without an army of his own any longer. He was undoubtedly a patriot, and I wanted to let him know that I did not think he was not worth talking to because he had no power.

H.H. Kung. As mentioned before, at my first meeting with Chiang Kai-shek, he specified that my primary contact in Chinese domestic matters was to be H.H. Kung. Though he is known by this name in the West, his full name was K'ung Hsiang-hsi. He was then minister of finance, while also occupying some other important posts in the administration. For financial matters as well as related policies, Chiang Kai-shek had much more confidence in Kung than in his brother-in-law, T.V. Soong. This is not surprising, for Kung came from an old Shansi banking family. Shansi, of course, had been the center of traditional Chinese banking. Kung went to Oberlin College, a small Christian college in Ohio.

On coming back to China, he went into the new kind of banking. In this way, Kung had an understanding of both the old-fashioned Chinese banking and the new style international banking. This gave him an ability to work with a combination of the new and old financial interests in China. The K'ung family in Shansi Province had been not only bankers, but also great landlords, and he was thus familiar with the politically extremely important landlord class, which was also influential in the banking business.

I got on very well with Kung. He was a nice person, and he certainly had much clearer ideas than T.V. Soong. Soong had gone to the United States while still very young. Chiang Kai-shek once said to me: "T.V. Soong has been so long in the United States that he thinks like an American—to my mind a not very intelligent American. You, Mr. Lattimore, you think much more like a Chinese than he does." My impression all along was that while Soong was anti-Soviet in a very simple-minded American way, Kung was much more old-style Chinese about the question.

Americans are apt to think in terms of crisis: "Here is a big crisis with the Soviet Union facing us. If we don't push them back they will keep on coming forward." In this way, we get our John Foster Dulleses talking about rollbacks and going to the brink. Kung's way of thinking would be: "Now, don't let China become involved in a situation in which China is used by the United States for anti-Soviet purposes. The Soviets are there and are going to be there for a long time. We must not create crises now that make relations with the Soviet Union difficult in the more distant future."

To add to these advantages over Soong, Kung's wife (Sung Ai-ling) was an elder sister of Madame Chiang (Sung Mei-ling), and the two sisters were very close to each other, while their relation with their elder sister Sung Ch'ing-ling (Madame Sun Yat-sen) was cool and distant. Within family politics, the two sisters were also very much against their own brother T.V. Soong, and Madame Chiang strongly backed H.H. Kung.

Hollington Tong (Tung Hsien-kuang). I have already briefly described how everybody knew that he was in the confidence of Chiang. Coming back from the United States as a newspaperman, he rose steadily as an "inside man" in the Kuomintang, and as a kind of spokesman without official rank he had the respect of foreign journalists, because if necessary he said, "I cannot answer that question," instead of inventing a false answer or evading the point. Foreign correspondents had the feeling that they were not lied to or misled by him, and if you told him something in confidence, he would not betray the confidence.

Recently I read somewhere that Stilwell described Tong as "oily and unreliable," or something of that kind. Nevertheless, in the words of British Ambassador Clark Kerr, who was a very good judge of men, Tong was "as clean as a hound's tooth." He was generally called "Holy" by the foreigners in Chungking, a kind of hint that he was entirely free of corruption. I met him quite frequently because often at interviews with foreigners, he would be Chiang Kai-shek's official interpreter, and Chiang often would ask me to check a particular translation with him.

Once I attended a dinner given by H.H. Kung in honor of an American mission which came out to examine the traffic situation on the Burma Road. The mission was headed by a man who was very important in the U.S. trucking business, especially heavy transport, including transport over bad roads. This man was a Jew.

At the table, Kung, trying to show off his familiarity with colloquial American, or American slang, referred to New York as "Jew York," which of course was an anti-Semitic remark.

At this moment, Hollington Tong intervened quickly in Chinese: "Mr. Minister, be careful. Our guest is from K'aifeng." The explanation here is that K'aifeng in Middle Ages was the most important Jewish settlement in China. Kung immediately understood the meaning. While T.V. Soong liked to give the impression that he knew how to behave like an American big shot, Kung liked to give the impression that he had easy familiarity with ordinary Americans without putting on the air of being a big boss.

Tong also had an eye on the future. His wife spoke good English; but he encouraged her to learn Russian as well, thinking: "Well, after the war the Russians are going to be important." He was said to have one family problem in the fact that he had a son who used political influence for financial advantage. What happend to the son I have no idea. All this was a part of the general Chungking gossip.

Ho Ying-ch'in. In Chungking, all the Chinese I knew that I could talk to with any degree of frankness agreed that Ho was the chief of the military right wing. He was a treacherous man and his loyalty to Chiang Kai-shek was very much in doubt. At the time of the Sian Incident, Ho advocated bombing Sian, which involved a great risk of Chiang Kai-shek being killed. I could never tell whether he had any ideology except for that of building his personal power by being at the top of the pyramid of officers appointed by himself. He had succeeded Chiang as the head of the famous Whampoa Military Academy, and this had enabled him to control promotions and appointments to build up a powerful clique.

Because of Ho Ying-ch'in's great influence in army politics, Chiang Kai-shek could not simply put him against the wall and shoot him. He was Chiang's chief-of-staff. The balance of forces in the Kuomintang was such that Chiang was obliged to balance one clique against another, taking into consideration, for example, who came from which province. While Chiang had among his confidential advisers men like Chang Ch'ün, who was in favor of reconciliation with the Communists, Chiang never completely adopted a policy of improving relations with the Chinese Communist Party.

On the other hand, Chiang never completely adopted Ho Ying-ch'in's policy of "Let's clean up the Communists." He was always wavering between conflicting pressures.

Ho was probably the strongest and the most influential Chinese Roman Catholic layman and was closely associated with the foreign Roman Catholic establishment in China, which at that time was extremely reactionary. Moreover, his estates were in a part of Kueichou Province which still had a considerable non-Han tribal minority. People said that if a big landlord had a surplus of Han-Chinese tenants, the thing to do was to go out and shoot some tribesmen and take their land for his own estates.

Kuo (Quo) T'ai-ch'i. He has already been mentioned as the person who nominated Hsieh Pao-chao as my secretary-companion. He told me that when he was Chinese ambassador to the Court of St. James's (from 1935) he was on the best of terms with Churchill. He modestly attributed this good standing not to his own skill as a diplomat, but to the fact that he never went to see Churchill without taking with him a box of the best Havana cigars. By the time I got to Chungking, he was out of office and living in a rather large group of comfortable cottages—almost a village—very close to the summer villa of Generalissimo and Madame Chiang. The inhabitants of this village, who were right under the eyes of Chiang's secret service, were all men who were temporarily out of Chiang's favor, because of intrigues or clashing ambitions, but might be reappointed whenever Chiang took a fresh look at his chessboard of persons and policies.

They had considerable freedom of movement. Thus Kuo was living there with one of the most beautiful girls I have ever seen, and he brought her over to call on me at the cottage where I stayed not far from the village but closer to the Chiang villa. As it happened, I had met the girl before in the United States where her friends were invariably rich and influential. After this meeting in Chungking, I never saw her again.

Chang Ch'ün. It was in the dugout where we took refuge during air-raids that I met Chang Ch'ün for the first time, and I became rather good friends with him. He was then the governor of Szechuan and was very much trusted by Chiang Kai-shek. At that time there were two major warlords in Szechuan, who were, I think, related to each other but were also rivals. They were temporarily "in suspension," but there was a danger that they might turn against

Chiang from the rear and open negotiations with Japan. It was accordingly important to have a trustworthy Szechuan man like Chang Ch'ün as governor of the province.

He was considered one of the Kuomintang's top experts on Japan. He had been in the same military academy in Japan with Chiang Kai-shek. According to rumor, Chang Ch'ün knew Japanese very well, better than Chiang, and his status at that time being senior to that of Chiang Kai-shek, he had more or less taken Chiang under his wing. Later when Chiang rose to the top, he returned the favor by using Chang Ch'ün as one of his confidential men. He was considered by Chinese generally as being the man on whom Chiang Kai-shek relied for analysis of the current situation in Japan. In the immediate circle around Chiang, he was the most earnest supporter of the United Front, being very definitely convinced that it would be a fatal mistake to direct the energy of the government against the Communists instead of against Japan.

I remember that once when he and I were sitting together in the dugout, we were talking about some of the differences between the Chinese and the Japanese societies, a subject on which I was, of course, very much an amateur. Nevertheless, in the course of a discussion on feudalism, we touched on the Chinese Communist use of the word "feudalism" as a cliché to describe all relationships between landlords and peasants in China. I ventured to say that the Marxist analysis of China as a feudal country was wrong and that the domination of the Chinese landed gentry, the people who were produced by the Chinese education system and who were the most powerful bureaucrats, was not "feudal." I also said that Westerners, when they used terms like feudalism, frequently failed to see the difference between Japan and China.

Japan had had a real and strong feudalism that lasted much longer than Chinese feudalism. In fact, the nature of early Chinese feudalism was still open to dispute, both as to how long it lasted and to when it changed into some other order of society. In Japan, on the other hand, even after the Meiji Restoration in 1868, and even though many institutions were legally changed, the spirit of feudal relationship lingered on very strongly, especially in agrarian relations, as did the feeling of duty and loyalty, on both sides, of the ruler and the ruled—some of this was what people today call "paternalism," namely the feeling of responsibility of the owner toward the man who works for him.

Sitting in the dugout was not exactly a seminar condition. The conversation started from the point of view that "here are Japan and China at war with each other. They are two different societies, and they respond in different ways to ideas of war, patriotism, loyalty, and the question of who should give orders and who should carry out the orders." After this discussion Chang Ch'ün said to me: "You are the only foreigner I have ever met who really appreciates the fact that China and Japan are not simply different in their political systems, but in the structure and character of their societies." He had probably not discussed such matters in great detail with many Westerners, but he seemed to have thought: "We are two men who can talk as men who understand each other, and we use the same terms in the same way."

Wang Shih-chieh. He was on one of the boards for the postwar economic planning for China and had a reputation as a sort of left liberal. He had a talent very valuable for his personal career, for being able to use a liberal vocabulary to justify conservative policies. As I remember, he was important in negotiations inside the United Front. He was publicly in favor of the United Front, but privately he supported the Kuomintang policy. I was not nearly as familiar with him as I was with Chang Ch'ün.

Chi Ch'ao-ting. I had already met Chi Ch'ao-ting at the IPR conferences. In Chungking, he was very much in the personal confidence of H.H. Kung and was, I think, already working in the Bank of China, which was a stronghold of Kung's. I do not know whether Kung and others knew that Chi was a communist. I had known, of course, that he was on the Left; but it was only a few years ago that I learned that he had actually been a member of the Communist Party. In the 1930s when I first met him, practically all Chinese university students were politicized. Both Chi and Ch'en Han-seng had warned me that among university students and cliques, after the original split in the United Front in 1927 and the civil war in Southwest China between the Kuomintang and the Chinese Communist Party, if you wanted to get somebody into trouble, you could just accuse him of being a communist. So they were very, very careful not to reveal their ideology or party affiliation.

I had met Chi Ch'ao-ting's father around 1935 in Shansi Province when I was spending a summer vacation with my family in a little mountain resort, not far from T'aiyuan. Chi Ch'ao-ting, who was still in the United States, had said: "If you ever go to Shansi, look up my father." His father was a traditional Confucian scholar who had also studied in Japan and later became commissioner of education for Shansi Province under Yen Hsi-shan, who was an anti-communist but at the same time was extremely careful not to fall under the control of Chiang Kai-shek. The Chi family was closely connected with Yen Hsi-shan's family and its interests. At the same time, the father was very close to and trusted by H.H. Kung, who was also of the same province.

He said about his son: "Ah, yes! My son is a bit of a leftist, of course; but nothing to worry about. When he comes back here from the United States and I explain to him all over again the true meaning of the Confucian classics, he will become a normal scholar." Chi Ch'ao-ting's father was what you might call in English today a "Left Tory," a mild conservative who had the attitude that: "Of course, students go to the Left, but when they get a job and have responsibility, they will sober up. They are not going to overthrow the government."

I do not remember whether it was before I went to Chungking and Chi was not yet back in China, or whether he was already in Chungking when I arrived. In any case, he once said to me: "If you meet my brother, be careful of what you say, because he is in Tai Li's Secret Service" (one of the most powerful of Chiang's secret service organizations). It is true that in China, traditionally, fathers often took care that their sons belonged to opposing factions for the security of the family, regardless of which of the opposing sides came out on top. In the case of the Chi family, however, the distribution of the sons in two camps seemed to have been due to chance rather than to family policy.

The Dilowa Hutukutu (Diluv Khutagt, according to the new spelling in the People's Republic of Mongolia). It was Hsieh Pao-chao's love of gossip that led me to find the Dilowa Hutukutu in Chungking. At one time he told me of a man who was head of the wartime office of the Council of Mongol-Tibetan Affairs, which was situated just outside of Chungking. This man was a Cantonese who had not the foggiest notion about Sinkiang, Tibet, and Inner Mongolia. I asked Hsieh how a man like that got put in charge of Mongol-Tibetan Affairs. His answer was: "Oh, that's an easy one. For years now, he is the man who's been getting pretty girls through the

back door for Chiang Kai-shek." For the Kuomintang Chinese, the
Mongol-Tibetan Council did not matter very much, and to be head
of the council was a kind of sinecure. Some of the Mongols and
Tibetans working in its office were collaborators of the Chinese,
but most of them were Mongol nationalists, though it was not safe
to say so out loud.

Having heard about the council, I paid a visit to this place to meet
some of the Inner Mongolian people, and to my surprise and joy I
found the Dilowa Hutukutu there. He had been one of the most
important "Living Buddhas," or Buddhist Reincarnations, of Outer
Mongolia. After the Mongolian Revolution of 1921 and during the
period of the "Leftist Deviation" (1929–32), he was tried and given
a sentence with suspension. When he was allowed to return to his
temple in West Mongolia, he escaped into Inner Monogolia as a
refugee. I had first met him in the 1930s in Peking. While we were
still in Peking, he often came to see us, and we asked him to be the
godfather to our son David, who used to call him "Wo de Fo-yie (My
own Buddha)."

When the Japanese occupied Peking, those who were especially
interested in Mongolia tried to win him over and make him a collaborator, taking him to Japan for a tour of Buddhist temples and so
forth. The old man, however, was by no means politically so naive
and felt that the Japanese adventure was not going to last long. So
he would not commit himself to the Japanese and managed to get
from Peking to Shanghai, then to Hong Kong, and from there to
Chungking.

I asked Chiang for permission to take him into my house as we
were old friends. Chiang had no objection, and the Dilowa
Hutukutu stayed with me all through the time I was in Chungking.
The Dilowa Hutukutu was a person who had no influence whatsoever in Chinese politics, and Chiang also must have thought:
"Now, after the war, the old question of China and Outer Mongolia
will open up again in one way or another. To have an important
Mongol like this, who feels that he has been well treated by my
regime and is well disposed to China, might turn out to be useful."

At home we talked in Mongol as the Dilowa had very little Chinese, and he was not in a position where he could learn much about
the real inside working of Chinese politics. This was another reason
for Chiang Kai-shek not to have any reservations about his living

with me. Though the Dilowa Hutukutu was a champion of Mongolian nationalism, given the situation in Chungking, we did not discuss politics but talked about Mongolia in a general way. I had no contact with other younger Mongols who were in Chungking, and I cannot even say what the Chinese would have replied if I wanted to see them.

Echoes from a Dugout

My house in Chungking was just opposite that of Wu T'ieh-ch'eng, also one of those most trusted by Chiang Kai-shek. He was the man who, as governor of Canton, suppressed the Canton Commune in December 1927. At the time of my stay in Chungking he was a sort of foreign secretary for maintaining contacts with the Overseas Chinese. Right up to the fall of Singapore to the Japanese, the Kuomintang was receiving important private funds to support its work from the Chinese, especially millionaires, in that city. This was of great diplomatic and financial importance for Chiang Kai-shek. Therefore, whenever such people came to Chungking, they stayed with Wu T'ieh-ch'eng.

In July and August of 1941, the Japanese air-raids were extremely heavy and frequent. Bombs fell all over Chungking and caused a great deal of damage. Chungking is built on rock, and people hollowed out caves in the rock for air-raid shelters. There was one especially famous and gruesome episode when the entrance to a cave collapsed when a bomb fell there, suffocating hundreds and hundreds of ordinary people. Nevertheless, so far as I know, there were no casualties among important people. The Chinese advance intelligence was good, and the air-raid alarm system was marvelously efficient. Japanese intelligence was also good because one day they obviously tried to hit the house where I was staying. Some bombs landed near enough to shake down a bit of the wall. Within hours, the Japanese-controlled radio broadcast in Chinese that the house of Adviser Lattimore had been flattened and he was believed to have been killed. Undoubtedly, there were some Chinese working for the Japanese.

Now, Wu T'ieh-ch'eng had a very superior dugout excavated right down into the rock. It was his personal bomb shelter, but it was very spacious and well fitted and known to be especially safe, so whenever there was an air-raid alarm, all sorts of important people came flocking into it. This was the dugout assigned to me, also. It had a little petrol power motor which ran a ventilation system as well as an electric light system. When we first went into the dugout, the air was fresh and clean. Even though the dugout was in solid rock, the pounding and shaking of the bombing, which went on for hours and hours—more than twelve hours at times, would in due course put the engine out. Then the lights would go out, and so would the ventilation. Candles were lit, but after a few more hours with no ventilation, the air would become so thick that even the candles were put out to economize on oxygen. There we were sitting in complete darkness, but people would go on talking, as there was nothing else to do.

The conversation was entirely in Chinese, and I was the only foreigner. If somebody turned to me and asked a question I would come into the conversation; but otherwise I kept myself as inconspicuous as possible with my mouth shut. It was not that I was trying to disguise my presence; I simply wanted not to be too intrusive or assertive. People talked as if there was no Chinese-speaking foreigner present; but then, one of the things that made life interesting in Chungking was that from the beginning, I was treated less as an American than as a "Chiang Kai-shek man." Of course, everybody knew who was there. In such a situation, people would think: "Since Mr. so-and-so is here, we mustn't talk about such-and-such." But there were permissible topics of conversation, and sometimes what subjects were not discussed was also significant. It could convey a kind of intelligence.

The conversation depended on who was there in the cave on any particular day. I once met one of the famous Muslim Ma's, Ma Pu-fang. He was governor of Ch'inghai and as such was important because he was semi-independent, and Chiang Kai-shek had no control over his territory. This Ma and his Muslims controlled much of the eastern part of Tibet, the rest being controlled by the Szechuan militarists of whom Chang Ch'ün was one. General Ma was down in Chungking on a visit, which was enough to make people talk very cautiously and delicately about problems of the frontier provinces and the future of Tibet.

At one time in the dugout there was a millionaire from Singapore who came up to Chungking from time to time. He always tried to insist that some of the donated money and medical supplies should go to Yenan. The Overseas Chinese on the whole were stronger supporters of the United Front than were Chiang Kai-shek's people. I met this Singapore man only once. He was arguing with Wu T'ieh-ch'eng that he should use his influence on Chiang Kai-shek to let at least some medicine through to Yenan. He said that the Singapore Chinese wanted to show that they did not forget that the Chinese Communists were also fighting against the Japanese for the Motherland, and it was scandalous that even basic medicines coming from the Overseas Chinese, the International Red Cross, and the United States, which were destined to be shared equally among the Chinese, could not get to Yenan. He kept saying: "At least a token amount of medicine has to get through to the Communists."

There is a very important point here that is often overlooked when people talk about the Overseas Chinese. Americans in particular are wont to wonder why a Chinese millionaire in Singapore should be "soft on Communists." In fact, during the interwar period, the basic mental and political attitude of the Overseas Chinese was: "Japan made a great advance in prestige as well as in power and wealth, and in countries like Malaya and Indonesia, the Japanese are treated like Europeans and Americans. They can join the clubs barred to other Asian peoples. (This was a great social test of colonialism.) If we live in Malaya under British rule, for example, our position will never be as strong as the Japanese until we have a strong government in China—that is, the government of a united country. Therefore we do not want to have the possibility of a strong government in China deferred and deferred because of civil war. We are in favor of a United Front by negotiation." It was as simple as that.

On the whole, the people who found themselves together in the dugout knew each other; and very often they talked about such things as postwar reconstruction plans. One would say: "Of course, the major economic help will have to come from the United States, which will be the only Great Power that will not be economically damaged by the war; and we must get them to help us." Then somebody would say: "We must watch our step with the Americans, because where their dollars go, their control goes also." Then another would say: "Yes, after the war the Americans will be the most dangerous imperialists." Still another would say: "That is nothing new. The Americans have always been imperialists. At the end of the war, we are going to restore a great deal of damaged industry in China and also expand our industry as fast as possible in order to modernize it. Now the problem is how to get American help without falling under its control. Don't forget. Americans are always talking about how they are not imperialists and never have been. In fact, they are the biggest hypocrites and the biggest imperialists of the whole lot. They are real b̶━━━." Sometimes they would even use very strong and vulgar words like *wang-pa-tan* (turtle's egg), one of the worst expressions for cursing somebody.

The danger as they saw it was that the Americans would say: "Yes, you can have this capital, and you can have these experts, *if* they are used in the following way." That would mean that the products of the new industry would feed into the American international economic system. It was a prophetic anticipation of what we call today the "multinational" economy. One thing to be noted was that although these Chinese were capitalist-minded, they were in agreement that in order to maintain China's economic independence, certain key aspects of the economy would have to be nationalized; this, of course, would not be welcome to the Americans.

In the complete darkness of the dugout, they were discussing their own problems with one another. It was not that they were trying to let me know what they wanted in an indirect way in order to have me influence Chiang or Roosevelt. I detected no evidence of any maneuvering of that kind. I suppose they considered me a friendly person and did not think that any information that I gathered would be used in a way hostile to China. Also, even though there were people hostile to Chiang Kai-shek in internal politics, they were all convinced that in international politics Chiang would do everything to get U.S. help while avoiding American control. He was a nationalist in that way.

Even to this day, very few Americans understand that the Chinese considered Americans to be imperialists. We delude ourselves with the thought that we never possessed concessions in China. It was true that we never had territorial concessions. What we did was to live in other people's concessions. We also overlook the fact that the first U.S. treaty with China established the most-favored-nation principle and also the principle of equal opportunity. As a result, every time the Germans, the French, the British, the Russians, or the Japanese got privileges of one kind or another from the old government of the Ch'ing Dynasty, the Americans enjoyed exactly the same privileges but without military action. It never dawned on us that to the Chinese that looked like a sly "me too" imperialism.

Another example, very important psychologically, was the famous Tsinghua University in Peking, which Americans frequently referred to as the Boxer Indemnity University, because it was founded with part of the surplus of the American share. Americans thought that this was a wonderful example of the pure unselfish generosity of the United States. The Chinese absolutely did not agree. Tsinghua graduates hated to be known as Boxer Indemnity students. They said: "If the Americans had really been generous, they would have said: 'We have collected too much money. Here is the rest of it. Take it back.' But what did they do? They said: 'With your money, we are going to found the kind of university in China which we think will be good for you. We will educate you Chinese in the way we think is right.' "

Among those people whom I met in the dugout, very few were primarily military. Planning for military action against the Communists as soon as Japan was defeated concerned army politicians much more than the type of civilians whom I met. These seemed to think that if China, after the war, could really get going on economic construction, that in itself would relieve the pressure of revolutionary support for the Chinese Communists. Discussions were much more in terms of those in favor of unrestricted private enterprise and the so-called bureaucratic capitalists, who were in favor of strict government control and planning.

In the darkness of the dugout, even the question of the United Front with the Communists would come up. In the dark, I learned that the problems of the United Front went far deeper than the few discreet mentions that one saw in the Chungking press, and that there really was more than one cleavage among each of the groups close to Chiang Kai-shek. Some believed that the United Front had been allowed to break down much too far, that it should be revived, and that it was possible to work with the Communists in a constructive way. They thought that if the Kuomintang carried on an active United Front policy, this would have such advantages that at the end of the war the Kuomintang would come out with much more prestige than the Communists, and the Communists would not be a real danger. The other major point of view was that the Communists were a permanent menace and that advantage should be taken of the war to tighten the blockade in order to starve them out and weaken them. Of course, there were a number of opinions between these two extremes.

I mentioned before that Chang Ch'ün, the governor of Szechuan, used to come to this dugout when he was in the capital. I was very much impressed also by what he said in the dark about the United Front. He was one of the few men high up in the conservative half of the Kuomintang who said that the United Front must absolutely be maintained and that there must not be a civil war at the end of the war. He believed that China could handle the war and the post-war situation only as a united nation. He was not, nevertheless, in favor of giving the Communists complete equality, but advocated multiple parties as the way to limit the power of the Communists, allowing other parties calling themselves democratic to take part in government so that they would draw away many who might otherwise support the Communists. There were also the National Salvation Movement—a kind of "bourgeois capitalist liberal" group—and various small cliques, often influenced by regional interests.

Listening to such conversations have a value that goes far beyond the words that might have been preserved on a tape recorder. The major importance of participating as well as listening is the overall feeling you get for the temper of the society you are living in—the internal agreements and disagreements, the tensions between the individual and the group. My lasting memory is that I was poor at the game of assessing theories and weighing them against each other, but sensitive to what men and women did and to the way in which they did it, and to their tone and manner in saying what they had to say—and to the timing of the moments when they fell silent.

Journey to Yunnan Province

In the autumn of 1941, some time before Pearl Harbor, Chiang Kai-shek asked me to make a journey to Yunnan Province to have a look at the Chinese end of the Burma Road. I was there from 15 October to 31 October. In July 1940, the Japanese had put pressure on Britain, already at war in Europe, to close the Burma Road, which had served as a route of supply to Chiang Kai-shek. Though the Burma Road was reopened after three months, an acute political question in 1941 was whether the Japanese would put a higher priority on a conquest of the British-Dutch-French colonial-imperial order in that part of Asia or swing aside into Yunnan Province, thus putting the squeeze on Chiang Kai-shek from deep inland as well as from the East China coast. By that time the Japanese were already in control of the Indochina end of a railway running into Yunnan.

Chiang Kai-shek was deeply concerned about these problems. He had already thought that the increasing Japanese pressure on Burma would bring Britain into the war in Asia. "Churchill is not Chamberlain," he said more than once. "Churchill is a fighter. His war plan must be first to break the German air assault on England. Then he will make a stand against Japan in Asia. Certainly that will bring the United States into the war." Thus he foresaw that Roosevelt's increasingly open support for Chuchill would result in the widening and deepening of a war involving Europe and Asia. In view of the Japanese defeat by Soviet-Mongolian troops at the northwestern frontier of Manchuria in the summer of 1939, which must have taught the Japanese militarists a lesson, it was supposed that the expansion of the war would not be precipitated by a Japanese invasion of Siberia.

It was in such circumstances that Chiang sent me to Yunnan. It was not an inspection. Chiang's idea was: "Go there and get a bit of education." He wanted me to see and understand the situation. On this journey, I was accompanied by Hsieh Pao-chao, who was absolutely delighted because, he said: "The life in Chungking is terrible. Unless you are in a very favored position, the secret police keeps tabs on you, preventing you from having an adequate sex life." He told me himself that all his life he had had only two really serious interests, drink and sex.

He often reproved me, until I told him to stop it, for leading a chaste life. He said that all the Americans with good jobs in Chungking, who had had to leave their wives at home, kept Chinese mistresses. It was necessary for my health, he said. Here, though he did not know it, he was echoing the opinion of Benjamin Franklin who, apart from being an original thinker, was at the same

time in many ways a typical man of the eighteenth century. In a letter to his son, Franklin admonished him not to neglect his sex life,
because a bit of sex now and then was beneficial to a man's health.

Hsieh explained: "Although Yunnan Province is now incorpo-
rated in Chiang's China, the local warlord, Lung Yün, has managed
to maintain a great deal of local autonomy. His own secret service
keeps Chiang's secret service under a certain amount of restraint.
So, you can have much more fun in Yunnan than you can in
Chungking." Sure enough, when we were in Kunming, he reported
that he had spent a wonderful night with a very nice college girl. He
said that in Kunming, as well as in Ch'engtu, there were "refugee
universities" for students who had fled from the Japanese, and
among them one could find girls who had been separated from
their families by the war and had to turn to concubinage or high-
level prostitution just to stay alive. He could get along all right with
whores, he said, when there was nothing else in sight, but it was
delightful to find, now and then, a nice, clean, educated, well-
brought-up girl whom one could "treat like a lady."

In Kunming I was, of course, received by Lung Yün, the governor
of the province. In order to explain what follows, I must point out
here that Lung Yün came from a very interesting social origin. Up
on the Tibetan frontier of Yunnan Province there was a non-
Chinese tribe, the Lolo, who had a great reputation as fierce war-
riors. At that time, instead of the Chinese being able to encroach on
them, it was they who from their mountain strongholds raided the
Chinese villages and captured peasants whom they carried off and
used as agricultural slaves.

Some of these Chinese got on rather well with the tribesmen,
and if so, and if they learned the language, they would even be
given Lolo girls as wives. As a result of this, there were quite a few
people who were half Lolo and half Chinese. Lung Yün was one,
and this had a lot to do with his maintaining as much independence
as possible from Chiang Kai-shek. At Lung Yün's headquarters in
Yunnan, all his personal bodyguards were tribesmen. The tribal
people could be easily distinguished because their average height
was greater than that of the average Chinese. You could tell them at
once by looking at them, even though they were in Chinese
uniform.

The governor had a dinner party for me, and before the dinner I was taken to a sort of private room for a talk. After the usual polite conversation that takes place when you meet somebody important in China, he told his military aide to go and stand at the door far enough away so that he could not hear. Then he asked me: "Do you know President Roosevelt?" "Well, yes," I answered. "I had an interview with him before I came to Chungking." "Do you know Churchill?" "No, I have never met him." "And Stalin?" "No, I don't; but you know, there is something very interesting about Stalin. He is not even a Russian. He came from a mountain tribe in the Caucasus mountains south of the Soviet Union; but he made his way up and now he is the top man in the Soviet Union."

"Oh!" he said and turned to his aide-de-camp: "Go out, close the door and stand outside. Don't let anybody come in." When the aide had gone out, he turned to me again and said: "Tell me more about Stalin." Westerners talk about inscrutable Orientals, but nothing could have been clearer. He was thinking: "If Stalin could do that, what are the prospects for *me*?" I simply told him that it was part of Soviet policy to give opportunities to members of minority peoples and tribes to take part in the general politics of the Soviet Union, and that they could rise very high and many of them had. I could hardly tell him exactly how Stalin got to the top position, because I had not known it myself at that time, except that Stalin had killed a lot of people, but so had other Soviet politicians.

On my inspection tour in Yunnan I saw and heard bits and pieces about the interaction between the central government, which was engaged in national defense against a foreign invader and was trying to consolidate its power, and various local powers which were trying to preserve their independence as much as they could. One of the stories goes back to the period of the famous Long March of the Communists, which started in October 1934. One of Chiang Kai-shek's tactics was to encircle a detachment of the Red Army, but not completely, leaving open an avenue of escape into a territory which did not yet acknowledge Chiang's authority. Then, in the name of pursuing the Reds, he would move his troops into that province. For Chiang, getting control of a hitherto independent province had a priority over exterminating the Reds who had fled into it. In the case of Yunnan, however, where Lung Yün was holding power, the Reds negotiated with him in advance. The negotiator on the Communist side was said to have been Chou En-lai.

The story went something like this: Chou said, "We are escaping under pressure from Chiang Kai-shek, and we have to cross your province. Now, if you hold us up, Chiang's forces will be hard on our heels and take your province away from you. Why not just leave us a way open? We only want to pass through and go farther to the Northwest. We won't rob, and we won't do any damage. We only want to go through as quickly and quietly as possible. Then Chiang will not have the excuse to enter your province in hot pursuit." Lung Yün saw the point, and the bargain was struck. This is not a story which I heard directly from Lung Yün himself, but through Hsieh, as a piece of gossip.

Not simply among the lower ranks, but perhaps right up to the middle ranks of Chiang Kai-shek's apparatus, if people got to know you and felt that you were a trustworthy character, they would gossip very freely about such things. It was rather a compliment, because their attitude was: "Here is a man who is not out for a scandal and not here to write some sensational report. He is a man who knows us Chinese and knows how things work. Therefore, we can talk to him as we talk to a fellow Chinese, as among friends."

While Lung Yün had made a deal with the Communists and let them go through his province without fighting, internally in his own territory his secret service was absolutely merciless toward anybody whom he considered to be a Communist. There were a number of military leaders of this kind in 1948 and 1949. At the last decisive moment in the civil war, if they surrendered their provinces and positions to the Communists without fighting, bygones were counted as bygones and they were perfectly safe, even though they might have the blood of hundreds of Communists on their hands. Fu Tso-yi, whom I have already mentioned in connection with Inner Mongolia, was an outstanding example. He surrendered Peking to the Communists and was given an important post in the new government, even though as governor of Suiyuan he had been quite merciless toward Communists.

After this meeting with Lung Yün in Kunming, we went by car down the beginning of the Burma Road and came to Tali, a very interesting city in a valley off the main road; it was almost like an oasis in the mountains. There was a small irrigated plain with rich agriculture and side valleys going up into the mountains. The local people there were called Pai-yi (White Clothes) by the Chinese.

There is a very good book about this region, *The Tower of Five Glories* (1972), by Charles Patrick FitzGerald. For anybody interested in minorities, this was a region and population worth studying, because the White Clothes were in the process of being assimilated into the general Chinese population. Men were leaving their villages for other kinds of employment and so had to learn Chinese. As a result, the male population was largely bilingual, while the women, remaining behind, were still mainly speaking only their own tribal language.

The White Clothes were also important because they were engaged in caravan travel both up to the Tibetan plateau and down toward Burma. The whole area was a crossroad of cultural exchange. It had also been a stronghold of the Muslims of Southwest China in the great Muslim insurrections in the second half of the nineteenth century, overlapping with the Taiping Rebellion. One of the most important Muslim leaders came from Tali in Yunnan. These Muslims were especially worth studying, and I was sorry not to have had the opportunity to do so myself. While the Muslims of Northwest China represented the Islamic influence that entered China along the caravan route from the Near East through Iran and Central Asia, the principal historical influence of the Muslims in Southwest China had come from Arabs conducting the maritime trade from the Persian Gulf into the Indian Ocean, around the Malay peninsula and up to southernmost China.

As Muslims they had special characteristics of their own. One intriguing possibility of Islamic influence has never, as far as I know, been investigated. In the fifteenth century, Cheng Ho of the Ming Dynasty, China's most famous admiral, reached India and the east coast of Africa. Chinese maps even show the Cape of Good Hope and the beginnings of the coast of West Africa. This Cheng Ho, an imperial eunuch, was a Muslim from Southwest China. Is it possible that his remarkable voyages were the result of "marriage" between Chinese shipbuilding skill (his ships were very large) and an Arab inheritance of maritime know-how?

I was only at the Chinese end of the Burma Road, where a permanent motorable road was being made largely by the ancient, traditional Chinese method of conscript labor of peasants from the surrounding countryside. They were working with picks and shovels, cutting through the hills, raking earth away from one place, carrying it in baskets and piling it in another place to fill in hollows. Forced labor was always the curse of China, giving opportunity to bureaucrats and local authorities in charge to cook the accounts by listing thousands of additional nonexistent laborers. As the road was an urgent wartime undertaking, the handiest to conscript were mostly Han Chinese, not tribesmen.

Many of the Chinese engineers were well qualified and were allowed to insist on efficiency and getting results. On the other hand, there was a lot of corruption in the actual handling of transport. There were infinite opportunities to juggle the figures for the supply and purchase of petrol, for the number of drivers employed, for the number of shifts driven. In such transport, it was also standard practice to sell some of what was being transported and report it as lost in an accident, or in addition to transporting official goods to contract with local merchants to carry their goods for payment. As we know in the United States, urgent wartime contracts enable money to fly on the wing of patriotism.

The question of appointing someone to head the whole undertaking led to a very interesting situation characterized partly by cooperation and partly by rivalry and competition. On the one hand, Chiang Kai-shek's direct appointees tried to push the local authorities to do the main job themselves, for if they could not use the local authorities to conscript labor and collect local supplies, the road would simply not go through. On the other hand, the central government did not want to leave the local authorities too much autonomy, because that would strengthen them and enable them to build up the always-longed-for local power base.

The man appointed was named Tseng Yang-fu, whom we joined up with in Kunming. He was Cantonese and had also been a student under my father and my uncle at Peiyang University in Tientsin. He then went abroad, I think to the United States, and came home a first-class engineer. Tseng also stood well with Chiang Kai-shek because when he was for a time mayor of Canton, he zealously followed Chiang's policies, especially against the Communists. He was part of the Planning Commission for the organization of engineering works in wartime China and planning for future engineering in postwar reconstruction and development.

I had become very friendly with him in Chungking. Even in war-ravaged Chungking, he lived in great luxury and had a first-class cook whom he always took with him on his trips. He had been appointed by Chiang Kai-shek and was already in Kunming when we arrived there. We traveled with him and I got to know him very well. Traveling with him meant living in luxury—and that was not easy in wartime China.

One of Tseng's private ventures was promotion of a nozzle for injecting the oil of *tung* nuts into diesel engines as a substitute for diesel fuel, which had become very scarce. By this and other enterprises, he made a lot of money and at the same time made himself popular with the landlords because *tung* oil, which had formerly been exported in large quantities, especially to the United States, could now no longer be exported because of Japanese control of China's ports. He also set up an efficient factory to repair and put into operation again broken-down machinery that had been rescued from Eastern China as the Japanese invasion advanced but had been damaged en route to Free China. The last time I saw him was after the war, when he came to the United States for treatment for Parkinson's disease. He stayed with us a few days. The treatment for this disease in those days was still rather ineffective, and he died soon after.

On our way back to Chungking we met another car which had in it two passengers, one Chinese and one foreigner. The foreigner was one of the various engineering and technical advisers to the Chiang Kai-shek regime. We stopped and Hsieh and the Chinese in the other car recognized each other. They exchanged the usual polite greetings, such as "Where did you come from?" and "How long have you been on the road?" The Westerner and I also exchanged a few words; but it was conspicuous that Hsieh did not introduce me to the other Chinese.

When we got going again he said: "That was Tai Li." Tai Li was the head of the Gestapo-like Bureau of Investigation and Military Statistics, the most important of the secret services under Chiang Kai-shek, and perhaps the most independent. Undoubtedly, Hsieh did not introduce me to him because he knew that Chiang Kai-shek would not like me to have anything to do with him. Very likely, I was under observation by his organization, and he would submit periodically to Chiang reports about who had come to call on Lattimore, and whom Lattimore went to see. I do not know whether Tai Li was corrupt or not, but it is certain that he was primarily a power man rather than a money man. He died just after the end of the war in a plane crash, which was believed to have been an act of sabotage in retaliation for the sabotaging, by his organization, of a plane carrying an important Communist.

Chapter Five

■

THE TWO SIDES OF THE UNITED FRONT

Generalissimo and Madame Chiang

Having known Chiang Kai-shek personally, I still think that he was a great man. He certainly was no saint, but neither was he a total villain. He was a man who was not only patriotic, but according to his own lights, revolutionary. He wanted to change Chinese society. He had a mixed career of great success and important mistakes, such as the 1927 coup d'état against the Communists. Because of this there was not in fact a united China to resist the Japanese aggression when the invasion of the Northeast came about in 1931. In spite of all this, Chiang Kai-shek was the rallying point in the war against the Japanese. In one of my conversations with Chou En-lai in Chungking, Chou himself said very emphatically that Chiang was essential to the resistance against Japan. While the Communists wanted him to be more effective in the national front, that in no way implied that they wanted Chiang removed from power.

It was not simply that Chiang sat back when he should have been active in resistance. He thought the way to save China was to create a trained, organized elite; and through this educated elite he intended to give the right orders to the common people and see to it that these orders were carried out. He did not show to the peasantry that he was offering them something of personal advantage to fight for. A part of his mistake was in the structure and the nature of his own background. He had been trained first in the old military academy in Paotingfu, then in Japan, and later he became the military head of the revolutionary, or semi-revolutionary, Whampoa Military Academy in Canton. He wound up with an army of professional officers, mainly from the landlord class, in command of troops who were badly paid, forced conscripts.

Unlike some other developing countries, such as the Latin American countries where the officer elite comes largely from the newly emerging bourgeois commercial and industrial families, in Chiang's China there were practically no commanding military officers who were of merchant or banking families. The officers regarded their soldiers simply as peasants in uniform, and they treated them in the same way that landlords treated peasants. This was a fatal error. At the same time within the Kuomintang, Chiang was saying to the landlord elements: "Don't be afraid. Your land is not going to be taken away from you and given to the peasants. Maybe the peasants should be given somewhat better treatment, and maybe the taxes and the rent they pay should be reduced, but landlords will never lose their possessions."

He also said once to me, however, that after the war China's agriculture would have to be collectivized in order to set free manpower for a planned new industrialization. Because of China's shortage of capital, land would have to be taken from the landlords without compensation. "Just the same as in the Soviet Union," he concluded, "only I shall be doing it, not Stalin."

Undoubtedly, Chiang was disappointed that Roosevelt had given him a kind of man quite different from the Harry Hopkins type that he wanted. In the circumstances, the basic relationships between Chiang Kai-shek and myself was one in which he thought of how he could use me in furthering *his* concept of a future China instead of just obliging Roosevelt, and how far I might be reliable for that purpose. Consequently, my reaction to what I thought I perceived in him was: "As Chiang Kai-shek has in some ways an antiquated mode of thinking, is there anything I can say or write that would modify his opinions and make them more practical in the modern world?"

Having discovered that Roosevelt had dodged his request, Chiang said to me: "You have traveled a great deal in the frontier areas. At the end of the war, when it comes to a question of a general settlement, frontier questions will be among the first to settle after the Japanese leave. This will involve the Soviet Union." This was how he wanted me to write separate memoranda on the postwar handling of the Northeast, Sinkiang, and Mongolia.

I had been interested in frontier questions for so long that I was sure that the future relations between China and the Soviet Union were going to be of world, not just local, importance. Therefore I was very much interested in what I might find out about the attitude of Chiang Kai-shek and his entourage on that question. So I spent a large part of my time on these memoranda.

In the paper on the Northeast, I emphasized specifically: "You must not only be the head of the state and head of the Kuomintang. You should also identify the recovery of the Northeast as one of your objectives. You should also make the people of the Northeast identify themselves with the Kuomintang and the government of China. Now you have your secret service people all through the Northeast. This is the time when you should recruit young Northeasterners. If you can, get hold of the people in the underground resistance to the Japanese. Smuggle them down here to Chungking. The Kuomintang has a special ideological indoctrination school for cadres. Put them in this school, give them favored treatment, and according to their abilities, promote them as fast as possible. Then when the war ends and your first troops enter the Northeast, they will be accompanied by people speaking with the accent of the Northeast. They will meet their old friends as representatives of the Kuomintang." Of course, the exact wording of my memorandum was much more polite than I have put it here.

My original texts were translated into Chinese, and I checked them carefully with the translator before they were presented to Chiang Kai-shek. Chiang thanked me for the memoranda but never made any special comments on them. Probably this again was a part of his forming his own idea of what I amounted to, and also to take note of such points as:

—These memoranda show that he knows something about the frontiers.

—Does the way he expresses himself correspond with the traditional U.S. policy regarding China's frontiers?

—Is this the kind of recommendation that is likely to have an effect on U.S. postwar policy?

In fact, however, my ideas were not of a kind that was likely to be popular or influential in postwar U.S. policy-making, and Chiang Kai-shek must have known it. Actually, when the war ended, among the first Kuomintang people who appeared in the Northeast, not a single person had the local accent.

The relation between Chiang Kai-shek and Madame Chiang was

something like that of political allies who do not entirely trust each other. I think that it was also for political reasons that Chiang converted to Christianity. He refused to be converted in advance, however, in order to marry a Christian wife, so it was some time after their marriage before he announced his conversion. They were Christian enough to maintain liaison with missionaries, especially the kind of missionaries who were influential in the United States. Madame Chiang very quickly realized the political usefulness of showing off their Christianity to get the support of U.S. voters. Probably in a great many Christian countries there are people of that kind who are more concerned with behavior in public than with the private thoughts that really guide conduct.

The value and importance of Madame Chiang has been greatly exaggerated, especially by Americans. They took her as the symbol of modern China, and there were those who were simple-minded enough to say that after all, Chiang Kai-shek was just a warlord by origin and did not even speak English, while his wife had an American education and spoke English brilliantly; therefore she must be the real brains of Chiang Kai-shek's government. Nothing of the kind. The two were united more politically than affectionately, I should say. While Madame Chiang did not do anything to stop people from believing that *she* was the clever one, in fact Chiang was able to make good use of her because of her standing in the United States. She did have a high standing, but it had only a limited value.

It is true that for a man like Chiang Kai-shek, half feudal and militaristic and half modern in his mentality, and in the China of that day with its mixture of modern and archaic elements, his wife and her relatives automatically formed political factions among themselves—competing factions, each with its own allies and rivals. Nevertheless, she certainly never controlled the planning or execution of either his international policy or his policy inside China, though such tasks of drafting cables to Currie were, of course, handled by her because they were in English and the code was in her hands.

I can remember occasions when Chiang Kai-shek, wanting to talk to me privately about important things, would invite me to spend weekends at his country villa outside Chungking. In the evening we would be sitting, three of us, on the terrace talking. The language used was a strange mixture of Chinese and English. Sometimes the Generalissimo asked me something and I replied in Chinese; then Madame would supplement what I said in Chinese with something which she had added. At other times, Madame would ask me something in English and I would reply in English; and before I could put my reply into Chinese for him, she would turn to him and say: "Mr. Lattimore says . . ." and give her own version of what I had said. I think she and I always talked in English and never in Chinese.

Having seen that there was a lack of total confidence between Chiang and Madame Chiang, I was naturally always very guarded in what I replied to her in English. The general pattern of these conversations in the evening was that Madame would dominate the conversation, and Chiang Kai-shek would let her go on and on until quite late. Madame would finally get tired and go up to bed. Then the Generalissimo would pull up his chair, and we would get down to serious talk.

In the kind of relationship that I had with Chiang, it was not my position to take the initiative in suggesting policies to him. I answered the questions he put to me. He knew that I was against dictatorship, and he knew that I was in favor of strengthening his position so that he could control the warlords, instead of being controlled by them. It must have been perfectly clear to him that I thought it inadvisable to try to use local warlords to crush local Communists.

Chiang's attitude to the Communists was very different from that of his wife. Madame Chiang had a simple-minded American anti-Communist and anti-Soviet attitude. It was after she had retired to bed that, to my great astonishment, Chiang said: "After the war the question of the Chinese Communists will have to be settled by military force, but the Soviet Union is different. We cannot negotiate with the Chinese Communists because the same words have different meanings to us and to them. But we can rely on Stalin. He keeps his word."

In fact, the Soviet Union never supplied the Chinese Communists as much as a revolver. All airplanes, guns, and ammunition went to Chiang. The Soviet line was that they were supporting

China as a nation against the Japanese imperialists, and in this situation it would be totally improper for them to do anything that could be regarded as playing Chinese domestic politics. Later, Chiang may have changed what he had to say about the Soviet Union and Stalin, and in his memoirs, which I have not read, I am told that he attributed the whole story of Chinese Communism to the Soviet Union. He was by that time totally dependent on Washington. I am only repeating what he told me in one of our tête-à-tête evening conversations in Chungking, quite soon after my arrival.

When I went to stay with the Chiangs at their villa, Madame Chiang often invited me for long walks, just two of us in the open country. We might have been under observation by security men using field glasses or something, but there was no bilingual person walking with us listening to every word. On one of these walks she told me: "Of course, our Soviet advisers are no good, because now that the Soviets are being attacked by the Germans, they need every competent officer they've got. So anybody we've got must be third or fourth rate." Eventually the Soviets got disgusted with the Chinese not making proper use of their advisers and pulled out their military mission. The head of the mission returned to the Soviet Union and became one of the heroes of the defense of Stalingrad, showing how fourth rate he was. This was the famous General Vasilii Chuikov.

One Sunday afternoon during a long walk I learned why Madame detested Ho Ying-ch'in. According to her, when the news came that the Generalissmo had been kidnapped in Sian, an urgent council was convened at the headquarters of the Generalissimo, attended by members of the inner circle in Nanking. The primary questions were: Should they bomb Sian? Or should representatives go there to talk to the mutineers? In that case, would they merely be captured, too? Madame Chiang said that in that situation, she wanted to go. The Australian adviser, W.H. Donald (previously adviser to Chang Hsueh-liang), was willing to go with her. T.V. Soong also proposed to go. For once she and her brother were in agreement that they must go up to negotiate.

Ho Ying-ch'in, however, said: "We must absolutely not try to negotiate. The first thing we must do is to bomb Sian." Somebody at this moment intervened: "If we bomb Sian, the Generalissimo may be killed, either by the bombing or by the mutineers in retaliation against the bombing." Upon this, Ho replied: "If he is killed that is too bad, but he is a soldier and he must take the chances of a soldier." Madame Chiang's interpretation was: "Ho hoped that my husband would be killed and he then would be in a position to seize the top military power." It is very important to remember that at the time when Madame Chiang was telling me this story, Ho Ying-ch'in was Chiang Kai-shek's chief-of-staff. This was the kind of multiple paradox that you got at that time in Chungking.

There was a very strong tendency among Americans to assume that because Madame Chiang had been so deeply Americanized, she must be completely pro-American, and that there was a strong American influence at the headquarters of Chiang Kai-shek. She, on her part, publicly supported the political legend that the United States was less imperialistic than any other country and was a true friend of China and all the rest of that line. Nevertheless, she was a curious combination.

She several times spoke to me very bitterly about her father, who had gone up in the world through working for American missionaries, having always been treated by the Americans as a Chinese of poor origin. He would travel in the interior and visit Chinese Christian communities, distributing religious materials and tracts. When he came back and reported to the missionaries in Shanghai, he would have to stand in front of the white people who were sitting. They never invited him to sit down. In other words, he was treated more like a servant than a colleague. She thought that the American attitude to herself also had always been: "Oh yes, she is clever, of course, but after all she is only a Chinese." She felt that the American attitude was racist and condescending, and she bitterly resented it. That was why, whenever she visited the United States, she insisted on top ceremonial protocol.

It was also what Madame Chiang told me during these walks, supplemented by gossip passed on to me by Hsieh Pao-chao, that enabled me to see something of the conflicts that existed in Chiang Kai-shek's family circle. As has already been mentioned, the relations between Madame Chiang and her brother T.V. Soong were strained, and they energetically disliked each other. Both of them were power hungry, and I suppose they competed for consideration as the top expert on the United States: not so much on U.S. politics as on inside knowledge about top people—who counted and who did not.

Another reason was that in financial and economic matters, T.V. Soong and H.H. Kung were rivals, and since Madame Chiang and her eldest sister Madame Kung were very close, they allied themselves against T.V. Soong. In financial matters, Madame Chiang relied entirely on H.H. Kung. Chiang Kai-shek trusted Kung, but not T.V. Soong, though the latter was useful in certain ways because of his much advertized U.S. banking and financial connections. For example, after the end of the European War, with the resumption of negotiations in Moscow between China and the Soviet Union, it was useful to be able to send T.V. Soong as his representative. That was a polite way of indicating: "You see, my representative is a man who is not merely my diplomatic representative, but also personally has high acquaintances in the United States." H.H. Kung could not have played that role as convincingly.

Madame Chiang was very much under the influence of Madame Kung, and politically Chiang Kai-shek had more confidence in Madame Kung, his sister-in-law, than in his own wife. He extended his confidence in Kung to Kung's wife. Of course, he knew all about the Kung-Soong rivalry and used it in his politics. In a city of malicious and contradicting political gossip, I was amazed by the almost universal dislike for Madame Kung. Everybody believed that she controlled one particular bank, through which she bought American dollars just before each new, steep fall in the value of the Chinese dollar.

One story, particularly showing personal dislike, was about her escape from Hong Kong after Pearl Harbor. She frequently visited Hong Kong for a bit of comfort and luxury and to do financial deals. On the news of Pearl Harbor, a special plane was sent down to rescue her and her entourage in the nick of time. She insisted that her favorite dachshund be taken along, but when the pilot said that the plane was overweight, one of her security guards had to be left behind. When the plane reached Chungking the first occupant to come down—according to the story, which ran through Chungking like wildfire—was the dachshund, while the security guard who had been left behind was captured and killed. Since there is no equivalence between the weight of a dachshund and the weight of a man, the insinuation of "sacrificing a man to save a dog" was purely symbolic of dislike.

The sister between Madame Kung and Madame Chiang, Sung Ch'ing-ling, was the widow of Sun Yat-sen. Having been always a supporter of cooperation with the Chinese Communists, she did not agree with her sisters. She lived apart in a comfortable house of her own; but it was something that rather resembled a luxurious house arrest, and people could not call on her freely. Madame Chiang was certainly the prettiest of the three sisters, though I would not call her a ravishing beauty; but she used her good looks, especially on foreigners, in a way more American than Chinese. People used to say in Chungking that "Madame Kung loves money, Madame Chiang loves power, and Madame Sun loves the people." My personal impression also was that Madame Kung had an extremely shrewd but unscrupulous, pecuniary mind. Madame Chiang was interested in power and influence and had a talent for intrigue. Madame Sun was the least clever of the three sisters, but a woman of complete integrity and simple honesty.

At my only Christmas in Chungking, in 1942, I was invited to their family Christmas dinner party. Though Madame Sun was a supporter of the United Front in a way that did not please Chiang Kai-shek, for the sake of family appearances, of course, she could not be ostracized. It was held at the house of one of the three sisters, and I was the only foreign guest. The relations between Madame Sun and the other two sisters were perfectly correct but by no means overflowing with sisterly love.

Chiang Kai-shek and His Government

Though in the West there is an exaggerated impression even to this day that Chiang Kai-shek was a dictator, he never really was one. Being a Chinese military politician who had come up on top, he had to keep balancing one faction against another. He had also to bear in mind the geography of China: "In which province did each important general have his power base in money and manpower, and how had his interests been affected by the Japanese invasion?" When he gave an order to a general, he had to think first: "Is this an order this man will obey, or will he sabotage it?"

One of the outstanding examples was Sheng Shih-ts'ai, the independent or semi-independent warlord of Sinkiang. He was by origin a poor boy who had been picked up by a rich merchant in Liaoning Province in the Northeast. He was educated and then sent to Japan where he graduated from a military academy. Coming back to Liaoning, he entered the Northeast Army under Chang Tso-lin. Having taken part in an anti-Chang mutiny, he fled inside the Great Wall and was taken up by the Kuomintang as a military man. Chiang Kai-shek was always suspicious of the allegiance of Chang Hsueh-liang and was very pleased to have a man who had inside information on the affairs of the Northeast and was independent of the patronage of the Young Marshal.

Later Sheng was sent to Sinkiang as a representative of the highest commanding staff of Chiang Kai-shek. This was a period of trouble with the Muslims, and Sheng got control of the situation. Then, after the Japanese invasion of the Northeast in 1931, many Northeast troops escaped into Siberia. The Soviets took them all the way round and sent them into Sinkiang. The official reason for this move was that the Chinese troops were being repatriated to Chinese territory; but in fact, the Soviets were presenting Sheng, who was taking a pro-Soviet policy at that time and was himself a Northeast man, with personal troops on whom he could rely. Having his best troops not from Chiang Kai-shek but from the Northeast, via the Soviet Union, helped Sheng to be more independent of Chiang Kai-shek. In 1934, he was made governor of the area; and from 1937, with the full Japanese invasion of North China, Sinkiang, bordering on the Soviet Union, became enormously important as a transport link for arms and munition from the Soviet Union to Chiang Kai-shek. This all the more increased Chiang's difficulty in controlling Sheng Shih-ts'ai.

Another interesting example of local warlords keeping their independence was that of Lung Yün, the governor of Yunnan, as has been described above. When Chiang Kai-shek staged his final attack on the Chinese Communists in 1934, which drove them out of Kiangsi and sent them on the Long March to Yenan, in a number of provinces the governors let the Communists pass through their territories without interference so as not to give the army of Chiang Kai-shek any justification to intervene.

On top of the problem of warlords whom Chiang had to leave in place as governors of their own territories, there were problems of the power conflicts within the Kuomintang itself, as in the case of Ho Ying-ch'in. Moreover, in a social system in which nepotism is important, you always have not simply those who benefit from nepotism but competition between those who benefit from it: so that X and Y may be beneficiaries of Chiang Kai-shek's nepotism, but the sons of X and the sons of Y may be in competition with each other for the succession to those benefits. I cannot say that I personally observed this, though I heard a tremendous amount of scandal in the form of gossip.

For Chiang Kai-shek, there was also the problem of getting the right kind of information. I have already mentioned that Madame Chiang had no confidence in the Soviet advisers in Chungking. The opinions of the Soviet advisers had to be filtered to Chiang Kai-shek through reports from his own General Staff, and the latter did not like to admit that they were militarily inferior to the Soviets and had to rely on Soviet advisers. Therefore they always depreciated the Soviet advisers in their reports to the Generalissimo. This was also because the Chinese military hierarchy did not want any military reforms that would weaken their own position in the military structure. In the Chinese manner, each general who rose to a high position tried to create his own power base by appointing his own men, largely his own relatives or people who had been his disciples at Whampoa Military Academy. Therefore, they were jealous of one another and jealous of the Soviets. In these conditions, how could Chiang Kai-shek get realistic reports?

In the Chinese General Staff, Madame Chiang intensely disliked some, and others were her confidential friends, though I did not know who were her favorites among the generals. As she, too, was in a position where she could not obtain objective reports, her military opinions largely came to her through H.H. Kung, who also had his private political structure with his own allies and rivals. He could not be a big political man without having military allies. In the China of that period, nobody could.

As there were so many competing factions in Chungking, it was Chiang's canny practice to use several channels of communication to guide his own Washington policy. One was his own Foreign Office; the second was his Ambassador Hu Shih and also T.V. Soong in Washington; and the third channel was myself. He always, and not only in an emergency situation, used more than one channel so that he could play off one faction against another.

Chiang did not have much confidence in his own foreign minister Kuo T'ai-ch'i, or his ambassador, Hu Shih, considering them as only part of the facade representing China as one of the democratic countries. Since I was working for Chiang Kai-shek personally, it would have been very dangerous for me to get into gossipy relations with the other factions, because that would have diminished my independence as an adviser to Chiang. I only talked with people under Chiang's orders about the things that Chiang told me to ask or talk about. I knew what the dangers were.

Like perhaps all dictators or would-be dictators, Chiang Kai-shek relied very heavily on secret intelligence. Also, as in all such situations, he kept several intelligence services going in rivalry with one another in order to avoid becoming captive of his own intelligence services. They would leak information on one another and in that way he would get to know what they were really up to. The best-known name in that game in China was Tai Li, but there was another group called the C.C. Clique, of the Ch'en brothers, Ch'en Kuo-fu and Ch'en Li-fu. They were a typical example of an ancient Chinese mode of career-making that survived into the modern age.

Suppose that in the China of earlier days there is a man who is wealthy or influential in other ways but has no sons old enough to continue in his footsteps. This man looks for somebody of lower birth but high personal talent, and he promotes the education and early career of this young man. For this purpose, it is essential to select a candidate from a clan which is not likely to become a rival of the clan of the patron. The idea is that the patron, having launched the promising young man on a career, will benefit when the protégé himself rises to position of power, as he will promote the careers of the sons or grandsons of his patron. This is the story of the relationship between Chiang Kai-shek and the Ch'en brothers.

When Chiang Kai-shek was a young man, he came under the patronage of a rich man in the Yangtze valley, who started as a landlord and later invested in more modern economic activities centered on Shanghai. His name was Ch'en Ch'i-mei, and he had enjoyed the favor of Sun Yat-sen. Ch'en Ch'i-mei, being a military man himself, saw that the military was going to be important in the new China, and so sent young Chiang Kai-shek to the military academy in Paotingfu and then to Japan to study military organization and tactics. As Chiang Kai-shek rose in power, in the proper traditional manner he promoted the careers of his patron's sons, who came to be known as the Ch'en brothers of the C.C. Clique.

I might mention here that Ch'en Li-fu was also a student of my father's when my father was teaching at Peiyang University in Tientsin. Ch'en Li-fu studied English under him, and then went to the United States and earned a degree as a mining engineer. Like so many Chinese potential technocrats of this kind, when he came back to China, I doubt if he ever went down into a mine. Instead, he embarked on a combination of bureaucratic career and political career. As Chiang Kai-shek rose in power, he and his brother became personal organizers and agents of the influence of Chiang Kai-shek, heading one of his several secret services.

The Ch'en brothers were in Chungking when I was there, but I only met Ch'en Li-fu. He invited me to his office and was very cordial—again in the traditional manner: "You are the son of your father and I am the student of your father. Therefore we have a brotherly kind of relationship." I had only one longish interview with him. He had worked up an ideology which was a combination of Confucianism and European authoritarianism modeled on Italian and German fascism, with a dash of the Y.M.C.A.-type of Christianity, for training a young elite to be Chiang Kai-shek's trusted cadres in the Kuomintang.

Parallel with this, he developed his political intelligence service, through which he organized a youth movement within the Kuomintang, and placed his own men in key positions in his intelligence service. In this way he would know very quickly if any faction was developing in the Kuomintang which might challenge the ascendency of Chiang Kai-shek. He impressed me as a smooth and able bureaucrat. At the end of the interview, he presented me with a photograph of himself with a complimentary inscription to be sent to my father.

In Chungking you had the paradox that on the one hand there were Chiang Kai-shek's secret services, such as Tai Li and the Ch'en brothers who were persecuting and tracking down leftists, and on the other hand you had a significant number of leftists who were being protected by highly placed people in the Kuomintang administration. I did not fully realize this at the time I was in Chungking, but looking back it seems to me much clearer what was going on. The general assumption of the top Kuomintang people, even before

Pearl Harbor, was that sooner or later the United States would be in the war. Then the primary work of defeating Japan would be done by the Americans. China must get ready for postwar planning. In every ministry that dealt with the United States and with economic matters of postwar development, there was somebody who was either a Marxist or a follower of Marxism. Chi Ch'ao-ting was an outstanding example. The last time I saw him was in Washington, after the war, when he was accompanying H.H. Kung as his private, confidential secretary.

What it is essential to understand about the Communists in "sensitive" positions under Chiang Kai-shek, the great anti-Communist, is that the Generalissimo and his most trusted supporters assumed that after the war China would be dependent on the United States not only for capitalist economic support, but also for capitalist expertise. That made it imperative to have experts who knew what made American capitalism tick. More than a text-book knowledge of capitalist theory was needed. China must know how, in the United States, capitalists as individuals rose to power, as well as how they exercised power. Who had studied that side of the world? Principally the Marxists, who were forever talking about "capitalist contradictions."

In order to remain intellectually independent of the massive American economic power on which it would be dependent, and also to be able to balance the postwar importance in Asia of the Soviet Union against that of the United States, China must recruit men who really knew how Marxism works. In some cases, a man who had studied at the London School of Economics under Harold Laski would do, but in some cases a suspected or even a known member of the Communist Party could be employed, if he were controllable.

Of course, the Kuomintang people did not want to be controlled by Marxists. There, once again, we go back to old Chinese ways: There are a great many Marxists in the Chinese intellectual world; and many of them come from good and powerful families. Appoint to research posts in every ministry young Marxists who are members of the old established and powerful families or whose own families owe their promotion and positions to patronage by great families. Because of the old and lasting Chinese tradition of family loyalty, these young leftists will not betray us. Their families will keep control of their sons, and through their families we can keep track of them.

Around 1975 or 1976, I saw in an American newspaper in Paris a quotation from Averell Harriman, once Roosevelt's ambassador in Moscow (1943–46), to the effect that he considered Stalin better informed than Roosevelt and more intelligent than Churchill. On my part, I think that sometimes Chiang Kai-shek was more far-sighted than either Roosevelt or Churchill. He was convinced, even in the first week of the Nazi invasion of the Soviet Union, that as the Soviets would eventually defeat the Germans, the Japanese would not honor the Berlin-Tokyo Axis and attack Siberia from the east to help the Germans in the west. As Chiang said to me: "In China, the Japanese are bogged down. They can't find a solution and win a decisive victory; but they need a victory of some kind. Therefore they will attack the colonial territories in the south. They are already established in Indochina, and they will create a diversion in the Pacific and get into serious conflicts with the Great Powers."

I would say that, in spite of everything, Chiang Kai-shek was a genuine patriot. He was highly nationalistic and was certainly responsible for holding China together at the critical moment, for example, of the defection of Wang Ching-wei to the Japanese in 1938. At that time, the defeatist pressure on him was very strong, and if he had not stood out against them, a considerable number of influential generals and politicians might have made their peace with the Japanese. I do not recall having met any individual who was afterward pointed out as being a Wang Ching-wei man. All I knew was the general allegation that there were other potential Wangs who would come out if the situation should get bad enough.

Of course, Wang Ching-wei was regarded as a traitor; but there were perhaps disappointed power-seekers in the Chungking regime who wondered to themselves: "If Chiang falls and Wang comes out on top, maybe I could get a better job." I am sure that Chiang Kai-shek suspected, or probabaly even knew, that there were people in Chungking who had underground contacts with Wang Ching-wei, though there would be no secret contact between Wang and Chiang himself.

Nevertheless, in spite of the inner rivalries, most people in Chungking, including rightists, such as Ho Ying-ch'in, agreed with

Chiang's main thesis that Japanese imperialism, having been contained in China, would be obliged to break out elsewhere, which would mean that China would have active allies, and these allies would win the war for China. Chiang Kai-shek's far-sightedness in this respect, however, at the same time proved to be the cause of his eventual fall, as we shall see later.

I can say that because of such a calculation among important Kuomintang leaders, no serious consideration was given to any possibility of coming to terms with the Japanese. I cannot say, however, how much the Chinese leaders knew about the internal situation in Japan, though this is an extraordinarily important question. I would say that probably one of those who knew Japan and who had the most influence on Chiang Kai-shek would be Chang Ch'ün. He indicated in his conversations with me that it was during his days as a student in Japan that he gathered his basic information and began to understand the class structure in Japan. Therefore later on, when other people would report to Chiang Kai-shek that in Japan Mr. X was on his way up and Mr. Y was on his way down, Chang Ch'ün would say: "That is because Mr. X belongs to this kind of family and this kind of social situation in relation to this kind of political movement, and Mr. Y belongs to . . . , etc."

I do not know whether there was any channel through which Chiang Kai-shek was obtaining any current information directly from Japan, although indirectly one can be sure that Chiang was getting information from the camp of Wang Ching-wei, the defector, just as Wang was getting intelligence from inside the Generalissimo's camp. In any case, I had no special reason to believe that Chang Ch'ün was able to follow what was going on inside Japan. What I did know, and thought important, was that very early in my stay in Chungking, he told me that Japan was following policies that would bring it into open conflict with European imperialist countries and eventually with the United States.

I was not in a position to know what kind of advice Chang Ch'ün was giving to Chiang Kai-shek; but I think he assumed, in the first place, that there would be in Japan, as in China, personal rivalries of cliques claiming power and control in one field of action or another. Certainly, the Chinese were much more aware of and sensitive to differences within Japan than the Americans ever were. The common American assumption was: "We are up against the Japanese militarists. They are absolutely solid. If General so-and-so is in charge, everybody carries out his orders click, click, click." In contrast, the Chinese realized that even if General so-and-so was commander-in-chief of the army, there were cliques in the army, and some would carry out the orders in one way, and others would carry them out in a different way. This kind of thing Americans seldom understood. I know this from having talked with people in Washington during the Pacific War when there were occasional meetings of the Office of War Information with representatives of the War Department, navy, and other related departments.

I do not think that in Chungking during the war years any decisions were made on the assumption that more liberal people might come into power in Japan, though I was not in China in the last year of the Pacific War. Certainly, there must have been very interesting debates involving people like Chiang Kai-shek himself and Chang Ch'ün and others, as they contemplated: "We are coming to the point where Japan is going to have to surrender. Given the people in power or close to power in Japan, who is likely to be the man who is entrusted with the mechanics of bringing about the surrender?" They would probably have had a pretty good notion of where Prince Konoe stood, for example.

Chou En-lai

At one of my very first meetings with Chiang Kai-shek, when he was telling me whom I should see to talk about what subjects, I asked: "What about the Communists?" "Oh, naturally you should meet them, too," he said. Obviously, he had waited for me to bring up the subject, hoping that he could detect what sort of directive I had been given in Washington. (In fact, the nearest thing to a directive had been an overall suggestion that a civil war in the course of a war for national survival would be disastrous.)

The Communists had an official delegation headed by Chou En-lai. I did not take any steps to make contact with them, however, but waited instead to see what would happen. What followed was rather amusing. First, I had a caller from one of the relatively independent newspapers. I think it was the *Takungpao*. At the end, the interviewer asked if I would meet people from other newspapers. I answered: "Why, certainly, yes. I shall be glad to meet and talk with anyone who comes." The next visitor was from a paper that represented some sort of in-between, "tolerated" group. When he came, I told him that this was not to be an interview for publication, "on the record," but merely a discussion in order to be acquainted with each other.

He also asked me if I would meet a man from another newspaper. The next man who came asked: "Would you meet the representative of the official Communist publication?" (There was, in these curious days, an openly published, modest, cautiously worded Communist paper.) I went through the same routine and answered: "Yes, of course." When the reporter from the Communist publication came, he asked, "Would you meet Chou En-lai?" "Yes, naturally," I answered, "but Chou En-lai is an important person. Perhaps I should call on *him*." "Oh, no, no," he said. "He will come to call on you."

I think the relations between Chou and the Kuomintang are best illustrated by this story of the chain of connections that led to Chou coming to call on me. It was typical of Chungking's network of political and personal contacts. Chou En-lai knew people who knew other people, who knew still other people. I already knew enough from the variety of contacts I was making to realize that it was completely misleading to think of a total, sharp cleavage between the Kuomintang and the Chinese Communist Party. There were all kinds of groups, though they differed among themselves, committed to the idea of compromise with the Communists in order to revive the United Front. They all had different ideas on how to go about it, but the idea that something could be done to improve relations with the Communists was pervasive.

Chou En-lai insisted he should call on me, because officially Chiang Kai-shek was the head of the United Front, and it was not fitting for the representative of the head man to be the first to call on the representative of the junior member of the United Front. This again is something that gets overlooked in the history of revolutions: At the period when a new revolution is trying to establish its footing internationally, it does everything to show that it is a civilized, not a barbarous revolution. In order to prove that they are not just murderous gangsters but people who understand the conventions of diplomacy, they are willing to play by the rules of the game. Subversion comes later, but only after the appeal for "normal relations" has been rejected.

When Chou En-lai came to call on me, he came alone, without an interpreter. My official interpreter-secretary, Hsieh Pao-chao, tactfully stayed out. We recalled that we had previously met in Yenan in 1937. At that time, Chou had made a distinct impression on me as a man who understood the world outside of China. Incidentally, I had heard that he had been studying English, and I knew that he had spent several years as a young man in France. Therefore, I began by saying: "Do we speak in English or in French?" "Oh, no," he said. "My English is very poor, and I have forgotten most of my French. In Chinese, please." I said: "Then you have to excuse me and help me out with my Chinese, which is not good enough." He said that would be all right, and from then on we always spoke in Chinese.

I said to him: "You know the circumstances in which I am here. I am recommended by President Roosevelt, but was appointed by Chiang Kai-shek, and I am working for him as his employee. If there are questions you wish to ask me, or matters which you wish to bring up, they should be brought up in that context." He said that he quite understood. His visit lasted about half an hour. There was no concrete discussion of any particular problem. He did not bring up anything that he would want me to report back to Chiang Kai-shek; and in our subsequent contacts in Chungking, I was never in the position of being a middleman, carrying suggestions from Chiang Kai-shek to the Communists, or from the Communists to Chiang.

We did talk, however, about the importance of the United Front; and I was able to assure the Chinese Communists that President Roosevelt was very much interested in the avoidance of civil war in China. Of course, everywhere in Chungking everybody paid lip service to the United Front, but still it was useful to have it on record that I had already said to the Communists as well as to Chiang Kai-shek that President Roosevelt was interested in avoiding civil war.

I think this was the only time Chou En-lai ever made a formal call on me, and I never went to the Communist Party office in Chungking; but I met him a number of times when there were important foreign visitors to Chungking and Chiang himself or some highly placed person would invite a foreign guest to dinner. On these occasions, to impress the foreigners that there was a United Front, Chou En-lai would be invited to attend. Undoubtedly, Chiang's intelligence services were trying to infiltrate the Communists, and the Communists were trying to infiltrate them. There must have also been a number of double agents. In that kind of atmosphere, it was much better to have somebody report to Chiang Kai-shek that Lattimore and Chou En-lai were at the same party and were observed talking to each other than to have it reported that Lattimore and Chou En-lai arranged a private appointment.

I remember one rather comical incident at one of these dinners when the famous American reporter, James Vincent Sheean, was in Chungking. The host was Ho Ying-ch'in, Chiang Kai-shek's chief-of-staff. Ho was known as one of the most reactionary generals and as one of the most important Catholic laymen in China. As a wealthy landholder in the province of Kueichou, he was friendly with the Catholic missionaries there. At that time, the famous Bishop of Nanking, Paul Yü Pin, was in Chungking. Ho had invited him as the other main guest. The bishop was originally a Northeast man, from Heilungkiang, and was very conservative, even reactionary. He had, however, refused to collaborate with the Japanese, and by the time of the all-out Japanese invasion in 1937, he was the Bishop of Nanking. When the capital was moved to Chungking he also came there, making himself the most conspicuous Catholic cleric in China. He was publicly against concessions of any kind to the Communists.

At the dinner, Vincent Sheean and Paul Yü Pin were needling each other. Sheean suggested that Catholics were a reactionary influence, and Paul Yü Pin was turning his remarks aside. As is well known, two of the most famous alchoholic drinks in China are Maotai and Meikueilu. The former was originally distilled in Kueichou Province and the latter in Shansi Province. The conversation turned to a discussion about which was better, the strong Southern drink or the strong Northern one. Chou En-lai intervened, saying: "Well, I really should be the authority on this subject, because I am the man who personally gave the orders for burning down both distilleries," the implication being that the Communists could reach into the heart of any province, including Ho Ying-ch'in's own Kueichou. The remark visibly did not please Ho Ying-ch'in, of course. Chou looked mischievous.

Various people around Chiang Kai-shek, especially this Paul Yü Pin and an American priest who was constantly with him, had been urging me to spread word in the United States that Edgar Snow was not only an untrustworthy and unreliable reporter on China, but actually also a Communist agent or spokesman. They argued that his *Red Star Over China* had done a great deal of harm to Chinese-American relations by promoting in the United States a feeling of too much friendliness for the Chinese Communists. I thought that Snow was an objective reporter; and I did not regard it as my duty to spread propaganda in the United States against one Chinese party voiced by another Chinese party; nor would Chiang want me to identify myself as a partisan.

On one occasion, I asked Chou En-lai: "What do you—not just you personally, but the Communist Party—think about Edgar Snow?" Chou's answer was: "From our point of view, Edgar Snow is an honest reporter. He sometimes gets things a bit wrong, but when he makes a mistake, he acknowledges it. We regard him as a genuinely liberal and progressive person. Of course, there is one thing that makes us a little nervous." I asked what that was. Chou continued: "He sometimes tries to explain things in China by saying 'from the Marxist point of view...' as if he had some Marxist authority for what he is saying. The point is that Snow is a man who, by temperament and by intellect, never in his whole life will understand what Marxism is."

Many years later, I told this story to Edgar Snow himself. He was very pleased with it. It is true that Snow, in some of his later writings, not only about China but also about the Soviet Union, would try to present things as if "in the way they appeared to Marxists," but I always thought that he was at his best when he described the way things appeared to him, or directly quoted what had been told to him by a Chinese or Soviet Communist. There one felt that he was an absolutely straightforward reporter.

Even at that time, Chou En-lai was very much a favorite among the foreign embassies in Chungking. This was because he was frank and open. Whenever he was asked a question that was too awkward to answer, instead of giving an evasive response, he would say: "Well, that is a topic which I am not prepared to discuss at the moment." As a result, the people had the feeling that when he was willing to say something, he was telling the truth and could be trusted. He was certainly a great favorite among the Americans, especially the military.

Chou said that in the existing constellation of forces in the Kuomintang, the Chinese Communist Party considered Chiang absolutely indispensable, and that though they had their troubles with him and disagreed with him about methods, they did not question his devotion to the cause of China's war of resistance. On his part, Chiang said that he considered Chou En-lai personally trustworthy, but of course he was under the control of these people up in Yenan. One of the items of gossip one heard in Chungking was that Chou was acceptable to Chiang for very personal reasons. According to this story, when Chiang was the military head of the Whampoa Military Academy and Chou was its political commissar, there was a mutiny of the leftist students of the academy that had actually put Chiang's life in danger. Chou had intervened and saved his life.

This gossip continued with the report that Chiang had repaid the favor: when Chiang turned against and slaughtered so many Communists in Shanghai in 1927, he had arranged to get Chou out of Shanghai on some sort of pretext and saved his life, but without alerting the Communists of the coming coup. Incidentally, since we are on the subject of gossip, I think I should stress one point here. In my opinion, interesting though gossip is, many people place far too much emphasis on individuals and explain things by personal rivalries, personal enmities, personal alliances, and so on. In contrast, the Communist tendency is to stress social class and class interests to the point of overemphasis.

I met Chou about half a dozen times. I suppose that one object of the Chinese Communists was to keep it on record, and keep it visible and known in Chungking, that the Communist regime was in touch with Chiang's American adviser. Certainly, Chiang also wanted me to be in touch with Chou. What this meant to both sides, in the odd topsy-turvy world of Chungking, was that in case of emergency they had a channel of communication independent of internal Chinese political intrigues. As it worked out, this channel never had to be used. I like, however, to flatter myself by thinking that while Chou had his directives from Yenan and I had mine from Chiang, it was partly because Chou and I developed a genuine personal liking for each other that things went well.

The broad distinction between my sentiments about Chiang and about Chou would be that Chou understood the modern world better than Chiang, and better, probably, than any other Chinese Communist of that time. I never consulted Chou on policy, and I never submitted a memorandum to him. All this kind of contact I did have with Chiang, and contact with Chiang was much more extended in time and involved much more frequent personal relations. On the whole, Chiang was a man whom I could admire, with certain very important restrictions; but I could not really say that I *liked* Chiang very much. On the other hand, my recollection of Chou En-lai is that he was a congenial spirit, the kind of man whom one could call *sympathique* in the French use of the term.

The last time I saw Chou En-lai in Chungking was just before I left there in July 1942 to return to the United States to take a wartime job. It was at a lunch given by the U.S. military attaché. Chou and I were there with several other Chinese and a number of Americans. There was a moment when Chou and I were left sitting on the same sofa, out of hearing of other people. I took the opportunity to say to him: "Mr. Chou, I am going home now. I should like to have your frank opinion. Do you think the time I've put in here as adviser to Chiang Kai-shek has been wasted? Has it been just a charade, play acting?" He said immediately, and very straightforwardly: "No, your presence here has, from our point of view, been useful. It has helped to maintain the status of the United Front."

The final impression left with me is that he must have been the greatest number-two man in history. One reason why he was as important as he was was that he had no ambition to be number one. He wanted to be with the Chinese Revolution, and whatever the decision of the Chinese Communist Party, he would do his best to execute that policy. He must, however, have had considerable personal influence on a man like Mao Tse-tung. If he thought that some of Mao's opinions needed modification he would not hesitate to say so, but in a way that would make Mao or anybody else listen to him.

All through my contact with Chou En-lai, he knew that I was not telling him everything, and I knew that he was not telling me everything; but as far as I can make out up to this day, neither of us told the other a direct lie. To a certain extent, there was a suppression of truth, but never any subversion of truth. There was a certain amount of *suppressio veri*, but no *falsificatio veri*, as the lawyers say. It was very much on the basis of that old feeling that I met Chou En-lai again in 1972 in Peking. I never, for example, expected him to "give me the lowdown" on the Cultural Revolution.

Chapter Six

■

THE WAR YEARS

Outbreak of the Pacific War

In late autumn of 1941, not only Chiang Kai-shek, but everybody in a responsible position in Chungking was very much concerned with the series of negotiations between the United States and Japan that was going on in Washington. I doubt that Chiang himself had ever thought of coming to terms with the Japanese. I think his calculation was probably based on reasoning that in the actual balance of power, both the Soviet Union and the United States would ultimately restrict Japan; and therefore it was more important to keep open lines of communication with Washington and Moscow than to try for any sort of deal with Tokyo. I personally was also against any form of agreement between China and Japan, which would nominally be an agreement between sovereign states but in fact would place China in a subordinate position.

In Japan, Prince Konoe, whom I met in Tokyo in 1937, had been appointed prime minister in July 1940, but in October 1941 he was replaced by the leading militarist, General Tōjō Hideki, as the first prime minister to take up that office without resigning from his military post. I think Konoe foresaw the danger of the continued Japanese intervention in China. But regardless of what arrangements Konoe and his friends might try to make with the Chinese to end the war, these efforts could not succeed because whatever terms Konoe might have proposed would be hardened by the militarists to the point that the Chinese could not accept them. In any case, if the Japanese side had hoped for this kind of possibility, I think it was wishful thinking.

158

Chiang Kai-shek said to me: "If there is any move toward détente with Japan, that will encourage potential Wang Ching-wei's here and weaken my ability to lead China against Japan." He was afraid that the Americans were going too far in the direction of appeasing Japan without sufficiently realizing the danger of Japan moving southward, and that they were not treating China's warnings seriously enough, thinking that these were simply aimed at trying to frighten the United States into a stronger line against Japan. Knowing that Roosevelt was really European-minded and was tremendously concerned with supporting Britain, Chiang was afraid that Chinese interests might be sacrificed for British interests. He also knew that since the Nazi invasion of the Soviet Union, China had fallen to Roosevelt's third priority.

Chiang Kai-shek discussed the matter with me in these terms. As he distrusted the State Department and feared that the people there would go along with the appeasement of the Japanese, he asked me to draft an urgent telegram to be sent to Washington. So I sent a telegram to Currie following the procedure laid down at the very beginning of my service with Chiang. Later this telegram was interpreted as an expression of my personal opinions sent on my own initiative to my personal friend Currie with the intention of influencing U.S. policy.

Nevertheless, as has been explained before, the actual function of the telegrams sent from me to Currie was not to express my personal opinions but to let President Roosevelt know through Currie what Chiang Kai-shek's views were. Following the way in which such things were done, it would have been indiscreet to say in so many words: "The Generalissimo would like the President to know the following, etc." I would not have agreed to send any message if there was something in it with which I could not agree; but I shared Chiang Kai-shek's conviction that any appeasement made by the United States would be disastrous to China.

Contrary to the impression of some people who think that I was much closer to President Roosevelt than I really was, I was in no way more informed than anyone else about the inside story of the negotiations that were going on in Washington. I do not believe, however, that the Japanese mission headed by Kurusu Saburō had been sent to the United States just before the Pearl Harbor attack in order to deceive the Americans. Nor do I think tenable the speculation that Roosevelt actually wanted Japan to launch such an attack to mobilize domestic support. It seems rather that aggressive elements in the Japanese army and navy thought that the time had come to take advantage of the war in Europe and the Nazi attack on the Soviet Union to make Japan's own effort against the colonial and semi-colonial possessions of Great Britain, Holland, and the United States in the Pacific. Japan had already established a strong position in French Indochina since July 1941.

In the beginning of December, I had been planning to go back to the United States on leave. One of the reasons for this was that I had a bad case of dysentery, and since there were no miracle drugs for this disease in those days, I needed to get to the United States for treatment. I suppose Chiang also hoped that I would come back from Washington with a report to him on what policies and what personalities were most influential in Washington. My departure had been all arranged for a week or ten days after what turned out to be Pearl Harbor Day; but a few days prior to that day I got a message from Chiang saying: "The situation is uncertain. As you have to fly down to Hong Kong to fly across the Pacific, it is better to wait for a while before you start."

I heard later that Chiang's intelligence services had reported to him that a week or so before the Pearl Harbor attack, smoke was seen coming out of the chimneys of the Japanese consulates in places like Singapore and other Southeast Asian cities. It looked very much as if secret documents were being burned. This in turn indicated that Japan might be about to do something drastic that would involve that part of the world in war.

Very early in the morning of 8 December (local time, 7 December in the United States), I received a telephone call, probably from Hollington Tong, saying: "Don't try to catch a plane to Hong Kong. The Japanese have attacked Pearl Harbor. This means that within hours or days they will also be attacking Hong Kong." The first information told me only that there had been a devastating attack on Honolulu; there were no details of what had happened. My immediate reaction was: "There will be a lot to do today. I'd better be fit for it." So, I went straight back to bed and went to sleep again. My wife always laughed at my reply to her question: "What did you do on receiving such information?"

I think it was about ten or eleven o'clock in the morning that I was summoned to a conference of the top people that was hastily convened to discuss the implications of what had happened. Chiang Kai-shek looked his usual impassive self, and in his usual way asked those present to give their opinions. I do not remember the exact number, but I should say there were between ten to twenty people, all of whom were high military figures and Chiang's most trusted political advisers. The first thing I said, when asked, was that a single disaster of this kind did not destroy the strength of the United States and that certainly the United States would be back in the war and would fight with even greater vigor. They knew that I had no immediate contact with the United States Embassy in Chungking nor with Washington, so they decided to wait and see whether there would be any message for me from President Roosevelt through Currie and what their own embassy in Washington would report to them.

One of the first questions at the conference was: "Does this mean that the Japanese will simultaneously mount a big campaign in China?" The answer was "No." Chiang was not exactly *pleased* when the Pacific War started, I suppose; but he certainly felt justified because his analysis of Japan's future move had been proved correct. He was, however, definitely pleased in one respect. Pearl Harbor meant that the United States was now not only officially but completely in the war. He thought that though the Allies would suffer severe losses in the Pacific and Southeast Asia, in the end they, principally the United States, would recover and defeat Japan.

Chiang Kai-shek never openly mentioned it to me, but with hindsight I think he probably rather wanted something to happen. The moment Pearl Harbor occurred, his calculation seems to have been: "This Japanese outward move has now brought the United States into the war. This will remove Japanese pressure from China. The United States is too strong to be defeated by Japan. This simply means that the war will be longer; but the war will be won, and we shall be on the winning side. The United States has let China suffer from Japanese imperialism; now let them do a bit of suffering."

Chiang was, in a way, very bitter, feeling that the United States did not fully understand China's suffering caused by the Japanese invasion. As the defeat of Japan would be assured by the U.S. forces, he went on to another conclusion. Instead of saying: "Now we must step up our activities to increase pressure on Japan on our side and hasten its defeat," his calculation was: "Let the Americans do the defeating. The thing to do for China is to engage in a holding operation and simply to last it out until the American pressure on Japan can be brought to bear." In other words, his long-term vision was to prepare his own position in China so that at the end of the war, instead of compromising with the Chinese Communists and with what remained of the United Front, which had already been pretty badly undermined, he would be able to compel the Communists and the whole of China to accept Kuomintang rule in the form in which he envisaged it.

As far as I can remember, Chou En-lai was not at that conference. If he were, I should have remembered. Very soon after Pearl Harbor, however, I discussed with him the implications for China of the United States now being at the war. Naturally, I did not say to him what Chiang Kai-shek was thinking and asked Chou his opinion about the new situation. I said to Chou: "In my opinion, this is an opportunity to attack Japan from its Chinese flank, not only to diminish the amount of power the Japanese can divert toward East Asia, but also to restore Chinese morale, because the morale of the people who are on the attack is always likely to be higher than the people on the defensive." Chou said that was exactly what he thought and this was the time for an active aggressive policy by China. I do not know whether Chiang and Chou discussed the new turn of events after Pearl Harbor, though I dare say it was not unlikely; but of course neither Chou nor Chiang discussed with me what the other had said.

I might go on to say here that Chiang Kai-shek's analysis of the situation, which had proved to be correct so far, after Pearl Harbor became the beginning of his disastrous defeat, because to take a passive attitude toward the war was in direct contradiction to the propaganda of courage, valiant resistance, fighting to the last, patriotism, and all the rest of it which the government was carrying on. If you supply that kind of propaganda and do not act on it, in the long run, the effect on the fighting troops is demoralizing.

On the contrary, the Chinese Communists, from Pearl Harbor onward, went more and more on the offensive, always harassing the Japanese as much as they could in the part of China where they were confronted by the enemy. In this way, they built up the morale of their armed forces. As a result, at the end of the war, Chiang's forces came out in the eyes of the people as passive soldiers, while the Communists and the guerilla partisans were looked upon as active fighters. In this way, the feeling of nationalism passed from the possession of Chiang Kai-shek into the hands of the Communists. They became regarded not merely as Communists, but also as active nationalists struggling on behalf of all of China.

On the other hand, the U.S. commitment to China of course rapidly became subordinate to the U.S. war in the Pacific, which first concentrated on naval warfare and then called for landings on the coast of China and Japan. Both Chiang Kai-shek and Washington agreed that the main effort in defeating Japan would be undertaken by the United States. A divergence emerged, however, between the view of Chiang and that of the United States about how the war should actually be conducted. Chiang wanted to hold his forces in reserve until the United States won the war in order to acquire a stronger advantage over the Communists in postwar China.

Nevertheless, the United States was more concerned about possible heavy casualties to their own forces in landings on the Japan and China coasts and wanted the situation to be prepared by the actions and efforts of China itself, namely, by destroying, or at least weakening, Japan's position in China before the time of the landings. Since the United States wanted a maximum effort by China to weaken Japan, they were much more in favor of an active United Front between Chiang's troops and the Red Army with its partisans than Chiang himself was prepared for. This contradiction, which strained the relations between Chungking and Washington, was there right from the beginning.

Very soon after Pearl Harbor came the news that two of the most important British battleships, the *Prince of Wales* and the *Repulse*, were sunk by Japanese air attacks off the coast of Malaya on their way from Singapore to Hong Kong (10 December). It became obvious that the British were going to lose Malaya and Burma. It was in these circumstances that Chiang Kai-shek received a visit from Field Marshal Lord Wavell, who by that time had been dismissed by Churchill from Egypt and appointed Governor of India. On 21 December, he came up to discuss with Chiang Kai-shek emergency Chinese-British measures based on Burma and India and what to do about stopping the Japanese advance.

Chiang Kai-shek launched out on a typical old Chinese tirade. At this meeting, there was a very interesting demonstration of a rather common psychological and political attitude among the Chinese. In spite of the Japanese invasion being in the forefront in recent years, the Chinese still cherished the old, old antagonism to Britain as the originator of foreign imperialism in China. This was Chiang's chance to take the high ground against the British. He said to Wavell: "You and your people have no idea of how to fight the Japanese. Resisting the Japanese is not like suppressing colonial rebellions, not like colonial wars. The Japanese are a serious great power. They have their own method of colonial war. Fighting against them for many years, we Chinese are the ones who know how to do it. For this kind of job, you British are incompetent, and you should learn from the Chinese how to fight against the Japanese." These were his actual words.

Chiang used very rough and insulting language. Then he told Hollington Tong, who was his most trusted interpreter, to translate this to Wavell. Tong thought that the language was a bit too strong and toned it down a little. When he finished, Madame Chiang spoke up and said: "That is not exactly what the Generalissimo said. You should put it this way." So she proceeded to give her own translation, which was even rougher and tougher than the Generalissimo's own language. Chiang Kai-shek, seeing Madame taking over and improving on Hollington's translation, turned to me and said: "Mr. Lattimore, will you please give the correct translation?" I cannot remember precisely what I said, but that was the toughest interpreting assignment I ever had.

While Chiang was giving his tirade, Wavell sat there politely. With the loss of the two British battleships so soon after Pearl Harbor, Wavell was not in a strong position. He did, nevertheless, quietly point out that it was the British who had resources in the form of artillery, airplanes, and other war materials, suggesting in this way that the Chinese should depend on the British in the conduct of war. This statement, of course, was also to be quickly undermined by the rapid Japanese victory and the destruction of the British regular forces in Burma.

In addition to the traditional rancor against the British, Chiang Kai-shek had, at that particular point, been especially exasperated by the British authorities in Burma. Up to the time when the Pacific

War started, the U.S. supplies to China had been delivered at Rangoon to be transported via the Burma route to China. Though these supplies were originally meant for China, the cargo of a number of U.S. boats coming to Rangoon had been held up by the British authorities there. Chiang Kai-shek had, through me and Currie, sent strongly worded telegrams to President Roosevelt, asking him, without much effect, to restrain the British from obstructing the transport of supplies to China. The official aide memoire on the Generalissimo's interview with Field Marshal Wavell is, of course, presented in a much more respectable form than it really was.

Resigning from Chiang's Service and Working in the OWI

My leave had been delayed by the outbreak of the Pacific War. I had not been able to recall the exact date of my departure until I discovered, among my long-forgotten file of Chungking documents, a letter from Chou En-lai dated 14 January, in which he wrote: "I was thinking of calling on you before you leave; but I deem it impossible now, since you are leaving tomorrow." So, it must have been 15 January 1942 that I finally left Chungking to return to the United States.

The journey took a roundabout route, as crossing the Pacific had become impossible. From China our plane flew over the hump of the Himalayas to India, from India across Africa to Brazil, and from Brazil finally back to the United States. On the same plane with me was Emanuel Fox, the principal U.S. Treasury representative in Chungking. He was on what was called the ABC Committee, consisting of a representative each from the treasuries of America, Britain, and China; they were involved in trying to stop the runaway inflation in China. I think he was being transferred to another job. We had seen each other off and on in Chungking. On that long journey with intermediate stops at various places, I became very good friends with him, but not in a way that would lead Fox, for example, at some committee meeting at the U.S. Treasury to say "According to Lattimore . . ." No Treasury man would have consulted me in that kind of way.

Though I had always thought that I was received by President

Roosevelt only once, just before my departure to Chungking in June 1941, among the Chungking documents I found a letter sent from Ruxton, Baltimore, where my house was, addressed to Madame Chiang and dated 16 February 1942. In this letter I wrote: "I have already seen the President, who gave me a very warm welcome." Somehow, I cannot remember anything about this interview. The most important thing about it was certainly not to provide any detailed technical discussion, but to assure the President that Chiang Kai-shek was not going to collapse and surrender to the Japanese and that there was no doubt about his determination to continue the war. At that time, I probably had not yet sufficiently realized that as soon as Pearl Harbor started, Chiang's attitude changed into letting the United States defeat the Japanese.

This letter also shows that I added a little personal note by writing, "By the way, he (John Davies) is also bringing you a pair of American walking shoes and some stockings which my wife got to go with them." John Davies, who had just been appointed the civilian aide and liaison man to General Stilwell, was about to leave for Chungking. Later, during the McCarthy days, even such a small present was suspected as my intention to "bribe"!

I spent a couple of months in the United States recuperating from dysentery. When I returned to Chungking in early October 1942, the house in which I had lived before was occupied by Stilwell. This fact seems to have given rise to a misunderstanding that Stilwell was a kind of successor to my office; but as has been repeatedly explained, I was an employee of Chiang Kai-shek while Stilwell was appointed by Washington, and his function was entirely different from mine. I was given another smaller house where I had the same secretary-companion, Hsieh Pao-chao, and could once again invite the Dilowa Hutukutu to come and live with me.

In any case, even before I went back to the United States, I had wanted to resign from the service of Chiang Kai-shek. Once the United States was officially in the war, the diplomatic interests, the Treasury and financial interests, military and naval interests, all had their direct channels to the Chinese government. If I, as an independent, anomalous adviser, remained there, I might be regarded by all the official channels as a nuisance and obstruction. As Pearl Harbor increased the worldwide importance of the concerted activities of the Allies, all Allied countries were strengthening their representatives in all different departments in Chungking.

While I was on sick leave in the United States, Elmer Davis, a very old and close friend of mine who had come up very high in the Office of War Information (OWI), said to me: "You are the man to head our San Francisco Office." He was a first-class journalist who had been a correspondent in Moscow and also in Hitler's Berlin. He also had translated books from French and was an American with thoroughly international qualifications. He wanted to get me for the Pacific-Asia side of the OWI. I was thinking about how I could gracefully resign my job and get away from China, because political intrigue was never my interest, and I did not have any ambition to become a political figure or anything of that kind. Moreover, I wanted to return to the United States and work for my own country in the war.

When I expressed my desire to resign soon after my return, Chiang Kai-shek said: "Oh, no. Circumstances have changed, but I still need you as my adviser." From his point of view, as I had been appointed by him and was on his payroll, I should remain as a retainer personally loyal to him. This, I suppose, was one aspect of the "feudal" side of his mind. It could also have been that at the back of his mind there was this calculation: "Although China and the United States are now full Allies, there are still delicate questions like the balance between the U.S. commitment to China's part of the war and the U.S. determination to defeat Japan first at sea and then by landing in Japan itself. In the course of this, there might be a difference in policy and the formal channels of communication might not work too well, and a man like Lattimore might again prove useful."

In the meantime, I continued to see Chiang Kai-shek, but not as frequently as before, and not so much on important matters. It was quite obvious by that time that Chiang was sitting back to leave the main effort to resist the Japanese to the Americans. I thought this was disastrous, but it was not possible for me to say so. The new development in the U.S. policy was sending General Stilwell to China, and he was urging Chiang to more military activity, using language that was objectionable to Chiang.

I could not put myself in the position of being Chiang's adviser in his service and at the same time backing up the policy of an Ameri-

can general whom he did not like. It would have been "counterpro-
ductive," as the jargon goes. I was never involved in military
questions like, for example, Stilwell's attempt to get Chiang to
make more use of Communist forces, especially Communist partisans operating behind the Japanese lines. It was because of this kind
of thing that relations between Chiang and Stilwell steadily dete-
riorated. I never had a private interview with Stilwell while in
Chungking.

I was working mostly with postwar problems, having a good
many interviews with H.H. Kung and with other economic postwar
planners. The Americans wanted the Chinese to get on with the
war, and the Chinese were already thinking much farther ahead
about what should be done after the war to create a position of new
importance in international politics.

Because of the reluctance of Chiang Kai-shek to let me go, I
finally had it arranged for me to receive an official request to return
to the United States to head the San Francisco Office of the OWI.
Chiang finally agreed to my resignation, thinking that it would not
be a bad thing to have a person who knew China well to be
engaged in the propaganda work for the Pacific areas directed
against the Japanese.

On 17 November 1942, I left China on the same plane with
Madame Chiang, who was going to the United States to launch a
propaganda campaign for China. Her attitude toward me had not
changed openly after Pearl Harbor. She still seemed to consider me
a part of the household, so to speak. Our plane flew by the same
roundabout route described above. When our plane landed, I think
it was in New York, meeting Madame Chiang was the famous
Harry Hopkins, the most intimate of the intimate advisers to Roosevelt, who was inside every major decision on international policy
as well as national policy in Roosevelt's government. When
Madame Chiang was received at the foot of the gangway by Harry
Hopkins, she immediately turned her back on me, and from that
moment on cut me dead.

Toward the end of Madame Chiang's triumphant tour of the
United States, she came to San Francisco and gave a public speech.
As I was already there since late December working for the OWI, I
attended the meeting. After the speech she gave a reception for
chosen important Americans, but I was not invited. I spoke to a

Chinese who was Chiang's public relations representative in San Francisco, saying, in a rather mild way, that I thought it was a mistake from the Chinese point of view not to invite to this reception the man who had been the personal adviser to the Generalissimo, because people might misinterpret it as a sign of a disagreement or trouble within his regime. He said: "I see your point. Come to the reception, and I will see to it that you are allowed in." So, I went and was in the file of people going past Madame Chiang to shake hands. When my turn came, she did not say a word to me, nor did she put her hand out. She looked at the next person coming up, acting as if I were not even there.

I do not think that the cold attitude of Madame Chiang was because she was angry with me for wanting to resign or anything. She thought that I was no longer useful and dropped me in the hope of getting hold of more useful people. I suppose she may have thought: "Here I am in the United States, putting on a big show. Lattimore has become an underling of Washington and not a principal person in it. Americans must not think that my public relations are in any way controlled by this particular American."

After my return to the United States, I had no special direct contact with Chungking. Only once I received a check through David Kung, the son of H.H. Kung, who happened to be in the United States, having just left Harvard or something like that. He presented the check as a "gift from the Generalissimo." During my service with Chiang Kai-shek, he had never offered me any presents. I thought it was correct not only to reject the gift, but also to report to Currie that the offer had been made.

Now, the OWI, in contrast to the OSS (Office of Special Services), was an open propaganda agency, though it is quite possible, considering the conditions of the time, that unbeknown to me some of the employees working under me in San Francisco were in fact OSS men planted there. I do not know very much about the setting up of the OWI; but what it was doing was conducting the civilian propaganda news service of the United States. We had liaison, of course, with the Allies, though I do not remember whether there was a Soviet liaison or not. Anyhow, the main divisions of the OWI were the war in the West and the war in the Pacific and China. The war in the West was handled from New York where they had their broadcasting facilities, and the war in the East was handled from San Francisco where we had our own broadcasting facilities.

About every three or four weeks I would go from San Francisco to Washington, and the top New York man would also be there. The head of the whole office was Elmer Davis, who had the personal confidence of Roosevelt and who had recruited me for the San Francisco office. These policy meetings in Washington would also be attended by military and navy intelligence people, with the representatives of the State Department as principal members. We would lay down the general lines for the immediate future about what should be specially emphasized and so on.

As frequently happened, the military intelligence people would have different ideas from the civilian people about the political emphasis in broadcasting. Then the matter would go right up to Elmer Davis. If he could not settle it, he would use his personal access to Roosevelt and tell him what the situation was. Roosevelt always agreed with him, and the directive came down. I remember an amusing incident at a regular top-level meeting in Washington. A member of our staff heard a couple of naval officers talking to each other, one of whom said: "We've learned how to handle this. It's no use fighting Elmer Davis on the way up, because he always has his way with Roosevelt. So what we have to do is to let him get his directive, and then sabotage it on the way down."

We broadcast in a large number of languages. In San Francisco we had programs in Chinese, Japanese, Malay, one or two of the Indonesian languages, etc. I do not think we broadcast in Russian. Some of our broadcasts may have been relayed from Hawaii. Naturally, we could not broadcast things that were considered military secrets. The Japanese had very extensive propaganda of their own about the Greater East Asia Co-prosperity Sphere. One of our main objectives all the time was to persuade people that they were getting the truth from us and mere propaganda from the other side. For example, when U.S. troops suffered heavy losses in some particular engagement, we did not disguise the fact. Broadcasting was our main activity, but we also printed leaflets to be dropped on enemy areas. We had to plan very carefully as to what to say in leaflets that were to be dropped over Japanese troops and what to say in the leaflets to be dropped over the Chinese or Malayan civilian population in areas occupied by the Japanese.

In our broadcasts to China, we were emphasizing the united

resistance of the whole Chinese people under their heroic leader Chiang Kai-shek, without going into actual political propaganda about the United Front. Everything we said, however, indirectly supported the idea of the United Front, but without mentioning the Chinese Communists separately. If there was a successful partisan action by the Communists against the Japanese somewhere in China, we said only "partisans" instead of "Communist partisans."

The texts for broadcast and leaflets were drawn up by the different desks. We had at each desk, as far as possible, a native speaker of that language. Our greatest difficulty was with the Japanese, because the U.S. military had evacuated all Japanese and Japanese-Americans from the Pacific coast and put them in camps in Colorado. When I came into the San Francisco Office, it was already a going concern, and I sort of inherited the Japanese who had already been tested and chosen. I personally appealed to the general who was in charge of the Pacific coast security, saying that those Japanese had been thoroughly screened and there would be no risk in letting them come to San Francisco to work for us. The general was very firm on the subject, and his reply was not only political but strongly racist. "All Japanese are yellow-bellied bastards, and they've got to be locked up until the end of the war."

Therefore, we had to send directives to these Japanese in Colorado as to what to write about; then the texts, having been checked there for political reliability by one of our people, had to be telephoned to San Francisco to be recorded for broadcasting. For that matter, we never had any live broadcaster in any language standing in front of a microphone and speaking; in war conditions, even an American broadcasting for the U.S. armed forces was never a live one. The broadcaster might make a slip or fault, so everything had to be recorded in advance.

At the top meeting of the OWI in Washington, the civilian people were largely people of newspaper background, like Elmer Davis himself, and they had their own ideas about what the public was ready to believe, but before any broadcast went out, there was military inspection for security purposes; it was at that stage that the military could alter the recording to be diffused. For one thing, we civilians did not emphasize atrocities, but the military were inclined to do so.

The military were not only obsessed with the idea that the entire

Japanese population in the United States, including Nisei, had been infiltrated before Pearl Harbor by agents from Japan, but were also convinced that some of them were active spies and all of them were unreliable. Moreover, the military were persuaded that no Japanese would ever surrender and all would die fighting. In fact, in this respect, you can say that the U.S. military were the victims of Japanese propaganda. Their idea was: "We are invincible. We have far superior armament and equipment. We are coming in, and we are going to kill you!" It was calculated to make the Japanese fight to the last.

We civilians were convinced that the Japanese soldiers, if they found themselves in a bad situation, and if their minds were properly prepared, could be persuaded to surrender. Our idea was to let it be seen that we respected them as brave men, and now that they had done their best and could not do anymore, it would be useless to resist. "Why sacrifice lives needlessly? Surrender, and you will be treated honorably." In fact, toward the end of the war, we got a good many surrenders. We had, of course, a monitoring service so that we knew what was being said from Japan on what subject, in order to decide what to say to counteract this. In our broadcasting, we never mentioned the name of Tokyo Rose, the young girl with a very charming voice broadcasting propaganda intended for U.S. servicemen, because that would convince the Japanese side that they were influencing us.

I had difficulty with an American who had been employed as a Japanese public relations man in California. He was a strong believer in the value of the authoritarian discipline of the Japanese military. Therefore, he always wanted broadcasts going out to Japan to say that Japan must, of course, be defeated, but the people who would be essential for maintaining law and order after the defeat would be the Japanese military in Japan itself. I always maintained that it was not our business to say that this or that particular group should be in authority in Japan after its surrender.

These were internal problems within the U.S. group of the OWI. But we also had difficulties with the representatives of the Allied countries. The biggest of the countries invaded by Japan was China, but it was by no means given a sole priority. As sub-director of the OWI, I had to review the entire situation of Asia and the Pacific regions. Resistance to the Japanese occuption was going on in various parts of Southeast Asia, and as the war went on, military action shifted here and there, and we had to follow that.

Therefore, at our regular weekly meetings for all heads of desks for various regions, there were also British, French, and Dutch representatives. Their duty was to keep an eye on our broadcasts to their colonial territories, now occupied by the Japanese, to assure that there would be no open conflict at the government level between U.S. policy and those of their own countries. They were in favor of the policy that would say that in Malaya the proper representative of decent government was the British, and in Indochina the French, and so forth.

Our attitude, however, was: "It is no business of the U.S. government to endorse the reimposition of colonial rule in these places." The foreign representatives then would protest, saying that we were being anti-colonial in a way that was really anti-British or anti-French. There would be occasional rows, always conducted in a polite language. The British representative, for example, would get up and say: "I really must protest against the wording of this broadcast about Burma." As far as I can remember, normally the draft written by an American would be shown to the colonial representatives, and they might object to this or that phrase. This would then come back to the U.S. head of the desk, who would sometimes accept the amendment and other times would say: "No, it has to go out as originally written." In such a case a protest might come up at the next meeting.

In the meantime, it was clear that Stilwell and Chiang Kai-shek simply could not get on. Stilwell had been, in the 1930s, the U.S. military attaché in Peking, and it was during these years that I knew him rather well. Most of the military attachés of foreign powers regarded a Peking appointment as just a round of cocktail parties, thinking that the Chinese Army was not serious and that the Chinese were not good as soldiers.

Stilwell, on the other hand, took every opportunity to go into the field, and during the Chinese civil wars he would manage to get up to the front lines to observe what was going on. Out of this came his conviction that the ordinary Chinese infantry soldiers were absolutely first-class military material. They could outmatch U.S. or European soldiers. They could endure hardship and difficulty. They were not demoralized by being wounded. At the same time, he formed another conviction that the Chinese professional army officer corps was hopelessly incompetent and inefficient. It was corrupt and could not be depended on.

Then in his reading, Stilwell came across the story about the suppression of the Taiping Rebellion and the part played by a British soldier of fortune named Charles Gordon, who organized and trained a Chinese military group, which became famous as "Chinese Gordon and his ever-victorious army." "Ha!" thought Stilwell, "The solution. Chinese soldiers with white officers!" The outcome was that Stilwell kept pressing to get more authority on the part of all the Allies—especially, of course, of the United States—and more authority for himself in the Chinese High Command.

What Stilwell was engaged in was the training of a Chinese elite force in Assam in India. They were to be trained not simply by U.S. officers, but also with U.S. noncommissioned officers, such as sergeants, who were closer to the Chinese group. They were to return over the Burma Road and help in the final defeat of the Japanese. The idea of training an elite Chinese national force would heighten the nationalistic morale of the Chinese. Nevertheless, this idea of an American-sponsored Chinese military elite might upset the British, because they might think that this was a dangerous example for Indian nationalism.

Stilwell's demand to obtain more authority in the Chinese High Command, of course, was not what Chiang Kai-shek was prepared to grant. The relation became so impossible that Chiang wanted to get as his military liaison with Washington somebody who would not only be his strong supporter, but who also was politically important in the United States. Roosevelt avoided that by sending Patrick J. Hurley, in September 1944, as his personal emissary to Chiang. Here was a man who supported Chiang Kai-shek out and out; but I am not saying that Hurley was a man with a strong base in Washington.

In Chapter 3, I already cited what Roosevelt is said to have pronounced at Hurley's departure for China. His was primarily a military appointment, but he was soon promoted to be the U.S. ambassador in Chungking. He got on fine with Chiang Kai-shek, as he was strongly behind the idea that the United States should give Chiang support of every kind, including military backing. In October, Roosevelt finally decided to withdraw Stilwell and sent out somebody who would be more friendly to Chiang's High Command. That was General Albert Wedemeyer.

It is on the record, for instance, that when Hurley received reports from young U.S. diplomats who were real experts on China, he treated the reports as pro-Communist propaganda and demanded the recall of several of these people. In point of fact, these were people who spoke Chinese and had many Chinese acquaintances. Several of them were in Yenan, and they sent reports that in the areas controlled by the Chinese Communists, the Communist regime got much more support from the peasants than the Chiang Kai-shek elements got in the areas controlled by them. This was an observation of facts. Nevertheless, these diplomats were actually recalled.

It is generally believed that Roosevelt, in the course of joint negotiations with Churchill and Stalin, was responsible for the idea that China, after the war, should be one of the Great Powers. My personal suspicion is that Roosevelt had a somewhat progressive attitude toward China, but it was also colored by an older conservative tradition that the Chinese were a kind of subordinate people.

In Roosevelt's grand scheme, after the war the Soviet Union would have to be allowed to hold a certain position in Eastern Europe. The main part of Europe, however, would be controlled and rearranged by Roosevelt and Churchill. In Asia, Eastern Siberia, China, and Japan, Chiang Kai-shek would be given a high nominal position, but the real decisions would be made by Roosevelt and Stalin. Therefore, when it was a question of Hurley demanding that some of his junior diplomats be recalled, Roosevelt would say: "That's all right. The war is still going on. But after the war, Stalin and I will take charge and straighten things out." In other words, that simply means that Roosevelt did not think that Hurley controlled or commanded any important political faction.

This compares with Chiang Kai-shek's projection of the future, which, so to speak, crossed with that of Roosevelt. Chiang also assumed that the days of the colonial empires were at an end. Both the Soviet Union and China had already suffered immense material damage. Both of them would be in need of U.S. economic help to rebuild and develop their economies. Therefore, the Soviet Union, even though ruled by Stalin, and China under Chiang Kai-shek would have a common interest in getting aid from the United

States in such a manner that they would not fall under U.S. control. This assumption provided for a degree of collaboration between the Soviet Union and China.

The Wallace Mission

In May 1944, when I was still in the Office of War Information, President Roosevelt sent a mission headed by Vice President Henry Wallace to the Soviet Union and China. There were two sides to the question of what the Wallace Mission was supposed to do. The official line was that it was to strengthen the coordination between the United States on the one hand and the Soviet Union and China on the other in the overall conduct of the war. For China, the policy of Washington was to try to get Chiang Kai-shek to cooperate more with the Communists so that the total war efforts of China against Japan would be more effective. One of the specific objectives was to negotiate and arrange for the stationing of what came to be called the U.S. Observer Mission in Yenan, popularly known as Dixie Mission (because of its location in "rebel territory").

The unofficial side of the Wallace Mission was related to the question of whether Wallace should once again be the official nominee of the Democratic Party to run with Roosevelt. At that time, in 1944, the end of the war was approaching, and international questions were of increasing importance. Wallace's reputation was not founded on any authority as a spokesman in international affairs. Therefore, nominally this mission was to enable Wallace to enhance his reputation as an international statesman qualified to accompany Roosevelt in the next election; but cynical Washington gossip maintained that Roosevelt, in fact, did not want Wallace with him in the coming election and was giving Wallace this opportunity to show himself a bit of a fool in international relations.

I have no idea why I was nominated to accompany this mission. The book that Wallace published on his mission, *Toward World Peace* (1948), which was ghostwritten mainly by a young man, stated something like: "When Wallace was organizing his mission, Roosevelt said that since he was going to China he must take Lattimore with him, as he was the man who knew what the situation was in China." As this young man seems to have read and admired things that I had published, he made me out to be a much more influential member of the mission than I actually was. In reality, my position was that of observer for the OWI accompanying the mission and not a regular member. It was, in a way, quite natural that somebody from the OWI should accompany the mission, because the official announcements made by the mission along the way would have to be coordinated with the external line through which the United States was speaking to the world.

Since it was wartime, we flew via Alaska to a Soviet airport at the northeast tip of Siberia near the Bering Strait. The local inhabitants were Soviet Eskimos. Then from there, we flew to Yakutsk. Here I began to get the measure of Wallace. In this area, we got in touch with the northernmost Soviet experiments in agriculture and livestock breeding as adapted to the subarctic. I became very quickly convinced that whenever it was a question of either plant breeding or animal breeding, Wallace knew his business.

The local Soviets knew about his agronomist reputation, and they did a great deal in showing him animal farms and vegetable farms. There, Wallace was absolutely down to earth. He would say: "No, no, you are doing it in the wrong way." There was one thing that particularly interested me because I entirely agreed with him. The Soviets were mad on crossbreeding, and their only notion of an improved type of horse, for example, was to crossbreed horses.

Wallace said to them: "That's wrong. Continue crossbreeding if you like, but you should in parallel have another way. Siberian and Mongolian horses are small, it is true, but they are very hardy. They are small because they are kept outdoors all the time, especially when they are colts. If you improve some of their living conditions and feeding, and pick out the best ones, then you will be able to breed by selection, and not by crossing. You will get larger horses, which have all the endurance and hardiness of original Siberian and Mongolian horses, much better than crossbred ones."

Wallace was also critical of their breeding chickens in the Arctic, where nobody had ever seen a chicken before. In all of the Arctic and Siberia as well as in Central Asia, the Soviets had specialized on the white Leghorns. Wallace said: "In this enormous area, you have different climates, different periods of sunlight. Why don't you try different kinds of chickens, which suit different conditions? Why make a standard chicken and produce a poor thing everywhere?" He showed himself a real expert, and the Soviets respected his expertise.

On this mission, John Carter Vincent was the representative of the State Department, and he took the attitude that I should be excluded from all official discussions which directly concerned U.S.-Soviet relations. That left me free. So while the other members of the mission were working, I had not only a wonderful but professionally very advantageous time. I was the only one in the Wallace Mission who was interested in archaeology and ethnology, and that was how I came to be friendly with A.P. Okladnikov, who was the head of the Ethnological and Archaeological Museum in Yakutsk. A pioneer archaeological explorer in the Yenisei and Lena valleys, he later became the top Soviet authority in Siberian archaeology. He personally took me around and showed me everything, including a sort of small outdoor museum like the famous one in Stockholm. In this one in Yakutsk, they had different styles of Yakut yurts, including eight-sided wooden ones built after the original felt tents. They showed me the interior, the human quarters, and the wooden pens for cattle.

From Yakutsk we went to Magadan on the Sea of Okhotsk. Magadan had historically been a very important whaling port, and we were shown, for example, the graves, dating back to the whaling ship days, of Americans who had died and were buried there. It was also the center of a big gold-mining operation. Later, Magadan became notorious as the main administrative center of a large group of Soviet forced-labor camps for political dissidents as well as criminals. It is said that one of the tasks of the Wallace Mission was to find out whether the rumor about the concentration camps in Siberia was true. As far as I know, however, the general directive of the mission in Siberia was to acquaint itself with the Soviet war effort, and whether the Soviets were able to mobilize supplies in Siberia to be sent to the western front, and not to say to them: "Are you doing this with slave labor?"

On this expedition, Wallace had as his interpreter for the Russian language a man named John Hazard. He was a lawyer who at some early stage had been sent to the Soviet Union to learn Russian, and he also had taken a law degree at Leningrad University; he was a magnificent interpreter. A very discreet man, he agreed with Vincent that I should be excluded from official meetings. Therefore, from the Soviet point of view also, I was low ranking. When we were taken out to be shown gold mines and other places, there would be a motor cavalcade. In the front car rode the top Soviet and Wallace with Hazard as interpreter; I would be several cars down the line.

It was already summer and very dusty, so that there were immense clouds of dust as we drove along. We drove past a number of wooden stockades which I could not see very clearly because of the dust. Hazard did not say anything to me at that time, but many years after the McCarthy business, I asked Hazard about this, and he said that driving in the front car he saw these stockades very clearly and asked the top Soviet with whom he was riding what they were for. The Soviet replied very honestly that they contained the concentration camps for criminal and political prisoners. Hazard said: "It was not my business to talk to you about it. So, I didn't."

It should be remembered that in 1944, the Soviet Union was our ally in the war, and its importance was fast increasing. The Soviets were becoming very important because the United States and Britain were delaying and delaying the landing on the French coast. Roosevelt wanted to reassure the Soviets that the United States was friendly. Pro-Soviet feeling in the United States was at its height, because the Soviet offensive on the eastern front was saving American lives on the western front of Europe. As a result, even conservative people had very friendly feelings toward the Soviet Union. Later, it was insinuated that I was covering up the reality in the Soviet Union, but I was totally ignorant about the actual situation. In any case, were Soviet envoys to the United States at that time told to go to inspect the U.S. detention camps for Japanese in Colorado?

After Magadan, we went to Komsomolsk, on the Amur; Irkutsk; and Ulan-Ude. From Krasnoyarsk we traveled partly by train and partly by car to visit the little village of Shushenskoe, where Lenin had spent his Siberian exile in 1897. On the way there, we stopped at one place instead of at another more important place. Years later I asked Hazard the reason, and he said: "The Soviets told me that the other place was full of Polish prisoners of war, and they were afraid that there might be an incident." It was about this time that we got the news of the Allied landing in Normandy (6 June 1944).

This, of course, added enormously to the feeling of U.S.-Soviet alliance and friendship. Then, via Minussinsk, we went to Semipalatinsk.

As I was not a regular member of the mission, I cannot say for certain, but as far as I could see, I do not think that Wallace was commissioned to do any formal negotiation with the Soviet Union. Nevertheless, at a great many social occasions at which people talked about politics, I became convinced that politically Wallace was a very wishy-washy person. He would say: "Ah, yes, you have your Soviet democracy. We have our progressive Roosevelt New Deal capitalist democracy. So, we both believe in democracy, and there are no problems we can't solve." I got the impression that it was not merely a diplomatically nice speech, but that he really believed it, and as an actual negotiator on tough problems where you had to agree about distribution of power and like questions, he would be inadequate.

From Semipalatinsk, we flew to Tashkent, to Alma-Ata, and on June 18 all the way to Urumchi. This was fascinating for me, because in two or three hours we flew over the route that had taken Eleanor and me nearly three weeks to ride on horseback in 1927. We left Urumchi very early in the morning of 20 June to fly to Chungking, but on the way had to spend two hours at an airfield not far away from Ch'engtu, because of reported low ceiling at the capital. On report of improving visibility, we took off again and finally reached Chungking, where the Generalissimo met us.

John Carter Vincent, though he was on very friendly terms with me on a personal level, was very strict about excluding me from the important negotiations in Chungking also. The following day, in the afternoon, Chiang Kai-shek, Wallace, and T.V. Soong moved into conference. Asked whom he wanted to be present, the Vice President said: "Only John Carter Vincent." Though I wondered what he brought me for, I thought Vincent's judgment was quite right and fair. I do not remember whether during the mission there were any occasions for me to write or issue statements. The job of the OWI was to make it known around the world, to both friends and enemies, that the relations of the United States with China as well as the Soviet Union were excellent and that everybody was united in pursuing the war against the Axis; but the very fact that the Wallace Mission was sent was quite enough for that purpose. Whatever he wrote later in his book, during the mission Wallace did not try to make much use of me, except for interpreting some of his conversations with the Chinese side.

One of the main purposes of the negotiations the Wallace Mission was conducting with the Chinese was to persuade Chiang Kai-shek to accept a U.S. military observer mission to Yenan. Nevertheless, Wallace could not go right up to Chiang Kai-shek and say: "I have come here to settle the problems between you and the Communists." What he had to say was: "I am here to discuss the best method of pursuing the war against Japan." Then in that connection the Chinese Communists could be brought in.

After nearly fifty years, I do not remember the details of what I was doing in Chungking; but my diary, beginning with our flight from Alma-Ata to Urumchi on 18 June 1944, was discovered after my return to the United States from Europe in September 1985. According to the notes I jotted down on the spot, my stay in Chungking went as follows.

Being excluded from these negotiations, I was free to meet a few old friends or sit around reading. Ironically, however, on 23 June, early in the morning, I was called for an unexpected interview with the Generalissimo for a before-breakfast walk with him in the garden. He made some friendly chitchat, then asked pretty bluntly what the Vice President's trip was all about. He obviously meant, in particular: Was the Vice President going to make a real drive to bring him and the Communists together? Having discussed this in advance with Vincent, I wanted the Generalissimo to bear the onus of any initiative in rapprochement with the Communists. Therefore, I went into quite a long speech. The points I tried to make were:

1. The primary question was Russia and not the Chinese Communists. Ever since the Russian Revolution, the people who matter in the United States have not been convinced that the Communists or Stalin were there to stay. At the time of the German attack, the most influential opinion was that Russia would collapse.
2. This U.S. attitude has undergone a complete reversal since

Stalingrad. Therefore, the political problem is to deal with the Russians before they try to deal with us on their own terms.

3. Simultaneously, a pressing question in the United States is reconversion of U.S. factories. The short-term problem is to avoid unemployment at the end of hostilities. Russia is one of the most promising immediate outlets for U.S. machinery and techniques. Therefore, U.S. business, finance and industry are pressing for an understanding with Russia, one which is good enough to allow economic confidence on both sides. There is not a whit of ideology in this.

4. China is an "of course" in U.S. policy. China will always be the main pillar of U.S. Pacific-Asiatic policy. But economically, China is a long-term proposition. Therefore, U.S. support of and participation in Chinese reconstruction must dovetail with participation in Russian reconstruction, which in initial stages will move faster.

5. Geopolitically, as a world power the United States is "maritime." We cannot link up with China in power politics except through sea power. It will take China a long time to develop sufficient sea power to do its share in linking up with us. In the interim, while China is building up its strength, friendly relations between China and Russia, of a kind enabling the United States to participate, is a requisite. We must face the reality that in both continental and maritime development, Russia will for a considerable time be definitely ahead of China.

6. Nationality politics. (I reminded him that this was an old and favorite topic of mine, and he nodded and smiled.) One of the things in Siberia which had most impressed me was the success of Russian nationality (minority) policy. Consequently, if Britain should follow a colonial policy which pushes toward Russia the people who stand between it and Russia, it is in for an unnecessary and overbalanced accretion of strength by Russia. China must avoid competing with Britain in retention of power over minority peoples and instead compete with Russia in making frontier peoples look to China.

At various points during this discourse—the longest uninterrupted speech I had ever made to the poor Generalissimo—he would nod agreement or indicate that I should go on. Then I asked him several questions:

1. Will the Russians enter the Pacific War?
   —Yes, as soon as they are assured of their position in the West.
2. What form will their intervention take? Are they likely to attack straight through Mongolia-Manchuria?
   —Undoubtedly.
3. When they do attack, are they likely to win important and rapid victories?
   —Yes.

I then shifted from question to statement: "If the Russians win important victories as soon as they come in, it will change the whole map of the Pacific War. Therefore, it is better for both the United States and China to have a clear understanding with them on cordial terms, before they come in."

(Of course, my long speech shows that I was far too optimistic about the continuation of the good relations between the United States and the Soviet Union as wartime allies and greatly underestimated the inevitability of a civil war in China after the Japanese surrender.)

I could only surmise that Chiang Kai-shek had this meeting and encouraged me to say my say to check on whether 1) what I had to say would in general confirm the conversations at which I had not been present; 2) the Vice President had been primed by me; 3) J.C. Vincent and the State Department checked with the Vice President and me; and 4) the Vice President represented only himself and his own "peculiar" or "advanced" notions or reflected an important new shift or trend in U.S. opinion or policy. Chiang talked to me very earnestly, and I remember having an impression that he wanted me to use my influence on this American mission, because he thought that those Americans were typical Washington men and did not understand that in the long range the Communists were a danger to China and that any attempt to increase cooperation with them, even during the war, was disastrous to the interests of China.

I suppose Chiang probably assumed that the mission would consult with me. What I had to assume was this: "The mission is excluding me from official political conference. If I volunteer and go to them to say, 'The Generalissimo said this or that,' they would think that I am trying to worm my way into the inside of U.S. policy, and I am not going to be as stupid as that." However earnestly Chiang might have hoped that I would strengthen the Kuomintang position within the negotiations, I was, of course, unable to do so. Nobody belonging to the mission told me, even in private conversations, anything about what was being discussed at the conference.

Later in the day, on casually entering Chiang's room, I found myself in the presence of Wallace, Vincent, Hollington, and another Chinese. At this interview, Hollington did most of the interpreting, but in longish passages, he was inclined to summarize and leave out a lot. When he did, I boldly filled them in. Chiang nodded approval and occasionally turned and asked me specially to interpret instead of Hollington. (Wallace had not told me anything about such a meeting to take place, but afterward he said he was glad that I had been present and that I had helped. I wondered if he was surprised.)

Evidently at this interview, the Generalissimo had made up his mind to show an attitude of generous cooperation, without waiting for pressure. He offered to give the U.S. Army the right to send observers—intelligence officers—into North China, including Communist territory. This was something the U.S. Army had wanted for a long time and in itself would make Wallace's trip a success. Linked, not too obviously, with this concession was a maneuver typical of Chiang. He made a long, detailed, and reiterative complaint that American critics—diplomats, the army, the press—were forever urging *him* to make terms with the Communists. Nobody ever told the Communists that they ought to come to terms with him. Nobody ever brought up such minimum prerequisites as the submission of the Communists to unified command and military discipline under him.

To my mind, this was Chiang Kai-shek at his most Chinese. He wanted desperately to have us mediate between him and the Communists; and he would accept almost any real terms if in the outward bargaining we would save his face by making noise about the degree to which the Communists ought to yield. Wallace completely failed to get this—understandably. I urged Vincent to hammer it home to him. I forget whether it was at this meeting or later, that Chiang, agreeing to the idea of rapprochement between him and Russia, preferred American mediation and was willing to hold a meeting on Russian soil—even in Moscow—if necessary.

My personal feeling about the Dixie Mission, as of 1944, was that since the United States was obviously going to be on the winning side, it was desirable to do everything possible not simply to strengthen the United Front between the Kuomintang and the Chinese Communist Party, but also to strengthen it in a way that would minimize the danger of civil war after the war. It would, however, be fair to say that on the whole I was rather sceptical of the Dixie Mission in the sense that this attempt at patching up the United Front would have any striking success. I was for the United Front, in principle, for the very simple reason that while the Chinese were fighting the Japanese, they should not also be fighting one another. On the other hand, the weakness of the American thinking behind all this United Front business was that they imagined that they could have more influence over the Chinese internal politics than in fact they really could.

In the United States, the liberals thought that their liberal thinking could make the Chinese Communists a little more flexible, while the conservatives thought that their way of thinking could make Chiang Kai-shek a little less rigid. I did not think so. I thought that the future of the United Front in China would be decided in China by Chinese factors. From what Chiang had said about Stalin and the Chinese Communist Party, I was sure that the Chinese Communists were not simply under the orders of Moscow, and I knew also that the Kuomintang armies were not under the orders of Washington.

After this interview, I went to the Chungking office of the OWI, where I learned that the Dilowa, previously said to be in Lanchou, was actually in town. When I went to see him, he was low in vitality and morale, but I had never before heard him so positive on the subject of Outer Mongolia. He said he knew Choibalsan and that he was a good and decent man. There were a few Mongols who had recently arrived from Peking, so I could get some news. The combination of news and views indicated that general sentiment in Inner Mongolia was now tending strongly away from both Japan and China, and was in favor of unification with Outer Mongolia. This went right up to De Wang. Some princes were against, but some higher-ups under them were for. Exceptions were probably the Mongols in Jehol and east of the Hsingan Mountains. In some places, there was general demoralization and uncertainty as to what to aim for.

Then before supper, I had a private talk with Madame, who said that she was responsible for the Generalissimo having me down early in the morning and getting me in on the conversations. She probed to find out: 1) Whether I was on an inside track with J.C. Vincent; 2) Why was it that my hand showed in speeches, but I was not put forward in interviews. She also asked about the effect of Chiang's *China's Destiny* in the United States. Chiang had written this book in 1943, and a portion of it was published in English from the Chinese Ministry of Information. (Its complete translation was published in the United States in 1947.) She said that she had advised against its circulation there. She revealed that she was planning to go abroad on the grounds of ill health *with Madame H.H. Kung*. This looked like an attempt to get away. She wanted the Vice President to comment on her health to the Generalissimo, which suggested that she was not sure of being able to get away on her own. She even pulled down her stockings to show that she was really sick. That part, at least, was convincing, for she did have some sort of skin disease.

The next morning, 24 June, I went down a bit earlier for breakfast and was joined by the Generalissimo, who proposed a walk. Then we heard that the Vice President was also out walking. So, we sought him out. The three of us sat on a stone bench. Perhaps noting Wallace's interest in minority and frontier peoples and thinking that the Vice President ought to know his thinking about this matter, Chiang Kai-shek said that while it was difficult to do anything during the war, after the war, Tibet, Outer Mongolia, and other areas would be given bigger and better autonomy than anything likely to be given to the British dominion states. In the situation we were in, I could not coach the Vice President then and there, but the point that should have been made was that "after the war" generosity for Tibet and Outer Mongolia would slack off along with "after-the-war" generosity for India.

After breakfast, before going out to the airfield, I found a chance to put Madame straight on why I had returned the gift of one thousand dollars, which David Kung had delivered from the Generalissimo, for she had hinted at it more than once during our conversations. She said she had never received my letter explaining my position on that matter.

On the Way Back from Chungking

From Chungking we flew to Kunming, where I had an attack of diarrhea and so missed a lovely chance to photograph the countryside. On arriving at Ch'engtu on 27 June, I went to the air force hospital for an examination. The verdict was: "No dysentery. Must have been chilled in the belly." I had slept very well the night before and therefore, feeling much better, spent nearly two hours in the Museum of Border Research Society. An excellent job of reorganization was being done by a young Harvard-Yenching man from Amoy, Cheng Te-k'un. In the evening, there was a state dinner given by Chang Ch'ün. The Vice President made a good speech, well delivered and well translated.

Szechuan, a heavily populated province, was perhaps the most important single area for the conscription of new troops for Chiang Kai-shek's army, as so much of China was under Japanese occupation. At the same time, it was regarded as a rather shaky province, for the old warlords still had their connections all over the province. Though they were rivals of one another, they had a common interest in not being completely controlled by the Kuomintang. If there was political disaffection in this area, it would seriously weaken Chiang's position. That was why Chiang had made Chang Ch'ün, who was himself a Szechuan man, the governor of the province.

While we were in Ch'engtu, one evening I received a mysterious message, an invitation to meet alone with one of the Szechuan warlords, who was supposedly living in retirement, having become relatively powerless since the central government had been installed in Chungking. That evening, a car was sent for me and I went to see this warlord, whose name was Liu Wen-hui. The Wallace visit sparked rumors everywhere that his mission included instructions from Roosevelt to try to renew and improve the relation between the Kuomintang and the Chinese Communists. What Liu was aiming at was to find out what the U.S. policy was regarding the Communists.

From the way he talked and the questions he asked, it was quite clear what sort of calculation was going on in his own mind: "When the war is over, the central government is going back to Nanking. Will there be a possibility that I can safely negotiate an alliance with the Communists? They are anti-Chiang Kai-shek and I am anti-Chiang, too. Maybe I shall be able to recover my lost influence in the province." In a very polite way, I made it clear to him that no such negotiations on the United Front had yet begun, and in any case I would have no part in them.

Here in Ch'engtu, another thing about Wallace played an important role. He was a physical health fanatic. In spite of his age—he was in his early sixties—he was proud of his physical vigor. Every time our plane stopped for refueling he would say: "Come on, everybody get out of the plane! Let's run!" We all had to run around the airfield. When the Soviets had discovered that he was crazy about volleyball, everywhere we went there was a volleyball team waiting, and he played with them. He wanted the other members of the mission to join, but I mutinied, as I would not do anything so stupid. This, however, was politically very valuable. Every time political negotiations became a little bit difficult, the Soviets would say: "Come, let's have a game of volleyball!"

The Chinese immediately found out the same thing. A man named Huang was sent from Chungking to meet us, whom foreigners in Chungking used to call the "Grand Eunuch." In spite of this nickname, he was the biggest, tallest, and broadest Chinese I had ever seen. He was an American-trained Y.M.C.A. man and spoke extremely fluent English. On returning to China, he had risen high in the Chinese Y.M.C.A. when Chiang and Madame Chiang started a sort of youth movement of their own, a weird mixture of Confucianism and the New Testament and the Y.M.C.A., for "physical fitness and pure thinking." He was much closer to Madame than to the Generalissimo and had great influence with her. I suppose this was the origin of his nickname. He quickly caught onto Wallace's weakness for volleyball and proposed a game everywhere.

As Chang Ch'ün was my old friend, I had said to Wallace: "You are interested in trying to avoid civil war between Chiang Kai-shek and the Communists. Fortunately, we are stopping in Ch'engtu. We will see the governor, whom I have already gotten to know very well. He is the only person close to Chiang who is against trying to solve the problem of China by civil war. If you want to get the ear of

Chiang Kai-shek, it is important for you to persuade this man of your views. He will relay your views much more effectively than your saying them directly to Chiang in a formal conversation. Then it will be a Chinese exercising pressure on Chiang and not an American interferring in Chinese affairs." Wallace said: "Yes, yes, I understand." Chang Ch'ün, of course, was very eager to have a good talk with Wallace. If the United States was going to succeed in getting a military observer mission in Yenan, any degree of personal rapport that could be created between Wallace and Chang Ch'ün would be valuable.

There was a very famous ancient Chinese irrigation system in Szechuan Province which was connected with a legend of a man who harnessed the water, built a dam, and joined streams together to fertilize the Red Basin of Szechuan, making it one of the most productive provinces in China. It was a triumph of early engineering, leading a river across a mountain slope and then opening it up to irrigate a plain. As Wallace was interested in water conservancy and grain conservancy, when he heard about it, he wanted to visit the place.

It was natural to take him out to see these things. Here Chang Ch'ün scored one point by having me, instead of the Grand Eunuch, with Wallace and himself in the same car. I was to sit between them to interpret for them. But the Grand Eunuch scored higher. Just before we started, he arranged a very strenuous volleyball game. Once we got into the car, I said to Wallace: "Now is your chance for a good talk." Then I turned to Chang Ch'ün and asked: "How do you want to open the conversation?" He and I exchanged a few words, and Chang Ch'ün started to talk. When I turned to Wallace to interpret, he was sound asleep, having exhausted himself with volleyball. He slept all the way to our destination.

Wallace woke up and looked out of the car. There was a mountain slope. Having been refreshed again after the good sleep, he cried: "Oh! Let's run up the mountain. See who can get there first!" And Wallace charged up the slope. When they came back, we had lunch, and of course no intimate conversation was possible. After the inspection, we got into the car to drive back. Another opportunity for conversation. Wallace, tired from scrambling up the mountain, was sound asleep again.

The next day, 29 June, I had had an opportunity to hear some criticisms against the central government and the Party. I was present at a meeting with the delegation of the Ch'ing Nien Tang (the Youth Party). They wanted "immediate democracy" in the form of freedom of speech and press, freedom of person, freedom of assembly and association, and also a greater representation in the People's Councils. They wanted greater discussions of issues right down to village level, which in my opinion, in view of their connections, meant representation of the local landlords rather than, in reality, the peasants. Though the Youth Party had a long history of right-wing anti-communism, for the moment their demands were united with those of the Communists. Their leader's analysis of the communist situation was:

"The Government says that the Communists have independent agricultural bases and armed forces and thus imperium in imperio. They must give these up and become an 'ordinary political party.' The Communists retort, 'Ordinary political party for what? People like the Youth Party are an ordinary political party and what do they get for it? Their press works only under a tight censorship, and they cannot carry their issues to the town, the village, the people, or the army. Their delegates to the People's Council are allotted, not elected. They are followed around by secret police and can at any moment be jailed indefinitely incommunicado, without trial."

The Youth Party leader's demands included democratization of representation for Communist and other parties, *accompanied* by nationalization of armed forces, so that they would be no longer in reality private forces of either Chiang Kai-shek or the Kuomintang. The Kuomintang cells and organizers were to be withdrawn from the army. The Whampoa monopoly should be broken, and the troops should be taught that they serve the nation and the government.

Coming away from this interview, I found the Vice President volleyballing and Chang Ch'ün wallflowering. This gave me a good chance for talk. I mentioned to Chang what I had heard from the Youth Party. His comments were: "Local militarists are 'bottled up,' and there was no danger of warlordism. Small parties like the Youth Party are really individual politicians who want to run around and talk until they are quieted with suitable appointments and subsidies for their newspapers and academies. The Communists are the only serious competing party. Administration and taxes and land distribution are real problems. If they can be straightened out somewhat, grievances on which the Communists are battening will be eased." Chang Ch'ün was all for rapprochement with the Communists, and he ended with what sounded like a sincere wish for me to come back.

Finally, the last morning came, and we were to make an early morning start to the airfield. Very early before breakfast, a message came to me: "Governor Chang Ch'ün is sitting in the foyer, waiting to say good-bye to Vice President Wallace." I let Wallace know that the governor was waiting for him. Then I came down and sat with Chang Ch'ün to wait for Wallace to appear. Just as Wallace came down the stairs into the foyer and Chang Ch'ün greeted him, the big window opening to the courtyard flew open, and the Grand Eunuch's head popped in, saying to Wallace: "Ah, we're in good time. The last chance for a volleyball game before you leave!" Wallace immediately ran to the window, put his hand on the window-sill, vaulted out of it into the courtyard, and played until it was time to start. Chang Ch'ün did not say anything, but he had a certain expression on his face, and I did too.

The Grand Eunuch, I suspected, was intentionally sent from Chungking to pop up and propose a game whenever there was likely to be a meeting of some sort at which Wallace would really get down to business with Chang Ch'ün. Chungking did not want to have Wallace enter into close contact with Chang Ch'ün, because when it came to the delicate question of the United Front and civil war with the Communists, Chang Kai-shek did not want any Chinese to have an independent contact with an American. The Grand Eunuch was entrusted with the work of preventing it.

On June 30, we flew back to Lanchou, reaching there about noon. There was the unmistakable feel of the Northwest, a wonderful feeling to me. There I overtook the Dilowa Hutukutu and had a good talk with him. Kansu was a very interesting place because at the time of the civil-war period, before the formation of the second United Front, this province, the former governor of which was Muslim, covered an important part of the motor route from the Soviet Union through Sinkiang into China. The governor's position was strategic as well as political. This resulted in a very curious bit of political manipulation.

Kansu Province at that time covered the Ch'inghai area of Tibet.

(It is now a separate province.) When a new Dalai Lama was to be discovered and appointed, the Muslim governor succeeded in making an arrangement with the Kuomintang government by which the governor was to allow Chiang Kai-shek's troops to enter his province to complete the encirclement of the Communists at Yenan and to block communication between the Communists in Yenan and Sinkiang, where Mao's brother was active. (This brother was later killed, in 1943, by Sheng Shih-ts'ai, the governor of Sinkiang.) In return for this, the governor of Kansu was given control of the negotiations leading to the selection of the next Dalai Lama so that he would be discovered in the Ch'inghai area of his own province.

Kansu Province had the principal economic access to Tibet in trade and exploitation of Tibetan resources. In Europe and the United States, Tibetan lamaism has always been distorted by an interest in mysticism and consultation of oracles and so on. The fact is, however, that from the very first Dalai Lama right up to the present one, no Dalai Lama has ever been discovered and appointed without political intrigue and manipulation. It is more than a religious event. It is also a highly political operation.

While we were staying in Lanchou, the military governor of Kansu was no longer a Muslim, but a man appointed by Chiang Kai-shek. One of the crazy aspects of Wallace was that he had a really dotty sort of amateur enthusiasm for Buddhism and Buddhist mysticism. So, when we had a dinner with the governor, a Tibetan lama was brought in, and the governor said we could ask him about Mongolia as he had traveled a great deal there. Well, there used to be a certain type of Tibetan lama whom you could recognize instantly as one who traveled around Mongolia collecting alms from ignorant superstitious people and getting very rich. This lama was such a comfortable, worldly looking character, really with corruption written all over him like smallpox.

Wallace began to talk to him in a very reverential manner. When the lama sat quiet for a while, Wallace said to me: "Do you think we can ask him what his innermost thoughts are at this moment?" This was too much for me. I said: "I can tell you that without asking him. At this moment he is wondering if he is going to bed with a small boy or a pretty girl." Poor Wallace! But it was closer to the truth than any Buddhist meditation, I can assure you that.

Wallace was interested in Mongolia because at one time he had been the chief American patron of Nikolai Roerich. This man, who had first achieved some fame as a scene painter of the Tsarist ballet theater, became attracted by Tibetan-Mongolian Buddhist mysticism. After the Russian Revolution, he went to Paris as an emigré, then to the United States, where his large-scale paintings based on Buddhist mysticism brought him financial backing. During the war, he visited the Soviet Union, went on to Mongolia, produced some heroic war paintings, and then returned to the United States.

After this, he went to Peking to organize an expedition to Lhasa to get more materials for his paintings. Whipping up an armed escort because of the bandit conditions on the way, he recruited from among the White Russian emigré population in Hailar and demanded arms from the United States Legation Marines in Peking. Naturally, the Marine Command said: "We can't do anything like that. That amounts to interference in Chinese politics." So, Roerich applied to Wallace to turn on political pressure, and the Marine Guard was compelled to provide modern American rifles to this gang of desperadoes tramping on to Tibet.

The Tibetans never allowed Roerich to get to Lhasa. They detained him and his men, but Roerich managed to have a dispatch sent out which was published in *The New York Times*. In this article, he complained that the barbaric Tibetans were holding them in seclusion at a very high altitude in spite of the fact that Mrs. Roerich, who accompanied him, had a weak heart and was suffering from a heart problem. Nobody even raised the question: "If she has that sort of heart, why did she ever start for Tibet?" Eventually Roerich and the others were released by the Tibetans and came down to India. One of Roerich's sons married a daughter of the famous Indian poet Rabindranath Tagore.

Because Wallace was interested in Mongolia, we had, partly when we were still in Siberia and partly through the Soviet Embassy when we were in Chungking, fixed up a friendly arrangement with the Soviets. Although the United States had no diplomatic relations with the People's Republic of Mongolia (former Outer Mongolia over which China continued to claim sovereignty), on our return journey we were thus able to land in Ulan Bator, nominally for a refueling stop, though Chiang Kai-shek would not have liked Wallace to have a direct contact with the Mongols. Instead of retracing all of the route we had taken on coming out, from Lanchou we flew over Ninghsia, the Edsin Gol, and the Gurban Saikhan Mountains to Ulan Bator.

When we landed and came down from the plane, there was a row of people waiting in an *assar*, the pavillion-style tent with the front open. They were looking at these strange Americans coming off the plane. Among the Mongols, I recognized from photographs Choibalsan, the prime minister, who had been one of the top leaders of the Mongolian Revolution of 1921. So, I stepped forward and addressed him, saying: "We must be meeting the celebrated hero of the Mongolian Revolution, Marshal Choibalsan." When he found that there was an American with the mission who spoke Mongol, everything just went perfectly. It was very fortunate for me that Roerich had interested Wallace in Mongolia. Otherwise, I would never have met Choibalsan.

In those days there were no hotels for foreign guests in Ulan Bator, and they put us up in the Tengriin Am (Heaven's Mouth) in Bogd Uul, the Sacred Mountain, to the south of the city. We were lodged in enormous white felt tents (*ger* in Mongol), only two men to each tent. I was sharing a tent with John Hazard, the Russian interpreter for the mission. In the middle of the tent there was a huge porcelain jar of the K'ang-hsi, or Ch'ien-lung, period, which would be worth thousands of dollars in any museum, filled with *airak*, fermented mares' milk. There was a ladle so that you could drink as much as you liked. When we went to bed at night and all the noise outside stopped, for the only time in my life I actually heard the bubbling of the fermenting *airak*—a kind of tiny buzzing sound.

We were to start for Siberia the next day, but bad weather turned us back, and we had a couple of extra days in Ulan Bator, to my great satisfaction. I visited the National Museum, and we were taken to see a Mongolian performance that was semi-opera, semi-theater. At that time, the Academy of Sciences was still very young. We were invited to meet with the academicians, and that was where I first met famous scholars of Mongolian literature, such as Rinchen and Damdinszren.

From Ulan Bator we went back to Yakutsk, and from there flew to an airfield in northern Canada, then to Seattle and back to

Washington. After our return to the United States, I had nothing to do with the mission. Nor did I know anything about what went on in the Democratic Party. In any case, as everybody knows, Truman, not Wallace, was nominated as the vice-presidential candidate. When Wallace attempted to form a new political party, I declined to join, in spite of earnest requests to do so.

Solution in Asia

In the spring of 1945, I resigned from the Office of War Information. The reason was very simple. We were obviously going to win the war before too long. The end of the war would bring on a very wide public discussion of "What now? What is the peace going to mean?" etc. I wanted to join in that discussion and add my voice to what was being said. This I would not be able to do properly as a government official. A special reason for my wanting to leave at this time, however, was as follows.

In the San Francisco office of the OWI, the representatives of the various colonial countries were always worried that our propaganda broadcasts about fighting for freedom and so on would infect their colonial population with the idea of gaining independence from imperial rule. It was curious that the Dutch, who had the reputation of being the most progressive of colonial rulers, in many ways were among the toughest in resisting any idea of the future independence of their colonies.

My analysis of the whole situation was that the relatively easy Japanese victories over the French, Dutch, and British in the early phases after Pearl Harbor had destroyed their prestige. As successful colonial rule depended largely on prestige, all the colonial peoples were looking around to find an alternative. While they, except for a few collaborators, did not necessarily accept the Japanese propaganda of the Greater East Asia Co-prosperity Sphere, they did say: "Look, these European rulers of ours can be beaten!" Apart from this situation in the colonies, the homelands of the British, French, and Dutch empires had been so badly damaged and weakened that they would not be able to mount a rapid, strong reoccupation of their colonial empires. Any protracted war to restore colonial rule would be a losing proposition. This was hardly something that I could write from within the government.

I decided that I must go back to being a non-governmental civilian. Luckily, just about this time I formed a connection with a small
agency called Overseas News Agency, which carried not just news
items, but also short opinion articles that were syndicated in various papers. This agency had begun, a good many years before, as a
Jewish telegraph agency. I would say that its owners were probabaly close to the socialist element in what later became the Israeli
government. At first I wrote an article for them once in two weeks
and later every week. I found them to be very congenial people who
were easy to work with.

My general line, so to speak, was pretty close to what had been
Roosevelt's line at the time of his death, namely that the wartime
alliance should be prolonged as an alliance of the victorious nations
to reinstate multiparty democracies instead of fascism and to convert from wartime economics to peacetime economics, which
would bring big problems of supply and demand, raw materials,
and industry, etc.

It was also during this period that I wrote *Solution in Asia* (1945),
which was published by Little, Brown and Company, as an Atlantic
Monthly Press Book. The title of the book was entirely the publisher's invention. I never did like it, because the ordinary book
buyer would think that I was writing about how to solve the problems of Asia; but the intention of the book was quite different. It
was to say that there could be no solution or stabilization of the
world problems unless Asia was also brought in. I was trying to
write about the Asian elements in solving world problems. Nevertheless, I did not have a good striking title of my own, a weakness
in arguing with the publisher. The book was written at the urgent
request of the publisher and in a very short time, in about six
weeks.

This book was reprinted by the AMS Press Inc. in 1975, and I
wrote in the introduction to the new edition:

When I was writing this book, I let myself go in being sarcastic
about "experts" who had made fools of themselves in their
analyses of Asian societies and politics. Now, thirty years later,
any one could make a fool of me by quoting passages from this
book—like my suggestion (p. 189) that after the war the Japanese
emperor "and all males eligible for the throne by Japanese rules

of succession and adoption should be interned, preferably in China but under the supervision of a United Nations commission, to emphasize united responsibility."

My proposal about the Japanese emperor raised a great deal of discussion after the war. It is often forgotten, however, that when I wrote this book the war was still going on, and I, like everybody else, knew nothing about the atom bombs. Judging from the way the Japanese soldiers were fighting in those Pacific islands, no one had ever thought that Japan would capitulate in that way, without any guerrilla-like resistance against the occupation forces. In Washington, there was a very strong element within the State Department which said: "With the defeat of Japan, there is a real danger of a wave of revolutionary feeling, and the Communists will become a powerful force." The pro-emperor clique in the State Department said: "We must therefore maintain the prestige of the emperor, and whatever reforms we bring about in Japan must work downward from the top, through us tutoring the emperor on what decrees to issue."

On the other hand, there was a very small, but often quite loud-voiced element in the United States which said that the emperor should be treated as a war criminal. That I thought was no good, because in fact all through the 1930s the emperor had been manipulated by the militarists. He had not actively inspired or organized the militarists, so that he was not a war criminal in that respect. My idea of interning him indefinitely was a sort of twentieth century adaptation of the idea of keeping Napoleon in exile. I did not mean that the emperor should be made prisoner, but should be exiled in order to avoid his being used as a rallying point of resistance by the defeated militarists.

I was also influenced by something that had been planted in my mind. Chiang Kai-shek had often complained to me that after the war the Great Powers would not treat China as a real ally; and they would try to regain as much as possible of their power in Asia, and China would be the victim of this. I thought that one way of establishing China, morally at least, on the same plane as the Great Powers would be to make China the place to which the Japanese emperor would be exiled—not necessarily for life, but for perhaps a cooling-off period.

I did not think that Communists would become very powerful in Japan after the war. I did not see the likelihood of anything resembling the First World War in which the defeated Tsarist armies fed the strength of the Bolsheviks in Russia. Neither did I have any reason to suppose that the end of the war in Japan would be like the end of the First World War in Germany. Both the Russian and the German cases involved troops in large numbers returning to their home countries while the war was going on. There had been continuous contact between the Russians in Russia and the Russian soldiers, and the Germans in Germany and the German soldiers.

In the case of Japan, the major war experience had been of the Japanese soldiers taken out of their own country, crossing the water, and being isolated among the people of the countries they occupied. The psychological condition of such men being taken back, again crossing the water, and suddenly coming in contact with the people of their own country, would be quite different from the previous Russian and German experiences.

These returning Japanese soldiers would be disillusioned by their defeat in an imperialistic war; but they would perhaps be more anti-officer than anti-emperor. This would mean that the basic drive in Japan itself would be toward the liberalization of the political institution rather than completely destroying the old and replacing it with something new in a revolutionary way. I also thought that the Soviet Union itself would not be making a heavy drive toward the export of revolution. When a Marxist party is actually administrating a large and powerful state, there are pressures that make them act sometimes as an ideological party and at other times as responsible governors of a large state.

My judgment at that time was that the Soviet Union, having suffered such appalling damage during the war, would be mainly concerned with healing its own wounds and restoring life in its own country. This could not be done by backing revolutionary adventures in China, Japan, or anywhere else, so it would be in favor of compromising and keeping a balance of power. As anyone can see today, forty years later, I was partly right and partly wrong.

Later, after the war, the same publisher asked me to write the sequel, *Situation in Asia* (1949). The most pertinent comment I can add now about this book is that while I was right in predicting the end of the old form of colonial rule, I completely failed to foresee the rise of the great mutinational corporations, which are very frequently in their own way a new form of colonialism.

It seems that I am often considered, especially in Japan, as violently anti-Japanese. Nevertheless, though I was anti-Japanese militarists, I was not really anti-Japanese people as a whole. In *Solution in Asia*, I pointed out, analyzing the modernization of Japan after the Meiji Restoration in 1868, that "the Japanese who conquered Japan created a remarkable dual system, combining a highly cartelized industry with an agriculture which preserved the social outlook of feudalism," and "the peasants, therefore, became the draft animals dragging Japan's chariot of the 'remarkable progress' which admirers abroad were so ready to praise" (1975 AMS edition, pp. 40–41). Because of the necessity to make the development of an internal market subsidiary to the development of markets abroad, the Japanese peasants had to be kept poor. I had learned this mainly from Sir George Sansom and Herbert Norman, personally and through their works.

After returning from Chungking, I was not very active in the Institute of Pacific Relations. I attended its conferences occasionally; but E.C. Carter was particularly interested in committee meetings and committee discussions. He was always trying to get me to come up from Baltimore, where I had rejoined the university, to participate in this or that committee meeting in New York. I did not want to go. I thought that such committee meetings were largely a waste of time. So, I would write back and say: "Sorry, on account of engagements here, I am unable to go to this meeting."

Instead of attending it myself, I would dictate to my secretary a memorandum of some sort and send it to Carter. The consequence was, by the time the Senate Committee got to examining the records of the IPR, they found in its archive a very large accumulation of notes and memoranda signed by me. From this it was very easy to put over to the public the impression that I must have been running the IPR, whereas the point was that I was avoiding the committee meetings.

I remember having attended the IPR conference held at Hot Springs shortly before the end of the war. It is very likely that postwar policy toward Japan was also discussed there; but I do not remember anything in detail. If I was really active, as has been held later by some people, I must have repeated what I had been saying

in my books and articles. As far as I remember, sometimes government people attended the IPR conferences and sometimes not. In
any case, it would not have been anything out of the ordinary that
some government people were at the Hot Springs conference,
though I do not remember who was there. By that time, all through
the war years, and not only just before the Japanese surrender, the
U.S. government had recruited people for the expanded wartime
bureaucracy. They had people from various universities who were
supposed to be experts on China, Japan, Indonesia, etc., and such
people would naturally attend conferences of that kind, without
actually representing official views.

After leaving the OWI, I had also resumed my teaching at Johns
Hopkins University, from which I had been on leave since my
departure for Chungking. Since my position there was Director of
International Relations, I had to think what was the best we could
do with rather limited financial means. I immediately began to
think of concentrating on Asia, in the first place on China, for
which I had my own resources, and for which it was easy to recruit
promising young scholars, including the kind of people who had
had intensive training in the Chinese language during the war. This
made it possible later, by 1949, as Chiang Kai-shek's regime was
collapsing and China became a major concern, for me to obtain
foundation help to invite three Mongols to come over and work
with me.

One of them was the Dilowa Hutukutu. The other two were
young men. Gombojab Hangin was from Chahar, a region to the
north of the Great Wall, and Urgenge Onon was from the northeastern corner of Inner Mongolia. My choice was mainly from geographical consideration, to have Mongols from two quite different
regions. Purely by coincidence, Gombojab was the young man who
was with De Wang when he came to see me in Peking in 1946.

Chapter Seven

■

BETWEEN
THE WAR AND THE STORM

The Pauley Mission

Shortly after the Japanese surrender, toward the end of 1945, a mission headed by Edwin W. Pauley was sent to Japan and China in connection with the question of whether Japan should pay reparations to the countries which had been under Japanese occupation. In the United States, there were differences of opinion on the matter. Some people thought that Japan should be forced to pay very heavy reparations. In the midst of the debate on this question, President Truman appointed a mission to Japan first to determine Japan's capacity to pay reparations and second to determine to whom the reparations should go. Pauley was a millionaire who was a political friend and backer of President Truman. I do not recall my first interview with Pauley, nor do I even remember how it came about that, for once in my life, I had considerable influence on the appointment of other members of the mission. Two of the men I nominated or proposed, probably at the suggestion of some friends, were David G. Jenkins and Martin Bennet.

David Jenkins was a New Zealander by origin, and I had come to know him first through the IPR, though we had never been close friends. As an economist, he was to take part in the economic analysis. As for Martin Bennet, I think my first contact with him was through Eleanor, because while I was away in Chungking she had worked for a time with the Office of Economic Warfare or something in Washington, and she had made the acquaintance of this man. He was a first-class engineer and also had great familiarity with statistics and statistical theory. His mother was a very left-wing radical, well back into the time of the First World War. So this man knew a great deal about radical left-wing thinking in the United States without himself being a radical. He was very down to earth and practical, the best man that I got on to the Pauley Mission.

Soon after we got to Japan in the beginning of November, and the mission formed its contacts with the MacArthur Occupation Forces, it became evident that there were two major guiding principles. One was that if Japan paid any reparations at all, nothing should go to the Soviet Union; the second was that if they should go principally to victims of Japanese militarism, anything given to China must go to strengthening Chiang Kai-shek, and nothing should be given to any of the marginal political groups in China, such as the National Salvation Movement. I remember that the Philippines was brought into this discussion as of special interest to the United States. Pauley himself was in close agreement with certain circles of the MacArthur administration.

I have no clear memory of what I did in the mission, but quite recently, in 1983, a Japanese postgraduate student, Miura Yōichi, dug up from among the documents released by the Freedom of Information Act a copy of the diary report which I had sent to H.D. Maxwell, who acted as Mission head in Pauley's absence. I had completely forgotten about all these things written during my stay in Japan, and having reread my diary after forty years, I must say that I find it rather good. Therefore, instead of my trying to remember what I was doing there, it will be safer to refer the readers to this contemporary document recording my on-the-spot comments on the situation which I found in Japan, which is included in *Report on Japanese Reparation to the President of the United States* (Box 21, Records of the U.S. Mission on Reparation, RG 59, National Archives).

There are two things I can add to the diary: I could not see any possibility of influencing occupation policy in Japan, and I could see that the major policy of the MacArthur administration toward defeated Japan was to preserve the imperial structure and make the emperor, as far as possible, an instrument of U.S. policy. As for the Japanese attitude toward the emperor, this was not inevitably one of reverence, as some Americans assured me. I was told an amusing story that after the surrender, rank-and-file soldiers in the Imperial

Guards referred to the emperor as the "defeated Grandpa." By the time I got to Japan, however, it was already quite clear that, given official occupation policy, any idea of internment of the emperor or suspension of the imperial system was no longer practical politics.

Since the time when I wrote *Solution in Asia*, the facts had changed, the situation in Asia had changed. So far as I can remember, my feeling was that under the new situation in which we were going to get an economically viable Japan, one which would be no longer a military power, the function of the emperor would be somewhat changed, and this was not a situation which could be altered by the speculations of a liberal like myself. It was a time for watching and observing, rather than a time for telling people what they ought to think.

I recall striking up a friendship with the head of MacArthur's intelligence service, Brigadier-General Elliot Thorpe. Later at one of the Senate hearings during the McCarthy period, he testified in my favor. There was also MacArthur's chief of counter-intelligence, whom I never met, who later tried to do everything he could to find out if I was connected with the Sorge Case in Japan. (Richard Sorge was a Soviet spy who made contacts with people highly placed in Japanese politics in the 1930s. He was arrested in 1941 and executed in 1944.) Of course, there was no evidence because I never had any connection with him.

Abiding personal memories are that I became very friendly with Herbert Norman, the Canadian representative at the MacArthur Headquarters, which one might almost call MacArthur's Court in Tokyo. I had known him very slightly when he had some sort of research connection with the U.S. IPR in New York. Norman was very friendly with Elliot Thorpe, and it was in Tokyo that I really got to know him. He was, I knew, extremely well read and well informed about Marxism, internationally and particularly as regards Japan.

I came to understand only later that this was a period when in Japanese intellectual circles you were simply not accepted as a first-class intellectual unless you know a lot about Marxist analysis, because class analysis was extremely important in analyzing the Meiji Restoration (1868) and the subsequent modernization of Japan. In addition to the fact that he was born and brought up in Japan, his understanding of Marxism contributed to the respect accorded to him by Japanese intellectuals. I rather doubt, however, that he ever could have been a rank-and-file Communist Party member receiving directives and been told to do this or that or to think thus or so.

An amusing story about Norman is that on one occasion, in the Canadian representative's residence, he had received a Japanese friend who had drunk too much and could not get home. So, Norman took him home in a car. As he knew that this man might feel that he had lost face, getting to his friend's home, Norman said: "Let's have another drink." Norman got so drunk that he had to be taken home. The score was even. I heard this story from somebody else, but it struck me as a very typical Norman story. He was a man who ranked very high in the intellectual life of the postwar period, and I had for him both respect and real affection.

One day Herbert Norman took me out to the country to call on a Japanese lawyer who was working in the Office of Military Intelligence in MacArthur's Headquarters. I had heard from Norman that in the 1930s this man was a lawyer who defended Koreans accused of subversive activities. MacArthur's headquarters employed a great many Koreans because they knew Japanese well and were considered as people who would likely be more favorable to U.S. policy, Korea having been a Japanese colony until Japan's defeat in the Pacific War. Some of these Koreans exploited their positions for personal advantage and took pleasure in humiliating Japanese who came in for interrogation, but whenever this lawyer came into the office, every Korean stood up and bowed respectfully.

This man was descended from a family who had become Roman Catholics in the period before the Christian faith was forbidden in the early seventeenth century. He himself was not a Catholic, but he knew a lot about the subject and told me about one of his ancestors who had made a pilgrimage to Rome and left a diary of his pilgrimage written in Latin. Apparently this diary was still in the family archives.

While I was in Japan, I had an interview with Shiga Yoshio, one of the principal leaders of the Japanese Communists, who had been imprisoned before and during the war and was released after the Japanese surrender. For a long time, I had thought that he was the one who told me about the difference between the Japanese Communists who had escaped to China to join the Chinese Communists and those who had remained in Japan and had been imprisoned. Those who had just come out of prison demanded a hard line, like the abolition of the imperial system, and they were astonished to find that the Japanese Communists returning from Yenan were telling them that this was not the time for such a hard-line policy and were calling for a compromise policy of multiparty democracy. This was probably because they were more realistic than their comrades who had been imprisoned and out of touch with reality.

According to my own diary, however, Shiga clearly declared that there could be no difference of opinion between him and his comrades who had remained in Japan on the one hand, and those who were still in China on the other. In fact, after discovering that my memory was confused about this matter, I learned that at that time, the end of 1945, the important Japanese Communists who had been in Yenan could not have been in Japan, as it was only in January 1946 that Nosaka Sanzō, the top leader of this group, returned to Tokyo. I must have attributed to Shiga Yoshio a story that I heard from someone else much later.

The Pauley Mission was supposed to be doing things like assessment of the industrial status and resources of Japan. A very important question was the amount of destruction that had been caused by the U.S. bombing. Here Martin Bennet, the engineer whom I had recruited for the mission, proved to be very valuable. The U.S. Air Force people were boasting about the scale of destruction that they had been able to inflict on Japan; but Bennet made surveys showing that, especially for heavy industry, when there had been a bombing that knocked down the buildings on top of the machinery, these ruins actually protected the machinery, and all you had to do was to pull away the bricks and stones, and there you had factories that were still capable of operating. The machinery was protected more by the U.S. bombing than destroyed by it.

In view of the bias of the mission toward using anything that could be got out of Japan for the benefit of Chiang Kai-shek's China, when we left Japan in December, we went to China. In China, the mission was subdivided. Several of us, including myself, went first to Shanghai and then to Peking, while another subgroup led by Martin Bennet went up into the Northeast (Manchuria). In Shanghai, I made a point of getting in touch with the local Soviet representative, because I still believed in the old Roosevelt line of continuation of the U.S.-Soviet cooperation after the war. Many years later, somebody produced some notes that had been recovered from our mission's wastepaper basket. These were the notes I had made about the dates for meeting this or that Soviet person in Shanghai. They were used in the attempt to link me up with Sorge. I suppose intelligence operations work in all directions, and at that time our wastepaper baskets were checked only with the idea of: "What are these chaps from MacArthur's headquarters in Tokyo up to?"

In China, though it was not *my* job, the mission was supposed to draw up an assessment of what damage the Japanese had done during the war in taking over Chinese industry, what new industries they had created or started, what the economic condition of China was as the consequence of the Japanese military occupation. I said "supposed to" because the means of carrying out such a mandate or directive were limited. We were supposed to consult with T.V. Soong about Chinese claims for Japanese reparations, a matter that was under the control of the T.V. Soong clique in the Chiang Kai-shek government. I do not remember whether the mission met Soong in Shanghai or in Peking; on that particular occasion, however, I myself did not meet him.

In Shanghai, but not so much in Peking, one thing struck me at once. The show windows of big shops on Nanking Road were stuffed with American electrical equipment which had become very short in the United States, and car sales places were full of shiny American cars. In the United States, everything, even irons for ironing clothes, was in short supply because of wartime production having been shifted to military equipment, but Shanghai was bulging with goods. This was the end of 1945. Though other things were difficult to date, a car you could date, and these were all 1941 cars.

This was politically very significant, for it meant that when the Japanese occupied Shanghai, they had said to some of the Chinese, "How about working with us?" and they got in reply: "All right. I'll work for you, but could you arrange to see that warehouse number so and so is sealed up?" Now, when the Japanese surrendered, the same stuff was all there. The same Chinese who had made the deal with the Japanese were now making deals with the Chiang Kai-shek people and were still there getting rich. This was to me the first warning sign that postwar corruption was likely to cripple the Kuomintang.

In Shanghai, I discovered one thing that would repay investigation if we could ever get at the facts. Very early, Chiang Kai-shek established connection with the German Reichswehr; not only did the Reichswehr have an important function in training the Chinese army, they also had their intelligence service, the center of which was in Shanghai. In the very complicated years when Hitler had not yet gotten complete control over the Reichswehr, some of the Reichswehr officers in China were by no means enthusiastic about him. With the establishment of the Berlin-Tokyo Axis, there was an intelligence link between Tokyo and the Reichswehr officers in Shanghai, and they undoubtedly transmitted intelligence information from inside Japan to Chungking.

Though I have no concrete evidence of this, I think it was quite possible that the link between the Reichswehr intelligence in Shanghai and Chiang in Chungking was never broken. I know, for instance, that after the defeat of Germany and the Japanese surrender, a number of important Reichswehr officers in Shanghai were smuggled out of China by Chiang Kai-shek's people and sent to refuges until they could safely return to Germany. I heard this through gossip about the White Russian mistress of the Russian intelligence service in Shanghai. After the Japanese surrender, she was taken over by the American head of intelligence service in Shanghai.

After about a week in Shanghai, three of us from the mission went up to Peking. One impression I had was how little Peking had changed; under the Japanese occupation, some good work had even been done in the restoration of temples, palaces, and old buildings. Both in Shanghai and Peking, there was a great deal of political blackmailing. In such cities, if somebody simply stayed there even without collaborating with the Japanese, he would be open to blackmail: "Now, you were here during the occupation. If you don't pay up so much, you will be accused of being a Japanese collaborator." We were in Peking only for a week, and in such a short visit with connections which were entirely limited to the reparations matter, it was impossible to make the kind of contacts that I needed to get some idea of what the Kuomintang and the Chinese Communist Party balance was like.

We had talks with Chinese bankers who more or less knew their business. But most of the Chinese, who were supposed to be in charge of industrial operations, were pure Kuomintang political appointees and did not know anything about running a factory. They did, however, know where you could sell a bit of machinery on the black market. I did not visit these factories personally and was not in a position to check on such matters technically. Nevertheless, I heard gossip about this sort of practice from Chinese sources. Having already some knowledge of the wide corruption spread through the whole Kuomintang structure, I was inclined to believe that there were many cases in which the Chinese officials who had taken over factories from the Japanese sold the machinery and put the money into their own pockets.

In the meantime, two members of the mission went to the Northeast. As it was the region where the Japanese had left all their industrial equipment, it was particularly important for the question of Japanese reparations. At that time, there was a great deal of talk about how much and why the Soviets had plundered industrial equipment in the Northeast. The Cold War had not actually begun yet; and the United States was not in a position to protest against what the Soviet Union was doing, because the U.S. doctrine for occupied territory and the Soviet doctrine happened to be exactly the same. That was: To the victors belong the spoils. When the Allies took Germany, anything that the United States wanted that was available in Germany the Americans took right out. It just happened that the United States was industrially much better equipped than the Soviet Union and did not want that much.

While accompanying the Wallace Mission, I had already learned that it was an illusion to think that in the Soviet Union, as a totalitarian state, everything was uniform. Especially in the war years, the Soviet Union's way of evacuating machinery from the west into Siberia was extremely uneven and irregular. Some operations were carried out with beautiful precision, others in a most chaotic and messy way. It seems that the same thing happened with taking machinery out of the Northeast. One of the two men sent to the Northeast was Martin Bennet, and his observations confirmed that there were factories where you could see that the machines had been ripped out of the factory in such an inefficient way that by the time they reached the Soviet Union, they would be scrap iron rather than machinery. In other places, the operation had been carried out with extreme efficency.

One example he gave was a hydroelectric dam in Kirin Province. He told me that for a large hydroelectric plant of that kind, a turbine was not just a turbine. It was a turbine which had been tailor-made and measured to fit that particular enterprise and could not just be taken away and put in some Soviet hydroelectric plant. The dam had been left without any unnecessary damage. In his opinion, the Soviet calculation was that in the end the Chinese Communists were going to prevail, and then those turbines would be brought back and put where they had belonged and do their proper job. It is quite conceivable that the Soviet Union did not want to have Chiang Kai-shek make the Northeast a strong anti-Soviet base with support from the United States.

The conclusion reached by the Pauley Misson can be found in its official report. In its broad outlines, it was: "Whatever political and economic rearrangements may be made within Japan, and whatever the restoration of economic relations between Japan and China and Southeast Asian countries might be, nothing should be of any benefit to the Soviet Union or to the Chinese Communists or to the liberal wing within the Kuomintang. Everything should go to the right wing of the countries concerned." Of course, I did not agree with this.

To me, then, the Pauley Mission was an opportunity to visit and see something of the conditions in defeated Japan and have a very brief glimpse of what was happening, or beginning to happen, in China.

During this mission, I had a personally gratifying experience. In Peking I found a man, Norwegian by birth, who before the First World War had gone to Siberia as a consultant to Siberian cooperatives on Scandinavian methods in the milk industry, such as making dried milk. When the Bolshevik Revolution broke out, he escaped into Mongolia and learned to speak Mongol very fluently. As he was an enormously tall man, the Mongols nicknamed him "Öndör Maidar" (the Mongol equivalent of Tall Maypole). During the Second World War, he was in Chungking working for British intelligence. After the Japanese surrender, he had come up to Peking to try to find out about the rivalry between the Kuomintang and the Chinese Communist Party for control of Inner Mongolia. He was desperately anxious to meet and talk with De Wang and went all over the place asking where the prince was, but it was impossible to get in touch with him. No one knew where he was.

I did not say anything to Öndör Maidar, but I thought that if De Wang was in Peking I would be able to find him. So, when I had a free afternoon I took a rickshaw and went up to Yunghokung, the famous Lama temple in Peking. I went inside and as soon as I saw a lama who was obviously Mongol and not a Tibetan, I spoke to him in Mongol and said: Are there any friends of the Dilowa Hutukutu here? My name is Lattimore, and I am a friend of the Dilowa Gegeen." "Oh, you are Lattimore. All right." So I was taken in and, with various people coming in and going out, we talked about this and that. After we became quite friendly, I said: "I wonder if it could be possible that any of the people I knew from Inner Mongolia are here." "Whom would you like to see?" "Sain Bayar, Chu Amban (governor) of Chahar, . . . I don't suppose De Wang is here, but it would be very nice if he were." "Ah," they said, "Nobody knows exactly who is in town." They were very vague, but added, "Telephone this number."

When I got back to the hotel, I telephoned that number. The answer was in Chinese, and I said: "*Mongol hün baihu?* (Is there any Mongol?)" The answer was: "I am a Mongol." I asked him whether Sain Bayar was there. He asked who I was. I said Lattimore. He said he would report and asked where I was staying. Then I went down to dinner. Halfway through the dinner, one of the waiters came and said: "There is somebody waiting for you in your room." So I went up, and there was De Wang with a young lieutenant-secretary at his side. By the way, though I did not know him at that time, this young man was Gombojab.

At that time, De Wang was uncertain as to what to do about the situation. His idea for the future was a kind of federated republic in which both Inner and Outer Mongolia, Tibet, and Sinkiang would be their own independent republics under the overall sovereignty of China. I rather agreed with his idea at the time. He wanted these ideas to be known in the United States. I said I would do what I could, but I knew it would be difficult. De Wang at that time had some illusions about the United States. The United States stood for self-determination, as had been proclaimed by President Wilson.

Already in the middle of the 1930s, De Wang had asked me: "Is there any chance that American influence can be brought to bear on autonomy for the Mongols?" I had to answer: "No, none whatsoever. The American doctrine is the integrity of China, and that is why the United States is against the Japanese occupation of the Northeast and the creation of Manchukuo. The American concept of the integrity of China is that Tibet, Mongolia, and Sinkiang are all part of China. You simply will not find anybody in Washington who can see or understand the problems of minorities in China." At that time, to most of the Americans, what was a Mongol? A Mongol was some sort of Chinese talking a funny dialect.

As has been described before, De Wang, being unable to resist the Chinese, had practiced the ancient tactic of slow-moving sabotage by carrying out Chinese orders, when he was forced to do so, as ineffectively as possible. Under the Japanese occupation, he continued the same policy. He never had any illusions about the Japanese. I learned later, though De Wang himself said nothing about it, that under the Japanese occupation of Inner Mongolia, he had a number of assistants whom he knew to be Communists in contact with the People's Republic of Mongolia. He did not care whether someone was a Marxist or of any other kind of political conviction. The only thing that mattered to him was whether that person was interested in the unity and future of the Mongolian people.

In spite of being a very high-ranking prince, De Wang was not against the idea of Mongolia becoming a republic. He was an honest man who had a real sense of devotion to his own people. As we see in the history of Mongolia, every time that Mongolian people nearly got something, they would be betrayed by some princes and high lamas selling out for their own personal advantages and to guarantee their titles. De Wang had been trying to unite and develop Inner Mongolia to give all the Mongols a feeling of being a part of the Mongol nation and not simply members of a tribe. Preservation of ranks and privileges of the princes was not his concern. That was the last time I saw him. Having tried some resistance against the Communist regime in the southwestern part of Inner Mongolia, he surrendered. I was told that, having been "reeducated," he worked in the library in Huhehot until his death in 1966. I think he was a very tragic figure.

The Civil War in China

While we were in China, General George Marshall was still trying to patch up the collapsing United Front. Marshall was a good appointment, because in his early career, when he was no higher than lieutenant-colonel, he had had several years of experience in China. Marshall was an immense improvement over Patrick Hurley and was even better than Stilwell. He attempted to negotiate a settlement in China that might prove to be stable. I had met him very briefly in the 1920s when he was commanding the U.S. 15th Infantry Regiment, which had been stationed in Tientsin for many years. The presence of the regiment was part of the Boxer Protocol to keep the railway open between Peking and the sea. Tientsin was a good observation point for the eternal civil wars of the 1920s; and it was also important for access from North China to the Northeast, including military communications as well as just ordinary transport.

I was following what was going on in China as far as I could in the whole period of the Marshall Mission and its final breakdown, which marked the beginning of the decisive civil war, in the autumn of 1946, between Chiang Kai-shek and the Chinese Communists. The supply of news was very irregular. There were several good correspondents sending good dispatches when they could get to the source of news, though they could not always do so. Therefore, the news was mixture, on the one hand, of hard facts about something that actually happened, and on the other of information heavily salted with speculation. In the United States, everybody was becoming a Kuomintang expert or a Chinese Communist Party expert.

When Japan surrendered, I could see that with Chiang as the head of the victorious government, the question of the Kuomintang and the Chinese Communist Party would move into a new chapter. It was no longer a question of maintaining a nominal United Front, but rather one of the division of power in China itself. I was worried about the United States getting involved in Chinese internal politics, in the form of providing U.S. transportation to move the Chiang Kai-shek troops by land and sea and air. I was one of those in the United States who believed that if friendly contacts with the Chinese Communist Party were maintained, this would strengthen the already existing tendency of the Communist Party, which was also nationalistic, to be more independent of Moscow. This, of course, ran against the doctrine that the Chinese Communist Party was nothing but a puppet manipulated by Moscow.

It will be interesting to recall here what Chiang had said in one of those late-evening conversations in Chungking, after Madame Chiang had retired. Knowing that President Roosevelt was for the United Front, Chiang wanted to counteract this with his own ideas. He said: "After the war, it will be impossible to settle on a coalition government with the Communists because negotiation with them is hopeless. The same word means this to me but means something else to them." Then he added: "The Soviet Union is different. You can do business with Stalin. He is a man who keeps his word." I was astonished by such a statement. Nevertheless, one can certainly say that Stalin did keep his word. For example, throughout the war, all Soviet aid of war materials to China was delivered to Chiang Kai-shek, and we know that the Communists were very bitter about this.

The Soviet argument would have been that they were supporting China as a nation. This went to such an extent that at the end of the war, when the Soviets invaded the Northeast and captured Japanese equipment, none was delivered to the Chinese Communists. I heard, however, that when the Japanese abandoned a village, the Soviets would collect the arms that had been left behind and let any Chinese pick up these arms and fight the Japanese, since they were regarded as on the side of the Allies. In this way, there is no doubt that a certain amount of Japanese equipment got into the hands of the Communists.

I remember one story that illustrates to a certain extent the general Soviet policy. After the war, when I was still writing a syndicated column, the great question at the time was whether there would be a real civil war in China. I went to the State Department once to see if they had any materials for release. There was a wire basket containing materials for journalists labeled "For use without attribution." That meant that journalists could use the information that they found in these papers, but they must not say that this came through the State Department channel. Among those papers I found a copy of a dispatch from a purported intelligence officer who had been parachuted into the Northeast during the short period when the Soviet armies were fighting against the Japanese. He was sent there to observe what the Soviets were doing and how rapidly the Japanese defeat was going. This man was evidently a member of the OSS, the Office of Special Services, which was one of the ancestors of the CIA.

He reported that he arrived at a village where the Japanese had just been driven out. The local Soviet commander called the village people together and said: "I am taking my men and going farther in pursuit of the Japanese. I don't have enough men to leave a liaison officer here in the village. But I need to have communication with the rear so that our troops coming in behind know where we are and what we are doing. Now, you have to elect such a person yourself to maintain communication."

The villagers, of course, had heard of Communists as people who were anti-landlord, and they replied: "The trouble is that the only men in the village who can read and write are the landlord and those connected with him, and you wouldn't want them." The Soviet officer said: "Whether he is a landlord or not is not my business. If you think you ought to keep an eye on him, do so; but I have to have somebody literate to whom we can send messages back."

At that moment in came a man, very dusty and tired. He cried: "Wait a moment, wait a moment. I am the advance man for the Eighth Route (Communist) Army. Don't worry. We will take over and make everything secure." The Soviet officer asked: "Are you a local man?" The Chinese replied: "I am not a local man. I am from the Eighth Route Army, as I have just explained." Then the Soviet officer told him: "This is the local people's business. You stay away. We don't need you."

On reading this report, my reaction was that the State Department was being very cowardly and devious. They were afraid that if they put out this kind of information and made it available to journalists as something coming from the State Department, the department would be accused of being pro-Soviet. So they put such stories in a basket for materials which journalists could use, but without being able to reveal the source. If I used it, I might be accused of being pro-Soviet. As I did not want to be a victim being tricked into using it, I put it right back into the basket. But today, historically, I think it is an important story.

During the war, I could never understand why Chiang Kai-shek did not realize that to have an enormous army and a tremendous propaganda of patriotism and yet not do any serious fighting would be fatal to morale. Of course, it was. At the end of the war when the Japanese surrender came, Chiang Kai-shek had an army with very, very poor morale. For example, Chiang had some good modern troops which had been flown to Assam to be trained and equipped there by the Americans. They were not flown back to China in time to be used against the Japanese. Instead, they were sent to the Northeast to stop the Communists from getting there. These soldiers were all from Southwest China, that part of China where Chiang Kai-shek was during the war, and so were filled with propaganda about fighting the invaders. They were spirited and well trained, but instead of fighting against the Japanese they were to fight against Chinese Communists.

The Communists had a very easy time, propagandizing those troops: "You come from Southwest China. What are you doing here fighting other Chinese? Let's stop killing each other. Come over to our side and you will be facing toward home. We'll help you get there." Many of these troops deserted and joined the Communists. Very often whole regiments surrendered with their officers and everything they had. Even the American newspapers had the news in detail that when the Communist forces finally entered Peking, they came in with hundreds of motor vehicles and motorized artillery, all brand new U.S. equipment which had been surrendered to them by the Kuomintang forces without fighting.

The general who was sent up for political and ideological policy to the Northeast by Chiang Kai-shek was a Southerner whom I had known in Chungking. When the Chinese Communists started on their Long March in October 1934, having been driven out of Kiangsi, this very general had been sent in to restore Kuomintang control over what had been the territory of the Chinese Soviet Republic. When this man appeared in the Northeast, the people said: "Ah, this is the notorious man of terror."

After the Japanese surrender, the landlords who had run away would come back with Chiang's troops, and they would demand back rent and back tax from the peasants for the period of the Japanese occupation. The peasants would appeal: "But we can't do that. We have already paid to the Japanese. They took it all, and we don't have anymore." Whereupon they were told: "You paid rent and tax to the Japanese? You are collaborators. Now, watch out! You pay, or you go to jail." If that sort of policy was applied in the Northeast, which had been occupied by the Japanese for fifteen years, one can imagine how people would behave. It is a fact that this kind of thing happened in many places in China.

I thought that the course of the civil war was showing that Chiang Kai-shek was being defeated by corruption and collapse within his own party and within his own army. This was where the Communists were much better. All through the war years, they encouraged guerilla warfare by partisans, involving local volunteer organizations, mainly of peasants, with the Red Army simply sent in to organize them. They were saying to ordinary people: "Not only can the Japanese be defeated, but *you* can do something about it." This was immensely morale building.

I was afraid already that the contrast between the Kuomintang inactivity and the Communist activity was going to work out badly for the Kuomintang. Toward the end, when the Kuomintang forces were crumbling, there were generals who were trying to get rich at the last minute to have some money to get out of China before the final defeat. So they pressed to be appointed the top commander. Chiang, however, appointed as top commander in North China Fu Tso-yi, who was known to be incorruptible. He had a very high reputation as an honest man who had never changed sides for pay and who was always loyal to Yen Hsi-shan, the warlord of Shansi. Being a Shansi man, Fu took Chi Ch'ao-ting, also a Shansi man, with him to Peking as a sort of financial and economic expert.

It was this Fu Tso-yi who finally surrendered Peking to the Communists without any resistance. By the time he surrendered Peking, however, it was all over, and the choice was either to defend Peking by force, involving street fighting and destruction, or give it up peacefully. Under the new government, Fu was given an appointment in charge of hydraulic projects like canals and irrigation. The use of water was intimately linked with the question of agricultural production and income, therefore, taxes.

I should like to add some anecdotes of the civil war period. After the Japanese surrender, I was looking for materials to write an article for Overseas News Agency about the possible breakout of a civil war in China. So I went to Washington and arranged to call on General Stilwell. By that time, the whole Stilwell episode had been closed, and he had no powerful political position within the U.S. military. He had been sidetracked into a small office, not even at the Pentagon but at an old barrack in Washington itself, and was doing nothing much except simply waiting for retirement.

That was where I went to see him. He said: "Well, Owen, can you tell me what's going on in China? What are the Communists up to? What are they going to do?" I replied: "I haven't any idea, but I am trying to write some articles, and I came to see *you* thinking that *you* might give me some information about the situation in China." He then asked: "Are you in touch with the Chinese Communists?" I said: "No, if I were, I wouldn't need to come to *you*." "Well," he said, "if you ever do get into contact with them, pass a message for me. Tell Chu Teh that I would be proud to come to China and shoulder a rifle as a private soldier under his command." Of course, it is well known that he detested Chiang Kai-shek; but remembering his old theory of Chinese soldiers with American officers, such a declaration coming from his mouth was quite remarkable.

In the early period of the civil war, when the situation of the Kuomintang was not yet so desperate, Chang Ch'ün came to Washington as a kind of special envoy of Chiang Kai-shek. I was surprised to receive an official invitation from the State Department to a reception for him at Blair House, the official White House guest house. I was told afterward and privately that when the guest list for the reception was shown to Chang Ch'ün he said: "I do not see Lattimore's name here." They explained: "Well, of course, Lattimore has nothing to do with diplomacy, and he does not belong here." Then Chang Ch'ün said: "He is the man I want to see." And my name was added to the list on his insistence.

So, at the reception I went down the line to shake hands with Chang Ch'ün. When my turn came he said: "When people start going home, don't leave until everybody has gone. I want to talk with you." In due course, he took me to a sitting room and told his aide-de-corps: "Close the door and stand outside. Let nobody in." Upon this he said: "The relations between China and the United States are going to be increasingly complicated, and perhaps increasingly difficult. We are old friends. Would you consent to write to me personal letters from time to time and tell me your absolutely frank opinion whenever something comes up in the United States that you think is important and that might have a bearing on China policy of the United States? I will give you a safe address."

I had my answer to that right away: "You do me a great honor to trust me in this way; but I think you will appreciate that having once worked officially for the Generalissimo, it would not be loyal to work unofficially for one of his ministers." Chang Ch'ün said: "I am disappointed, but I quite understand. You are a good Confucian." He never did join the new Communist government, and I never met him again.

As I mentioned before, when the Chinese were talking among themselves in the air-raid shelters in Chungking, they called the Americans the "most imperialist bastards of the lot." Most people in the United States, however, had the illusion that they had never been an imperialistic nation. Nevertheless, some of them did understand what it was all about. One such was J.W. Foster, a very important man in his time. He had been a senator, secretary of state, and also a U.S. judge at the International Court of Justice at The Hague. He happened to be the maternal grandfather of John Foster Dulles. Soon after the Boxer Rebellion (1900) and the U.S. war with Spain, which ended in U.S. occupation of the Philippines, he wrote a book called *American Diplomacy in the Orient* (1903).

In this book, he explicitly justifies the use of gunboats to protect missionaries, saying that the power of Confucian class in China must be broken, because otherwise China could never be made Christian. Then he records a conversation with some British expert on international affairs. The Briton said admiringly: "You Americans are the ones who know how this enlightened imperialism must work." Of course, he belonged to the generation in which imperialism had not become a bad word, and capitalism and Christianity were supposed to go hand in hand. So he believed that the old system in China had to be broken in order to allow the development both of U.S.-style capitalism and of U.S.-style Protestant Christianity.

Missionaries spread the misconception that the Chinese regarded foreign missions as a benevolent operation, and most Americans never understood how the Chinese associated the missions with imperialism. Missionaries were allowed to reside in the interior of China, while other foreigners were limited to the Treaty Ports. This right of missionaries was itself based on the imperialist treaties. In about 1947 or 1948, when Chiang Kai-shek's position in the Northeast was crumbling and the Communist forces were beginning to enter the Great Wall, the U.S. consulate general told all the missionaries along the railway lines between Tientsin and Shanhaikuan to evacuate to Tientsin for shelter from the war. There were quite a number of them, and in their way they had been very progressive and had done a lot to develop China, for example, by fruit farming on poor land that was not good enough for growing grains.

At that time, I got a message from a Chinese pastor attached to one of these U.S. Protestant missions. He had been sent to the United States to attend a theological seminary for higher training as a professional Christian pastor. He came to see me and said: "Would you please go to Washington immediately and use your influence to put an important matter before the State Department?" He told me that as soon as these missionaries got to Tientsin, they had to report to the U.S. consulate general to be interviewed and asked: "How many Reds are actually in your district? What is the state of the Kuomintang forces?" From the consulate general, this information immediately went to the U.S. Military Intelligence, which was in liaison with Chiang Kai-shek.

In the eyes of all the Chinese of that district, this proved that missionaries were in fact an imperialist agency intervening in the domestic affairs of China, and it was also proof of the Communist accusation that missionaries were imperialist spies. This kind of story would absolutely never appear in any ordinary American newspaper, but I knew China well enough to understand what the Chinese pastor pointed out. At the same time, I also knew that if I had gone to the State Department and said that, or written the story in a document, they would put it on one side as "pro-Communist stuff!" I had to say to the pastor: "I am very sorry, but I have no influence whatsoever with the State Department."

There was a man who was quite active in China Lobby propaganda during the Korean War. His father was a Protestant missionary on the Fukien Coast. In order to prove that not only he himself but his whole family were red-blooded, hundred-percent American, he told how his father would go on tours in the interior visiting mission outputs, and when he came back to the coast would immediately report to the nearest U.S. warship in the Fukien port.

According to their ideas, it was natural and right for missionaries to keep the military forces of their country well informed. Many of them were too unsophisticated to think what they were really doing to the Chinese.

One of the prominent figures in the China Lobby was a man who had made a fortune in the business of having linen made and embroidered in Ireland to sell as a semi-luxury product. Then at some point before the Pacific War he was denounced by the progressive left-wingers for running a sweated industry in Ireland, employing girls and women at very low wages. So this man shifted his operations to China. He himself was a Jew, but he largely used the girls in orphanages run by Roman Catholic nuns in China. Selling the embroidered linens at high prices in the United States, he got rich very quickly.

Here is a very important difference between the United States of 1940s and that of the 1960s. Though today, of course, the Left Catholics are a very important force in the United States, in the 1940s, as far as I know, there was no such thing as a Catholic Left in the country, and all the U.S. Catholic establishment was right wing. So this Jewish millionaire, profiting from sweated labor in the Catholic nunneries in China, was a natural ally of the right-wing Catholic Lobby, which linked up with the right-wing Catholic Lobby in China.

This man had a publication in which he sang the praises of Chiang Kai-shek and blasted the sinfulness of the Chinese Communists. He had joined the IPR fairly early, and at one of its meetings had tried to get motions passed to turn the IPR from being a semi-academic organization that tried to analyze the politics and economics of Asia in an objective way into an instrument of propaganda for the Right against the Left. I suppose this happened during the war years, and though I did not attend that meeting, I know that his motions were rejected. From then on, he began to hint, and later on assert more strongly, that the IPR was an instrument of the Soviet Communist world conspiracy. He was one of those very active in the McCarthy accusations. I do not think I ever had any direct or indirect contact with him.

I think it has to be made very clear right at the beginning that nobody ever tried to recruit me to work for the China Lobby. The people who formed the China Lobby were all enthusiastic volunteers who came forward of their own accord, thinking now they must support Chiang Kai-shek. The mere fact that I did not come forward like that made me suspect in the eyes of the China Lobby people. My position had always been that it would be disastrous for the United States to get involved in the Chinese civil war supporting one side against the other. Even before the end of the Pacific War, seeing the increasing involvement of the United States only on the side of the Kuomintang, in June 1945, I wrote to President Truman presenting my view. Truman received me on 3 July; but this interview did not last more than three minutes. To put it briefly, Truman told me that there were well-informed experts in the State Department and they knew what they were doing. Thank you, Mr. Lattimore. Good-bye.

While I was still in Cambridge, England, around 1979 or so, I received a letter from John Emmerson, who had been in the State Department and was driven out of it during the McCarran period. He asked me whether I had visited President Truman twice in 1945, at the behest of Dean Acheson, to register opposition to the continuation of the monarchical system by Japan after the war. I replied that as far as I remember, I had never in my life met Dean Acheson and that I did not see Truman twice, but only once, and that once was not at the behest of Dean Acheson and had nothing to do with the Japanese emperor.

In any case, there is an episode, which I heard later and which illustrates my relation with the State Department. After the war, the State Department set up a system of having Asia specialists from the academic world act as consultants who would be invited now and then to committee meetings at the State Department. One friend of mine in the department proposed my name as somebody to be invited as a consultant, and the reply that came back to him from Secretary of State Dean Acheson was: "Lattimore is a journalist and not a scholar. So we do not need him." That shows how much influence I had.

In the beginning of October 1949, however, a three-day conference was convened by the State Department. (This was quite different from the more-or-less standing body of academic consultants mentioned above. After my return from Chungking, I had never been consulted by any official quarters on China policy.) There were about twenty-four or twenty-five people, including myself. Now, it often happens with all kinds of governments that they write to a number of people who lecture or write articles and say they are about to have a conference on such and such subject, and they will greatly value your participation and opinion. So you all assemble. Then, the spokesman, say of the State Department, puts before you what is really the department's own or the Establishment's point of view. The idea is that you are flattered because you have been consulted, but you go away talking about the opinion that has been given to you rather than the opinion you gave.

A record says that out of the twenty-five people assembled, seventeen were in some way connected with the IPR. It is quite possible, because it was in general a conference on China policy or Far Eastern policy as a whole. Consequently, the IPR connection was not surprising. An amusing thing about this conference is that one of the participants was Harold Stassen, once a hopeful candidate for the presidential election. At that time, he was an active politician in Minnesota, his own state. He kept getting up and leaving the discussion in order to show what an important person he was. He would say: "Excuse me, Mr. Chairman, but I have an important engagement with this or that important person." Then he would go off and come back after a while. So, there was a large period of the conference when he was not even there; but he later gave testimony in the hearings, saying that the man who talked most at this conference was Owen Lattimore. He was not even there to hear me if I had spoken, and when he *was* there, he had a great deal to say himself instead of listening to what other people had to say.

I remember writing somewhere, watching the downfall of Chiang Kai-shek, that Chiang was a great man and had done great things, but like all other great men, he had his limitations. I would still say the same thing at the present day. I thought that he was sincerely trying to make China a great country. However, in some ways he continued to be rather medieval-minded, which handicapped him in trying to carry out modern programs. As I have already said, he was not, or could not become, a dictator. I do not think that he was a thoroughly feudal figure, but he wanted to make himself the dominant personality within the new China. For example, in his conversation with me he said: "After the war, China will have to industrialize. This will include a great deal in the way of nationalization. The new industrialization in China will draw population from the rural areas. Therefore, rural economics as well as agricultural production will have to be changed. For that we will have to collectivize and create state farms, just like the Soviet Union. Only they will be *my* collectives and *my* state farms, and not like Stalin's."

The China policy of the United States certainly failed. There were, as usual in situations of that kind, many reasons. Right up to the Pacific War, the U.S. investment in Asia was small and was limited to a few things like oil and oil refineries and so on. Consequently, the U.S. business community that was taking notice of what was going on in Asia was not as large as that of, for example, Great Britain. Even the academic Americans who studied Asia were on the whole weak in people who had done their primary study in Asia itself. There was a strong tendency, if you were going to be an Asia specialist in a U.S. university, to build up your career on the study of diplomatic documents, treaties, and so on. The number of people who had a real contact with and feel for the life of the people in Asian countries was very limited. It worked both ways, of course. Those whose careers were based primarily on the life and the experience in Asia, like myself, were weak in academic preparation.

In this situation, a very high proportion of the publicity in the United States about a country like China came from missionaries, and missionaries coming home from China would go on lecture tours and talk about the glorious possibilities when all China became Christian. In an atmosphere like this, when Chiang Kai-shek and the Kuomintang people finally had to take refuge in Taiwan in December 1949, the question of "Who let the United States lose China?" became a hot issue, as if China had ever *belonged* to the United States.

The Storm Breaks Out

One episode I must mention of the period before the outbreak of the McCarthy storm was during the IPR international conference in India in December 1949. I do not remember anything special about this meeting; but I do know that what impressed the American delegation not a little was that when I arrived at the airport a day or two later than the main group, waiting for me at the airport was a personal aide to Prime Minister Jawaharlal Nehru, who said: "Come along with me. Mr. Nehru wants to see you." So the fact that I was rushed out of the airport and taken straight to Nehru made quite a sensation. I think it was the first time I met Nehru in India. He considered me a kind of representative of the American progressive opinion that he wanted to cultivate.

The U.S. ambassador in India at that time, Loy Henderson, was very anti-Nehru. He had a typical American attitude that India was starting off with too much of a government program and this was socialistic, and socialism was the top of the slope down which you slide into communism. As a matter of fact, I first met him when he visited Kueihua when I was there in the 1930s. He was interested in what I had to say about the economic and trade conditions, the Suiyuan Railway and the caravan trade, and so on, and we became quite friendly. He wound up as ambassador in Moscow before going to India. He was regarded as a reliable anti-Bolshevik, having been in the Allied Intervention after the Russian Revolution. During the intervention he had met his future wife, a woman from the Russian Caucasus. She was so anti-Bolshevik that, living in Moscow as the wife of the ambassador, she would not buy things like fresh vegetables in the Russian market. Everything had to be brought in from Finland.

He was interested in Central Asia and Mongolia and had a very valuable private library, mostly of the old Tsarist books about that part of the world. Eventually when he retired, he moved to Spain and died there. I wanted to get hold of his library for the Mongol project which I started at the University of Leeds in 1968, but when I heard of his death, I was too late, and John Krueger had got the library for the Ural and Altaic Studies at Indiana University.

Now, in India, as I had already known the ambassador, we began on a very friendly footing. At some kind of official reception, however, when I was standing talking with him and another man, Nehru came up and, putting his arm through mine, said: "Come along, Lattimore, I want to talk to you." The ambassador was infuriated as Nehru snatched me away. Nehru then took me into a little room and introduced me to two men. The first man was an engineer and one of Nehru's principal Indian advisers on the post-independence Indian economy. The second was a very interesting man whom I think was born in Russia. He was of Jewish origin and had emigrated after the Russian Revolution to Germany, where he spent some time and became an employee of General Electric in the United States.

Even before Roosevelt recognized the Soviet Union, certain American economic contacts with the Soviet Union were permitted for companies like the Ford Motor Company. There was a famous project of constructing a hydroelectric dam in the Soviet Union, and this man, knowing Russian and being an electrical engineer, was sent to the Soviet Union to work on this American Soviet project. After this, he returned to the United States and continued to work for General Electric. Later, he went to Israel to work as an expert on the Dead Sea Project. Nehru then invited him to India as his personal economic-technological adviser.

The four of us sat down and talked until two or three o'clock in the morning—an intensely interesting conversation all about problems of development: what are the social consequences of a development program, how can it be handled in a balanced way, and so on. I wish I had had a tape recorder. By the time I got away, I was so tired that I went straight to sleep; but I should have sat up and written a diary account of the whole thing. The last time I saw this man was in England. By that time, he was already ninety years old or a little more. When I asked him: "What are you doing now?" he replied: "Oh, I have taken up atomic physics. Enough to keep you doing something new, or else you get old."

This was the time when the cease-fire between India and Pakistan involving the division of Kashmir was being negotiated. Nehru knew that I had passed through Kashmir years ago and wanted me to go up there to see the situation. Therefore, after the IPR meeting, with Nehru's blessing, in fact at his request, I made a visit to Kashmir. When I was there, the man still dominant on the Indian side of Kashmir was Shakha Dura. Later he and Nehru fell out; but at this time Shakha Dura was a big man, and Nehru wanted me to meet him, so that Shakha Dura and his entourage would be able to give me the Indian view of the Kashmir quarrel. This visit was extremely interesting.

The final collapse of Chiang Kai-shek was in December 1949, and at this time I was still actively running the Page School. The Page School was rather heavily concentrated on Asia, especially China and Central Asia. I already had programs on my Central

Asian Seminar and my Mongolian Seminar with the Dilowa Hutukutu and the two younger Mongols. As of 1949, there was no propaganda coming out from the Page School in favor of Chiang Kai-shek. As far as Chinese internal politics were concerned, we were trying to find out who was scoring goals and who was losing goals, so to speak.

In the spring of 1950, I was approached, again not on my initiative, to head a United Nations Mission to Afghanistan. It was to be an exploratory mission to find out what could be done in the way of international support for the modernization of Afghanistan's economy. I had with me an extremely able Canadian agricultural expert, another very interesting man who was born on the island of Mauritius, and another man, a self-educated person who came from a working-class family in London.

In Afghanistan, we dealt largely with the minister of economics. He had been born near the Afghan frontier with the Soviet Union and had known Russian from childhood. In the period of the Bolshevik Revolution, he had helped a lot of White Russians escape the revolution via Afghanistan, taking an economic tribute from them as they passed through. So he had become a wealthy man, but he was also careful to maintain good relations with the Bolsheviks. He even got to Leningrad and met Lenin himself. Later, he had been either ambassador or consul general in Berlin at the time the Nazis were in power. Consequently, he had good German connections also, and between the wars there had been a great number of German enterprises in Afghanistan.

It was while I was in Afghanistan that the storm broke out on me. When I had set out with the U.N. Mission, I was not aware of any hostile criticism against me. Facts have been very much distorted since, because over and over again it is said that Lattimore had to come racing back from Afghanistan to face the accusations made by Senator Joseph McCarthy. It is not true. Instead of abandoning my work in Afghanistan and flying back to the United States, I stayed on until my mission was completed, though no more than a week elapsed from the moment when I first received the news to the time I left Afghanistan. I cannot remember how long the mission stayed in Afghanistan, but my impression is that the telegram about McCarthy's accusations came toward the end of my stay there, and the most important negotiations with the Afghans had already been completed.

I went back, at the end of March, as planned, not a day earlier. I knew that I was on the blacklist, so to speak, of the China Lobby; but I had never really heard of McCarthy and did not know how serious a political figure McCarthy might be. He might be just a loudmouth shouting nonsense, or he might be a person with a political following in the Senate. I had no way of knowing. Up to that point, he had been active to a certain extent attacking American communists and fellow travelers in the United States; but he had not been particularly associated with Asia. At the time the telegram arrived in Kabul, saying: "Senator McCarthy says you are the principal Soviet agent," my immediate reaction was: "Who the hell is this guy McCarthy?" Of course, I knew that an anti-communist atmosphere had been growing in the United States, and I also knew and disagreed with the common assumption in the United States that the Chinese Communists were controlled down to the last detail by Moscow.

In fact, as early as 1945, when I went to Japan with the Pauley Mission, there had been hostile articles, one at least in the *Los Angeles Times*, suggesting that I was a man who was too friendly to the Soviet Union. At that time, nobody in the United States thought that the Chinese were capable of anything as modern as a communist revolution won by a Chinese Communist Party. So they must be slightly half-witted puppets of the Russians, and the whole thing was to be explained from Russia, and not from China.

Probably I was picked out by McCarthy partly because of the China Lobby, but even the most superficial preliminary inquiries would have shown that I had no influence in the State Department; I was a university professor; and I had no high-up political friends. This means that I was wide open for the wildest kinds of accusation. This, paradoxically, illustrates the importance of being unimportant. I suppose McCarthy knew that I was not that important; but I was an easy victim because in attacking me he was in no danger of being confronted by some formidable institutions or persons that would come to my defense. Certainly, from a very early point in the whole business, McCarthy was in touch with the man who had made a fortune by embroidery done by Chinese orphans and who was one of the leaders of the China Lobby.

Three or four years previously, I lectured during the spring term at Rutgers University in New Jersey. That was at the time of the annual meeting of some important society, either the National

American Newspaper Editors' Society or perhaps the National Newspaper Publishers' Society. This was a huge organization, and somebody on a paper on Long Island got in touch with me and invited me to give a luncheon speech to this crowd. So, I gave them a speech dealing with the difference between received respectable opinion and independent personal opinion.

In my speech, I used as an example those articles that I had written for the *Saturday Evening Post* and *The Times* of London shortly before the Japanese attack at the Marco Polo Bridge in 1937. In those articles, I said that China would eventually hold out while the received opinion was that the Japanese military would cut through China like a hot knife through butter. At the end of the speech, I was given an ovation from all those hardened newspapermen. This later caused several people to write articles about how Lattimore had anticipated by a decade or so what had come to be respectable opinion, and Lattimore got into trouble from being too right too soon.

One of the main accusations against me was that I was responsible for the United States losing China. That was one of the absurdities of the 1950s—that the United States *lost* China. How can you lose something that you never had? They accused me of influencing, or trying to influence, U.S. opinion in favor of the Chinese Communists. It is very significant, however, that McCarthy did not say that I was the principal agent of the Chinese Communists, but that I was the principal *Soviet* agent, as it was received opinion that the Chinese Communist Party could not but be controlled by Moscow.

There were all these allegations about my influence in the State Department, but how can you prove influence when there is no such a thing? In the course of hearings of the Tydings Committee and the McCarran Committee, a lot of people lost their jobs, but publicity in the newspapers about them was not as great as the publicity about me. This is one of those paradoxical things which you can explain by the fact that the lack of evidence about me was one of my greatest difficulties. If a man had worked for the State Department, there would be a record like this year he was appointed here and the next year he was appointed somewhere else. I was a private individual known for my opinions but never having held any office that had any influence within the government; and this very fact made it possible, beginning with McCarthy, to make the charges all the more sensational.

As the details of what I went through during the Tydings Committee of the Senate are found in *Ordeal by Slander* (1950), I am not going to repeat the whole story here. The Tydings Committee ended up with the conclusion that not only was I innocent of what McCarthy had tried to assert, but that McCarthy himself was guilty of, I forget the exact wording, something like a fraud and something else perpetrated on the Senate and the people of the United States. It was an outright condemnation of McCarthy. So I thought that the thing was finished for good. But this came up again a few months later.

By that time, the secretary-general of the International IPR, Edward Carter, had retired. He had taken the files of the IPR to his summer house in Massachusetts and had stored them in a barn as he had the intention of using them for a history of the IPR. One of the McCarthy men found out about the existence of the documents and reported to McCarthy, who drew this to the attention of Senator McCarran. On 8 February 1951, the FBI illegally seized these documents, and this was the beginning of the McCarran hearings, which started in July. Among these documents there were many letters which I had written to Carter in order to avoid going to IPR committee meetings, as has been mentioned before.

The hearings at the McCarran Committee were much tougher than those at the Tydings Committee. Several times I have been asked why I do not write the sequel to *Ordeal by Slander*. The main reason, perhaps, is that the case was "dropped" without having come to a definite conclusion, and it might not be appropriate to write about a case which is, in a way, "pending." In the hearings, many people came up to testify that Lattimore was identified as this or that; I did not have the recourse of suing such people for libel, because they were not stating things on their own but merely giving sworn testimony before a Senate Committee, which had immunity. By the time my case was dropped, to write another book on it was like whipping a dead horse. I just did not feel like it. If at that time I had written a sort of second *Ordeal by Slander*, it would have been regarded as self-serving and would have provided a springboard for other people to dig up all the accusations, saying "Ha, ha, he says he is innocent. But according to sworn testimony. . . ."

In any case, Dr. Robert P. Newman of the University of Pittsburgh is now writing my biography centered on the period concerned, making full use of papers from the FBI, the army, and the State Department which have been declassified and made public by the recent Freedom of Information Act. They give the inside account of the Lattimore persecution. Therefore, readers who are interested to know what was taking place in those days and the political and social background can find the full and well-documented story in Dr. Newman's book, more than what I can remember now after so many years.

All I can say now is that in the course of the hearings, what I had said or written was brought up now and again, taken entirely out of its original context. For example, a letter I had written to Carter in July 1938 was made much of for the word "cagey" it contained, and the letter itself came to be known as the "cagey letter." Cagey is American slang, originated in the behavior of animals in a cage. The word was picked out of my letter to show that I was a suspicious character. My meaning was: "We should be careful not to say or do anything that could be misunderstood or misconstrued." But in the hearings, it was interpreted as if I had meant "Let's not do it in a way that will let people guess what we are really up to."

At another time, I was asked all of a sudden whether it was *before* or *after* my nomination by President Roosevelt as the adviser to Chiang Kai-shek that I met Umanskii of the Soviet Embassy. As I mentioned in Chapter 3, by a slip of memory I answered that it was *after* the nomination. By the time I met Umanskii, my nomination had become definite, but had not yet been officially announced. Nobody is expected to remember correctly and in detail all that he did more than ten years ago when he is questioned suddenly about it. This, however, was construed as my trying to hide some conspiracy with the Soviet Union. As they could not prove that I was a Soviet spy, they accused me of perjury.

Incidentally, it was through a funny episode that I discovered that my telephone was tapped. One day, before I had any idea about the storm that was to break out on me, I was asked to translate some telephone conversations in Mongol. It turned out to be my own conversations with the Dilowa Hutukutu. What happened seems to be that the FBI had tapped my telephone, but they could not find anybody in Washington who could translate these conversations for them. Then someone, who did not belong to the FBI and did not know the origin of the recordings, said he knew a man who could do the job. So, it was turned over to *me*.

Even in the declassified FBI papers, some important points are suppressed for reasons of security or some such thing. At the same time, the policy of the FBI when they released these documents was to delete anything that would enable you to identify actual people, so I have no idea of who or what he or she might have been; but these documents show that all sorts of informants, including some woman who seems to have been one of my neighbors, came up to the FBI with their stories about me. One of the most fantastic reports was that given by another woman. She twice reported to the FBI that in about 1940 she had been to Mexico and had interviewed the assassin of Trotsky in prison. According to her, he had said that he would never be hanged because he had a powerful protector, who was in a strong position in Washington. Who was this man? Lattimore! The story was so fantastic that even the FBI did not take it seriously.

Before the McCarran Committee, one or two people said that there was a strong preliminary evidence that I might have been connected with Sorge and it should be followed up. But quite obviously, there was nothing in the file to be followed up. There was a hope, I think, that through Sorge's Japanese connection something against me might turn up. Though I was mostly connected with China, one or two people of Dōmei, a Japanese news syndicate, who were involved with Sorge may have known me. The fact that there was no evidence, however, could be held against me as a proof that I was so deeply buried underground.

In these memoirs, I do not want to be bitter or vindictive about anybody. After all, all people are to a certain extent molded by the times they live in; but if I were to be bitter I could be bitter about Karl Wittfogel, because he tried and to a certain extent succeeded in using me to advance his own career. In one of his testimonies at the Senate committee, he said that at the time he came to China he was still a secret communist, and he could tell by the way I talked that I was also a secret communist. He never said that I confessed to him that I was a communist. John Fairbank, in his autobiography *Chinabound*, writes that I had helped Wittfogel to enter the United States; but in fact he had entered the United States and received an American grant for research in China, where I first met him. Here I must say that John Fairbank had sent the galley proofs of his book for me to check, but I could not send him corrections in time for the final printing.

I think Wittfogel's very bitter attack on me during the McCarthy days was to protect his own position. He had been a member of the German Communist Party but had disagreed with it and left it. There were all kinds of actual ex-communists, or people who had been very close to communists, who were trying to save their skins by denouncing others in order to demonstrate or prove how deeply anti-communist they were. Somebody once said Wittfogel had for a while been in a Nazi concentration camp. Like a good many ex-communists who remained this way or that way Marxists, he was convinced that McCarthy was a sign that the United States was going to become fascist, and there would be new concentration camps; and he wanted to make sure that this time he would be on the safe side of the barbed wire instead of the inside. What Eleanor had said about Wittfogel in the 1930s turned out eventually correct.

As for Freda Utley, who also testified against me, she never tried to use me for her own career. I first met her in 1936 in Moscow when I accompanied Carter who was trying to get a Soviet group of scholars interested in the IPR. Freda was present at one of the lectures I gave in Moscow. Eleanor and our little boy David had gone ahead to England to wait for me. At the end of our visit I took the train from Moscow, and at the channel port in Holland I ran into Freda Utley. She had a little baby in her arms and was having trouble getting her luggage through. I helped her a bit to get her on the train to London. She told me then that she was leaving the Soviet Union because her husband, a Russian, had got into political trouble and had disappeared. He was in trouble not because he was a principal figure of any kind, but because he had been a secretary or assistant to somebody more important who had been purged. But Freda Utley had been allowed out because she still held a British passport, so she returned to England.

After that, she entered on a long campaign, which must have

been intellectually and psychologically terribly frustrating; she attempted to show that she was a completely reliable Stalinist-line communist, and therefore her husband should be released and allowed to rejoin her. She went out to Japan and wrote a book called *Japan's Feet of Clay* (1936), which was very much in the standard Stalinist line of analyzing the Japan of those days. In the early years of the all-out war between Japan and China, she went to Hankow, and there she strongly supported the Stalinist version of the new United Front between Chiang Kai-shek and the Chinese Communists. After this, she came to the United States and did a round of public lectures to groups which were in favor of boycotting American shipments of scrap iron and other materials of military value to Japan.

As Eleanor and myself were engaged in the same kind of activities, I think we arranged some of the lectures she gave. At one time, we went to Washington to have dinner with other people who were interested in the anti-Japanese imperialism movement, and Freda was with us. She told me that she had been trying and trying in vain to get in touch with the Soviet Embassy, and as she knew that I knew Soviet Ambassador Umanskii, who had once attended an international meeting of the IPR, she wanted me to telephone the Soviet Embassy. She was desperately anxious for an opportunity to call on him and talk about the problem of her husband. I succeeded in reaching Umanskii from a public telephone booth and said that maybe he knew the name of Freda Utley. What Umanskii said over the phone was: "That ▓▓! Never!" At any rate, my failure to get an appointment for her convinced her that I was in the pocket of the Soviet Embassy.

So after the war, having given up all hope of ever getting her husband released, even without knowing what had happened to him, she had joined the China Lobby and was working for Chiang Kai-shek and against the Chinese Communists. She was, so to speak, correcting the record of the time when she had made pro-Communist and pro-United Front broadcasts and lectures. Denouncing me was part of all this. I had not been successful in helping her, and she became more and more psychopathic. Such a person could easily imagine, as sincerely as a psychopathic person can, that I had deliberately misled her about my political affiliations. She is a person for whom I feel deeply sorry as a victim of the 1930s and 1940s.

When the storm broke, there were various people whom I had considered merely acquaintances who suddenly appeared as strong supporters. The law office Arnold, Fortas & Porter took over my defense free of charge. There were other people whom we had considered as good friends who simply disappeared, and there were also those who testified against me.

There was one case of a man, a university professor, with whom I had discussed the collaboration between the Page School of International Relations and his department. He was Catholic, and it turned out that he was what is called in America a "populist," which means that he was against the rich being too rich and the poor being too poor. He came from one of the western states where everybody hunted. In Maryland, however, the shooting of ducks, in migration seasons along the Maryland estuary, for example, was controlled by a few rich people who owned this or that section of the shore, and they acted together so that they reserved the shooting to themselves and kept outsiders out. This made this man furious. As soon as I knew that he was radical in this sense, I asked him some questions to find out how radical he was in general.

Later, he used the fact that I had asked him such questions as evidence of my being a communist agent seeking to recruit him. One bit of the testimony he gave was that when he was invited to an outdoor party at my home in Maryland, John Service, the State Department man who was also one of the guests, said that he had a document that he wanted me to examine. This document was a denunciation of the United States by Mao Tse-tung, and in it he used a couple of phrases in his Hunan dialect which Service had not been able to identify in a dictionary. So, he and I went up to my study, and I got my dictionaries out, and we tried to find the correct translation for the bad language used by Mao Tse-tung, which said something like "the Americans stink like an ancient corpse." This university professor later reported to the investigation that Service and I had gone away to examine in private a classified document.

During the McCarthy period, I ran into Harold Isaacs at an academic meeting in Philadelphia. He told me that the FBI had been after him to see if they could get any derogatory information about me. I asked him what he told them. "I told them," he replied, "that you were too intelligent to be a Stalinist, but didn't have the guts to be a Trotskyist."

There were also fortunate by-products of the McCarthy accusations. For a great many years I had not had any word from the Barretts, who had given me very important financial support in the early stage of my career, but got furious because I published academic books and took up a university job. When the McCarthy attack started, they packed up from California, where they had been living, and came to Washington to attend every hearing. They were absolutely delighted. The old man thought: "Ah, Lattimore is not behaving like a university professor at all. He has some guts. He is fighting!" In this way, we became great friends again.

Another person who turned up was one of my best friends at the British Public School, Ian Black. We had edited a school magazine together, but after my return to China in 1919 we had lost trace of each other. Thanks to McCarthy, he found my name in the newspaper and wrote me from Paris where he was living with his French wife, Raymonde. We renewed our friendship in the early 1950s, when Eleanor and I spent about one year in Paris for my lectures at the Hautes Études, though unfortunately Ian died shortly before I moved to England in 1963. Still later, in the 1970s, I rented a flat in Raymonde's house in Paris for a few years.

Now I think that I was too naive and optimistic about the situation in the Soviet Union. My first visit to the Soviet Union was in 1936. Of course, I knew that there were critics of the Stalin trials and others who supported them very strongly on the grounds that the people who had been condemned had been justly condemned, and so on. I was aware that in the world press there were pros and cons. But I did not go into it very deeply, because it was not my professional interest. I did feel, however, that in this period, the Stalinist policy on minority peoples in Central Asia, Stalin himself being of a minority people, was better than the Japanese policy in Manchuria or the Chinese policy in Inner Mongolia.

During my first visit to Moscow, I stayed with an American, who was a very good correspondent. He started life, I think, as a teacher in Cairo and then had become a free-lance journalist and joined the *Christian Science Monitor*. As its correspondent, he had spent several years in Tokyo and then in Peking. By the time I got to Moscow, he had been its correspondent for more than one year there. Obviously, with his experience he was the man who knew what propaganda was, and he certainly, at that time in 1936, had not yet become convinced that the Stalin trials were an enormous fake, and this considerably influenced my opinion. My article in *Pacific Affairs* saying that the Stalin trials would help ordinary people to protest against their government was, in large part, based on articles by this man. Afterward, he attended one of my hearings in Washington, and I met him when we were all going out. He said: "You said what you said was based on articles by me. But you certainly went farther than I meant anybody to go."

People may ask me why I wrote many articles and reviewed many books on the Soviet Union. It was because of Soviet policies toward minorities, as I have mentioned above. I was not interested in Marxism in itself, but I was interested in what was going on there. For example, I was not trying to examine from the point of view of "Would Bukharin or Trotsky have done this better?" because that was a hypothetical question. There is a tendency among some people to believe that if you write about a certain subject and do not condemn its ideology, you must be partisan to it. There is too much tendency with us to compare political controversies inside of the Soviet Union with controversies between the Republicans and the Democrats in the United States. That is not the point. You have to compare what happened in the Soviet Union after the revolution with the situation under Tsarism. The primary comparison is between Russia's past and Russia's present. Having grown up in semi-colonial China, my comparison is always how the life of ordinary people has changed after the revolution.

Moreover, the original revolutions took place under quite different circumstances in Russia, in France, in America; and you cannot expect revolutions to proceed in purely democratic waves that overwhelm purely wicked preceding dogmas. A revolution is not a tea party. Here I am quoting not Stalin but Mao Tse-tung. Therefore, concerning the purges in the Soviet Union, I thought in terms of the old, old saying that a revolution devours its own sons. There are bound to be struggles for power among the different people who had led the revolution. In this context, I should not have said one lot was more "democratic" than the other. I should have said that one group either had a more popular following, or was more tolerated by the people, than other groups. I was not in a position to judge, and I should not have written or spoken as if I were in such a position. But what I did not see was the degree to which the Soviet press under Stalin was able to whip up the idea of greater popular support and popular approval than actually existed.

With the McCarthy business, I was not dismissed from my university, but I was not given any assignment for lectures. The Page School was closed, and our Mongolian research project was wrecked beyond repair. The Dilowa Hutukutu eventually moved to New York, where he was looked after with tender care by American friends interested in Buddhism until his death in 1964. The two young Mongols had some difficult years, but Gombojab, who was able to get a university assignment, is now a professor at Indiana University. [Gombojab died in the fall of 1989.] When I received an invitation from Leeds University in England to build up a new Chinese department, I made it a condition that I could bring Urgunge with me to teach Chinese and Mongolian languages.

This invitation from Leeds University came in 1962. It was a part of the new program for Asian studies: Chinese studies in Leeds, Japanese studies in Sheffield, and East Asian studies in Hull. The idea was that while the classic approach in these areas had been mostly very general studies called Sinology or Japanology, the new approach was to require the students to specialize in one other discipline as well as the language. That is, they were to be not Sinologists, but specialists in Chinese history, politics, sociology, etc., with adequate training in their respective academic fields. I moved to Leeds in 1963 and continued to work as head of the Department of Chinese Studies until my retirement in 1970.

■
APPENDIX

The following three memoranda were presented by Owen Lattimore in 1941 at the request of Chiang Kai-shek. Two were written immediately before and after the outbreak of the Pacific War, and the memorandum on the Northeast is one of the three that Lattimore wrote soon after his arrival in Chungking in July 1941. They are not likely to be included in the official archives, where Lattimore-Currie (Chiang-White House) correspondence can be found.

The Northeastern Question in the Near Future

A. Probable Direction of Japanese Diplomatic Pressure
1. If Japan decides not to risk war with the United States, she will necessarily have to renew and try to prolong the diplomatic conversations in Washington. For this, a new topic of conversation is required. The most convenient topic is Northeast China.
2. If Japan is willing to continue with the conversations, then it means that Japan is already contemplating the possibility of defeat. Already, Japan's attempts to acquire additional territory and power have been rebuffed. From now on Japan must try to arrange, in case of defeat, to retain as much territory and power as possible.
3. For this kind of negotiation, Japan has only two fundamental arguments.
   a) America and Britain must, for the sake of their own interests, prevent revolution in Japan.
   b) America and Britain must, for the sake of their own control of the world balance of power, maintain Japan as a guard against Russia in Northeast Asia.
Under both of these arguments, Japan will demand that America and Britain must enable Japan to maintain a special position of some kind in Northeast China, either through international recognition of the puppet state of 'Manchukuo,' or through some kind of mandate which will preserve control of the Northeast for Japan.
4. China must face the fact that these Japanese arguments are fundamentally acceptable to the majority of the American State Department and the majority of the British Foreign Office.

B. China's Method of Defense against Japan's Diplomatic Strategy

1. Because of the Stimson non-Recognition Doctrine and the Roosevelt-Churchill Atlantic Charter, America and Britain cannot recognize "Manchukuo" without the consent of China.

2. Therefore an attempt may be made to put pressure on China to agree to multilateral negotiations in the course of which China will consent to recognize either:
   a) "Manchukuo"; or
   b) some kind of mandate over the Northeast, nominally international but actually giving real strategic, economic, and political control to Japan.

If China's consent could be secured, the way would be open for America and Britain to recognize and participate in either alternative.

3. However, as long as war is actually going on, nobody can force China to agree in advance to any such arrangement.

4. China's attitude should be based on the recent declarations of the Generalissimo regarding the Northeast. These have met with universal popular support and have been formally endorsed by the People's Political Council. The Chinese Government cannot go back on these declarations without shaking the confidence of the people. Therefore the Generalissimo's statements constitute, together with the Stimson Doctrine and the Atlantic Charter, a general denial of the validity of territorial aggression and puppet govenment since the aggressions of Germany and Italy in Europe and Africa, and of Japan in Asia.

5. In view of this, if America and Britain are worried by the threat of revolution in Japan, they must also take into consideration the danger that if the eventual peace terms are fundamentally unjust to China, the Chinese Government may not be able to keep the domestic situation in China under control. Revolution against the feudal and militaristic government of Japan would not affect the growing strength and stability of the Chinese Government. On the other hand, the fall of the Chinese Government would mean chaos throughout Asia.

6. Therefore China, if diplomatically urged to agree to even partial appeasement of Japan, can fearlessly stand on the principle of refusing to agree in advance to any terms that in the slightest degree diminish China's territorial integrity and political sovereignty. Without any danger to her own interests, China can insist that the peace terms between herself and Japan must be part of a general world settlement negotiated after a clear military defeat of all the Axis aggressor nations.

7. In the meantime, after the arrival of Litvinov in Washington, it is probable that an attempt may be made to frame a general anti-aggression pact. China should strongly support any such pact, provided it specifically recognizes China's full territorial integrity and political sovereignty. As a subsidiary to any general pact, China could willingly sign a supplementary treaty with Russia mutually guaranteeing the integrity of each other's territory along the entire Sino-Soviet frontier.

C. China's Domestic Policy Regarding the Northeast

1. Each step taken should be regarded as a logical outcome of the declarations already made by the Generalissimo. It should be made clear that

the Government is following the unmistakably expressed will of the people.

2.   Both in China and abroad, it should be repeatedly made clear that China's claim to the Northeast is not a claim for additional territory, but the maintenance and defense of a territorial integrity which has always existed.

3.   Both the American State Department and the British Foreign Office undoubtedly believe that Japan can somehow withdraw from China as far as Shanhaikuan, and yet somehow continue to maintain her hold on the Northeast. China, with a deeper understanding of both Chinese and Japanese psychology, knows that even before the Japanese troops have been withdrawn as far as the coast and Shanhaikuan, the whole structure of Japanese government will collapse. Once that happens, Japan cannot hold the Northeast or even Korea.

4.   Therefore China must protect her own interests by refusing to agree in advance to any compromise with Japan. Then, the moment Japan collapses, China must seize de facto control of the Northeast. Negotiation will then be easy; but it will be even easier if China has already signed a general non-aggression treaty with the ABCDS powers, and a subsidiary treaty with Russia.

5.   The first preparatory step in China should be the setting up of a Northeastern War Area. The military headquarters of this area should be established as close as possible to the Northeast.

6.   Liaison should be established between the new military headquarters and the guerillas in the Northeast. Everything should be done to intensify the activity and extend the area of Northeastern guerilla activities. It should be recognized that guerilla warfare in the Northeast differs somewhat from guerrilla warfare on other fronts, because of the impossibility as yet of beginning regular warfare.

7.   In connection with the new military attitude, the existing provincial governments of Liaoning, Kirin and Heilungkiang should become more active, especially in gathering information and issuing propaganda.

8.   Suitable [Kuomintang] Party and guerilla leaders who have actually been working in the Northeast should be brought to Chungking and publicized on a national scale as the men who have actually been maintaining the struggle for unity with China during the period of Japanese occupation.

9.   The Party should at once begin a program of national publicity, so conducted as to have a noticeable increase in intensity month by month.

Japan's Probable Next Move
Chungking, 10 November 1941

These are my own speculations:

Many Chinese continue to believe that Japan's next major move will be against Siberia. This belief is based on the assumption, sometimes not expressed in so many words, that Russia will be defeated so badly that she will be the easiest victim in sight.

My belief is that Japan has three alternatives: a) an all-out offensive to finish China; b) the offensive against Russia; c) a southward offensive against, or to embarrass, Britain and America, and perhaps China as well.

The first alternative is less and less probable, because in view of the development of the world situation as a whole, Japan could not win enough from China, in time, either to enable her to influence a world decision in favor of herself and Germany or to save herself from defeat if Germany is defeated. Nevertheless, if firmly enough checked in other directions, Japan might try a last big offensive in China. This would probably be aimed at the T'ungkuan passage.

The second alternative depends not only on Japan and Russia, but also on Germany. I do not think this is generally enough realized. Not only in her position as an axis power, but in her position as a danger to the countries which are enemies of Germany, Japan is now more and more dependent on German pressure—almost on German orders. I do not believe Germany will want Japan to attack Russia. It is not likely that a Japanese attack on Siberia, if the Germans are going to win west of the Urals, would make that German victory easier and cheaper by enough to make Germany urge such a course on Japan. If, on the other hand, the Germans are going to be defeated west of the Urals, then Russia is strong enough so that an additional Japanese attack in Siberia would not turn the scales.

It follows that even for the purposes of the German campaign in Russia Japan can be more useful to Germany by moving in some direction other than that of Siberia. If Japan can force America and Britain to concentrate men, ships, planes, etc. in the Pacific area to guard against a sudden Japanese attack, less American and British supplies will be available for aid to Russia.

Also, Germany undoubtedly holds a lower estimate of the Japanese army, navy, and air force, separately and in combination (especially the army), than is common among American and British experts.

This leads to another conclusion: Germany will prefer to use Japan as a threat, rather than allowing her actually to go to war against Britain and America, as long as possible. If Britain and America were once at war with Japan, they would be forced to try to dispose of her as quickly as possible, in order to free themselves to attend to Germany. They would, in fact, defeat Japan with a rapidity that would surprise themselves much more than it would surprise Germany. Germany would then no longer have the advantage of having Japan to force Britain and America to hold land, sea, and air forces in reserve.

If Japan's most useful function is to worry America and Britain, at what point will she apply pressure? In this decision Japan's own choice becomes more important, and Germany's pressure less decisive. Japan will naturally want to apply pressure at the point which promises the best combination of two advantages: 1) profitable appeasement if she succeeds in bluffing the British and Americans so that they will not fight; b) the best chance of victory, or the least chance of defeat, if Britain and America should decide to fight.

The choice of areas is: Philippines; Netherlands India; Singapore; Thai; Yunnan. In all of these areas except Thai and Yunnan, there is too little chance of a successful bluff and too much danger of a fight on terms not advantageous to Japan.

As between Thai and Yunnan, Thai offers the best chance of a successful bluff. Therefore, if a preliminary bluff against Yunnan were to fail, Japan might fall back on the maneuver of bluffing Thai, as a way of filling in time while still hoping for a Geman victory as the last-minute miracle of salvation. However, there would be one serious disadvantage in attempting to bluff Thai after the failure of a bluff against Yunnan: if Japan made a bluff against Yunnan and then backed down, it would be because Britain and America backed up China. If they had succeeded in making Japan back away from Yunnan, Britain and America would feel very much encouraged in also calling Japan's bluff against Thai. Moreover, even a successful bluff against Thai would neither solve Japan's economic shortages, nor settle the war against China, nor put Japan in a definite and decisive position for defeating the British at Singapoe or the Dutch in Netherlands India.

Therefore the most likely Japanese pressure is against Yunnan. Britain MIGHT take the risk of letting Japan cut the Burma Road, hoping that even if this were to lead to the final defeat of China, at least the consolidation of the victory would occupy Japan so long that she could not make a decisive attack in the Netherlands India-Singapore region until the British and Russians, backed by America, had got the Mediterranean-Near East-Russian situation in hand. If Britain were to take a sufficiently frightened and weak stand, America might refuse to act alone to save China.

Even if Britain and America were to back China to the point of actually fighting (perhaps only with air forces), the help given might be "too little and too late," enabling Japan to cut the Burma Road after all.

Final conclusion: there will be increasing Japanese threats against Yunnan, probably followed by actual invasion.

Hedged bet: if the American and British reaction to the mere threat should be so prompt and strong that Japan would not have time to get a running start in actual invasion, the change to a Thai bluff would be all the more unlikely. This in turn would mean that Japan's last desperate resort would probably be an all-out offensive on the main China front. This, for a number of reasons of terrain and politics, would probably mean T'ungkuan.

Consequences to China of the New War Situation

1.   Ultimate victory for China has been assured by the outbreak of war between Japan and America and Britain. Nevertheless, for the next few months a new and serious economic situation will prevail in China, which may have serious political consequences.

2.   The Burma Road may be cut by the Japanese. In any case, the shortage of military supplies, gasoline, machinery and ordinary economic commodities will certainly become increasingly severe.

3.   The first Japanese successes cannot result in a defeat of America and Britain, but they have already resulted in a considerable loss of American and British prestige. In Chungking, where there is more information and where more people have expert political and military knowledge, this does not matter so much. Outside of Chungking, where there is much less detailed information, rumor will certainly exaggerate the British and American losses. The result will be a considerable increase of pessimism among the Chinese public. Japanese and Wang Ching-wei propaganda will take full advantage of this. When combined with increasing economic hardship, the political consequences may well be dangerous.

4.   The chief center of danger is among the landlords and gentry, especially those who are associated with local militarists and those who have already been engaged in unpatriotic speculation and hoarding. These are the classes of people who have already provided the greatest number of traitors for the Japanese and Wang Ching-wei. More of them may now try to get into touch with the Japanese.

.   5.   This kind of danger exists in Yunnan, Sikang [sic, Sinkiang?] and Szechwan. In the Northwest, it also exists in Kansu and Ninghsia, especially among the Moslems, who are in the rear of the Government armies in Shensi.

Suggested Steps to Meet the New Situation

1.   Every effort should be made to increase production, so as to relieve the economic situation. The previous proposal for a loan from the American Treasury, for internal use in China, should be pressed more vigorously than ever. The prospects of getting such a loan, partly for stabilizing prices and partly for increasing production (which will also relieve prices), are better than ever.

2.   Demands are already being made, in certain quarters, that the Government should cut down expenses, "in order to save money." These demands should be firmly resisted. Certain kinds of longterm expenditure may perhaps be cut down, if they do not result in immediate production or strategic advantage, but all expenditures which result in immediate large-scale employment or immediate production should be maintained and even increased. The demands for a general deflationary policy should be treated as a more or less open but quite unjustified attack on the Government's recent financial policy.

3.   Strong steps should be taken against hoarders, especially those who are landlords and who are also associated with local militarists. The recent arrests of hoarders in Szechwan are an excellent step in the right direction.

4. Resentment among the landlords and other hoarders, even when they have the support of local militarists, will not be dangerous politically if the Government, at the same time, takes prompt and effective measures to relieve the economic burden of the people. This will result in increased loyalty and support for the Government on the part of the nation as a whole.

5. The Northwest road should be vigorously developed as a substitute for the Burma Road. The engineering difficulties are not nearly so great as on the Burma Road. Transport is the main problem. This can partly be solved by the increased use of camels, as well as by the increased production of gasoline.

Methods of Carrying Out the Steps Suggested Above

1. As much cargo as possible should be got in over the Burma Road in the next few weeks.

2. Owing to the shortage of labor in Yunnan, any extra labor that is needed should be transferred from the construction of the Burma Railway to the operation of the Burma Road. Preparations should be made at once, in case of emergency, to stop work on the Burma Railway altogether and to transfer its engineers and skilled workers to other parts of China.

3. The oil refining machinery now lying in Burma should be transported at once to Kansu, to develop the oil wells already existing there and to increase the production of gasoline and diesel oil within China. This machinery should be given priority of transport on the Burma Road even over military supplies, with the exception of aviation supplies.

4. The Industrial Cooperatives should be rapidly increased in number and the Government banks should supply capital for them and fresh capital for the most productive of the existing Cooperatives. It will certainly be possible to get American backing for this policy.

5. American backing will in itself be to a certain extent an insurance against Leftism in the Industrial Cooperatives. As a further safeguard against Leftism, Cooperatives which are financially successful should later be allowed to reorganize as private capitalistic enterprises. In any case, the present situation is different from the previous situation, and if the Government vigorously takes the lead in expanding production through the Industrial Cooperatives, the credit will go to the Government and not to the Communists or any other Leftists. The result will be increased support for the Government among the masses of the people.

6. Existing trade agreements with Soviet Russia should be maintained and expanded, and any new agreements that are possible should be signed. By developing transport in the Northwest, a situation will be created which will before long facilitate a new, joint American-Soviet-Chinese Lease Lend agreement.

It can be foreseen that in the near future America will not be able to send supplies to Russia in large quantities except through Vladivostok or some other Pacific port. This will make Soviet war against Japan absolutely necessary.

When that time comes, America will be able to demand that Lease Land supplies be provided for China also by Russian cooperation. Owing to war traffic on the Amur railway, it will not be possible to transport American supplies from a Pacific port all the way by the Trans-Siberian and Turk-Sib railways to the beginning of the Northwest Road in Sinkiang. It will be possible, however, to arrange that in return for extra American supplies to Russia, equivalent Russian supplies should be delivered to China from the Soviet factories in South Siberia and Russian Turkistan.

It would probably also be possible to get from the Russians a certain amount of captured German equipment. It should be noted that it is easier to transport tanks over the Northwest Road than over the Burma Road, because the mountain passes are not nearly so high.

7.   China militarily should take advantage of the situation as a whole to prosecute the war. Politically, she should take advantage of the situation to reduce the Communist danger. Increased cooperation with Soviet Russia is militarily a necessity, and politically it will mean that during the immediate future the Communists will not dare to make trouble.

For the longer, future, cooperation with America, especially through the proposed loan, will be a reinsurance against Communism. While America has no interest in interfering in internal questions in China, she certainly does not want to see a Communist China and does want to help to establish a China that will both be completely independent and in its domestic government completely stable.

Submitted through Madame, 14 December 1941. No Chinese translation.

INDEX

247

248 INDEX